A Monk's Tale

A Monk's Tale

By Muni Natarajan

This book is dedicated to
Satguru Sivaya Subramuniyaswami,
my teacher, my friend and
my second father

Introduction

While I was a monk, I served as a waiter, a printer, an artist, a writer, an editor, a musician, a farmer, a beekeeper, a teacher, a priest, a yogi, a swami, a cleaner of toilets and a frequent traveler of the world. I survived two hurricanes, one earthquake, an attempted robbery at gunpoint, a 41-day water fast and the death of the man this book is really all about—all while striving to maintain a perspective that the "I's" experiencing all of this were but seeming.

My name is Muni Natarajan. For 37 years, I lived in a monastery dedicated to the practice of yoga. The head of that monastery, Satguru Sivaya Subramuniyaswami, was my spiritual teacher. We just called him "Gurudeva." This is what he wanted.

Gurudeva is gone now—or so we say. He passed away in November of 2001. After I left the monastery in February of 2007, I was often asked what it was like to live as a monk. As I responded to this question, I discovered—by observing the facial expressions of those who where listening—any time spent living as a monk in Gurudeva's proximity formed a unique story worth telling.

I was also often asked about what I was taught while I was a monk. Since Gurudeva was central to both the life I lived and the teachings I absorbed while I was in the monastery, my responses to questions about that life and those teachings focused upon Gurudeva.

Gurudeva reformed our lives into a practice of yoga and our monastery into a greenhouse for the development of character. Every moment was valued as a means of learning and growing. Every experience was treasured as a foray into discovery.

Since it would be impossible to provide in any one book a complete account of all that might occur during any extended period of time, *A Monk's Tale* will only focus upon an assortment of chronological events that I feel will give some overall sense of what it was like to live the life I lived for 37 years.

If some of what you read here seems further fetched than fiction, please know every ounce of it is true—with one exception. The names of most of the people mentioned have been changed. This I have done to protect the living, respect the dead and honor the loved.

The Life Begins

First Sight

I first saw Gurudeva in Hawaii on the island of Oahu, striding swiftly toward a public library in Honolulu where he was scheduled to give a lecture on yoga. It was a hot, tropical, Sunday afternoon in late June of 1970. The two of his monks he had chosen to travel with him on that day were hustling to keep up.

I instinctively waved to him from across the street even though we had never met in person. He waved back like he was hailing an old friend. As I walked up to him, I felt unusually calm, considering how long I had anticipated this first meeting.

Movie star lean and handsome in his all-white outfit, he beamed a broad smile as we shook hands. The strength of his grip surprised me and accentuated the power of his presence. Even though he slumped slightly in a stylish sort of way, his long, muscular legs made him seem taller than his six feet, two inches. His shoulder-length hair was salt-and-pepper grey, combed straight back. Although his eyes were dramatically piercing, his body language was smooth, easy and friendly.

"Nice to see you," he said. He spoke with such a relaxed familiarity I almost expected him to say my name, even though I knew he didn't know it. I stammered out an awkward "aloha" as his two monks stepped forward to yield their introductions and inquire about me. All of this happened quite politely in the space of about three minutes as we sauntered into a classroom-size hall adjacent to the library.

For about eight months, I had been working as the house drummer for Don Ho at the Polynesian Palace in the Cinerama Reef Towers hotel of Waikiki. Don Ho was easier than easy — a soft, benevolent man, forever kindly in his own laid-back way.

I will never forget that uncommonly happy and carefree period of time in my life. During the day I would draw with pencil and ink, paint with watercolor and oil. At night I would play music. I was living in a paradise of sorts, no doubt about it. But such living wasn't why I had come to Hawaii. I was there to see Gurudeva.

I had first heard about Gurudeva some two years before, while I was attending Indiana University in Bloomington. There, I was introduced to his teachings in yoga classes conducted by one of his students.

In the several phone conversations I had with Gurudeva during that time, I expressed my sincere interest in the monastic program he had established in his Hindu monastery. During those phone calls, he urged me to come to Hawaii to meet him personally and to see the land he had just purchased for his monastery/church on Kauai. So there I was in Hawaii, finally, fulfilling the first of those encouragements.

To my surprise, the two monks—not Gurudeva—delivered the scheduled talk at the library. Although they took turns speaking with a coordinated ease that was most pleasant to observe, I had to resist an inclination to turn around and look back at Gurudeva who was sitting behind me. After all, I come to see and hear him, not his monks.

When the talk was over, a few of the approximately 40 attendees left. Those who remained tried to look casual as they—like me—waited to talk with Gurudeva. One by one, each took a turn. I figured if I placed myself last I might be allowed more time for a conversation that didn't feel rushed by others waiting. When it finally looked like my chance to visit might be coming up soon, one of the monks held his wristwatch up in front of Gurudeva to indicate it was time to leave. My heart sank.

As Gurudeva passed by me on his way out of the room, he touched my arm ever so lightly. "Would you like to chat for a minute?" he asked. Before I could nod "yes," we were moving gracefully through the front door of the building out into the shade of a nearby tree. The two monks disappeared to arrange transportation, and Gurudeva turned to give me his characteristically undivided attention.

Now was my chance to talk, but my mind was blank. Still, I felt impelled to say something. Just as I was about to blunder my way into an awkward babble, Gurudeva spoke.

"You could quite easily move your awareness into the source of all that exists right now because you've only just been introduced to the very idea that is possible," he said. "It will become more difficult later as you learn more about it." This was the first of a great many unexpected answers to unasked questions I would receive from Gurudeva through the 30 years that followed.

When the monks returned, Gurudeva invited me to join him for lunch. About fifteen minutes later, ten of us from the lecture were sitting huddled around Gurudeva at a table in a nearby vegetarian restaurant. It was a delightful experience. There we were—sipping spicy tomato soup, munching delicious avocado sandwiches and talking about "looking at the world from the inside out," "holding mountaintop consciousness" and "living with the feeling that nothing is happening."

Just as I was wondering to myself, "Is this man from another planet?" one of the ladies at the table asked Gurudeva what he thought about extraterrestrial life. Gurudeva turned to me and said, "Actually, I came here from another planet, but I think I got the wrong address." Everyone at the table laughed—except me. I thought he was serious.

Innersearch

During our conversation right after the Honolulu lecture, Gurudeva had asked me if I might be interested in attending a two-week yoga intensive at his monastery/home on the island of Kauai. The event, entitled the 1970 Hawaii Innersearch, was scheduled to begin only ten days hence. I happily consented, seeing this offer as an opportunity to make my first pilgrimage to "the garden island" where Gurudeva lived and worked.

At the time, this travel/study program, informally referred to as "Innersearch"—which combined classes in Eastern spirituality and yoga with sightseeing—was a fairly new venture for Gurudeva. During later years, he and his monks would conduct a great many of these mystic tours, traveling primarily to India, Sri Lanka, Singapore, Malaysia and Japan, but also to Nepal, Tahiti, Thailand, Australia, New Zealand, Russia, England, France, Germany and the Netherlands.

I joined the 1970 Hawaii Innersearch not as a paying student but as a member of what Gurudeva called the "Taskforce." The four of us on this program lived in monk's quarters, trading work and service for room and board. Although we attended some of the ongoing Innersearch classes, we spent most of our time sweeping, cleaning, setting up tables, moving chairs, serving food and washing dishes.

Because the resident monastics were also performing these daily chores, we taskforcers had a great opportunity to see what monastic life was like by closely observing the monks themselves.

Gurudeva's monks were constantly "working with themselves," as they put it—striving always to subdue negative emotion, restrain frivolous conversation and maintain "control of awareness."

Understandably, the two weeks of Innersearch passed quickly. Although we labored hard, it was not hard labor. There was magic in the air. Absolutely everyone felt inspired in one way or another.

It was a joy to attend Gurudeva's Innersearch lectures. I loved his simple clarity and hands-on pragmatism. Within the first minutes of his first lecture, he defined the ultimate goal of yoga as the fundamental purpose of life.

"You're here to realize the Self," he proclaimed. "There is no other reason for your existence on this Earth. You have lived many lives, all for this one purpose." As time went on, I came to realize this was his pivotal message to every spiritual aspirant he met—from the wholeheartedly sincere to the vaguely curious.

It did not take time to get to know Gurudeva. It took sincerity. For those who knew him well, his manner was purposeful but informal. For those who did not know him well, his manner was kindly but formal. Yet, every life he touched was changed for the better, even though such change might not have been immediately apparent.

The teachings conveyed during the 1970 Innersearch classes consisted of principles and practices. In the free time between classes, students gravitated into two camps. One camp discussed the principles. They were the thinkers. The other camp jumped into the practices. They were the doers. The doers could have used more thinking, and the thinkers could have used more doing.

The thinkers were forever asking questions like: "If seeking Self is the central purpose of life, why are most people seeking just about everything else instead? And what is wrong with this diversified seeking that seems to be society's norm? What is wrong with all of those other obviously valid life-pursuits—like finding a good job, getting married, raising a family and becoming a responsible member of society? Aren't these at least as important as seeking Self?"

The doers were forever calling such questions "negative nitpicking." It was their contention that just putting the teachings into practice should supersede the time-wasting cultivation of critical thought.

Certainly, those doers must have been surprised to hear Gurudeva apparently condone the nitpicking by saying, "Let your mind try to disprove these teachings." Yet just as certainly, they must have also been encouraged when he added, "Just remember, one of the biggest obstacles to Self Realization is an overdeveloped intellect."

Toward the end of the Innersearch, the doers were thinking more, the thinkers were doing more and Gurudeva was observing it all. While we were learning from him, he was learning from us.

As I pondered Gurudeva's central theme of Self Realization, I discovered what I recorded in my yoga journal as "a long-awaited zest for life arising from a worthwhile quest for the intrinsic essence of all."

Admittedly, I was a charter member of the doer camp. All I ever wanted was to start right away preparing for monastic life, since to me being a monk meant—to my way of thinking then—devotedly seeking Self Realization. When I enthusiastically made my ambitions clear to Gurudeva, he surprised me with a warning.

"Take it easy." he said ever so calmly. "This isn't a race. There's plenty of time."

Vows

I stayed on Kauai after the Innersearch to talk more with Gurudeva about becoming a monk. During those talks, Gurudeva was calm, balanced and objective. He did not push me away, nor did he pull me in.

"Your dharma is your highest life path," Gurudeva said during one of our more intense conversations. "It is, for you, an optimal way of living determined by your inherent nature as that nature gets filtered out into your everyday experience. Although your inherent nature is pure, simple and good, the body you were born into is an instinctive animal with a thinking mind.

"The body and mind are not bad. They serve a very important purpose. Their purpose is to provide a vehicle for the fulfillment of a fundamental desire we all have to experience all that life has to offer. Following desire, we move away from our pure, inherent nature until finally we have had enough and want to move back. My question to you now is, "Are you moving away, or are you moving back?" If you are on your way back, you will do well as a monk.

"Even if you have a keen interest in following a monk's dharma, you'll still have a backlog of unresolved karma to deal with, and we are prepared for that. What is important right now is your intention.

"In a broad sense, what we are calling 'your karma' is your past, the sum total of all you've done through many lives. If you've made a lot of messes, your karma will be heavy and clouded, and your dharma will be unclear. If you've done well in cleaning up your messes, your karma will be light and your dharma will be obvious.

"To understand your karma so you can determine your dharma, study your tendencies. What do you have a tendency to do? What is the nature of your desire? Ask yourself these questions honestly. Then, finally, ask yourself this question: 'Is it my dharma to be a monk?'"

I hesitated.

"Give it a little time," he said, gracefully alleviating my immediate confusion. "Meanwhile, let's talk a little bit about yoga. I know that's what's really on your mind."

I had to marvel at Gurudeva's cool expertise in working with people, his easy way of moving in and out of sensitive conversations.

"In a deeper practice of yoga we strive to be aware of being aware," he said. "This is easy to accomplish if you don't complicate your effort with too much thought. Just mentally say to yourself, 'I am aware,' and be aware. Then, mentally say to yourself, 'I am aware that I am aware,' and be aware that you are aware."

I shut my eyes and tried to do as he said. It seemed like maybe I was doing it. Then I thought to myself, "Maybe I'm not doing it."

"Don't doubt," Gurudeva said, answering a question just starting to form in my mind. "It's simpler than you think. Awareness is backed by a certain feeling—the feeling of *being*. Yoga is simple, but it's not easy. Just take it one step at a time. Progress on the spiritual path, as in life, comes through a great many little successes. There are many little realizations on the way to the one big Realization."

To round out this introduction to monastic life, Gurudeva had a couple of senior monks guide me through the structure and function of Saiva Siddhanta Church and its school, the Himalayan Academy. They were kind as they patiently answered my unsophisticated questions.

Once Gurudeva felt I had caught the general gist of what life in his monastic order would be like, he left the path choosing to me. At no point did I get the sense from him that I should or should not be a monk, or that I was or was not suited for monastic life.

In the end, I was still unwavering in my commitment to live the monastic life. None of the people I worked with back in Waikiki could believe I was giving up a happy, easy and lucrative professional life for what appeared to them to be a stark existence of renunciate austerity. Yet, in my mind, there was no going back. I wanted to be a monk.

8

So, Gurudeva gave his blessings for me to begin a six-month program called the Aspirancy. This half-year dose of monastic life was designed to give a young man a chance to settle into a monk's way of living long enough to get past what Gurudeva liked to refer to as "a natural fascination with novelty."

At the commencement of this Aspirancy, I took two vows: the vow of humility, a promise to fit into monastic life "like the nameless one," and the vow of purity, a promise to be celibate while remaining physically and mentally virtuous.

Lifetime monks take three more vows: the vow of obedience, a promise to live by the rules of the monastery and directions of its guru; the vow of confidence, a promise to not divulge private monastery information; and the vow of poverty, a promise to embrace a renunciate life in which all sense of personal ownership is relinquished.

On the Move

After my initiation into the Aspirancy, life suddenly got busy. Within days, I was on a plane to California with instructions to live at our San Francisco center while serving in the Silent Ministry, a monastic program in which monks worked incognito as waiters in restaurants.

Waitering is a humble enough job—and far more difficult than those who have never tried it might suspect. Adding in the demands of Silent Ministry made it even more challenging. In addition to being good waiters, we Silent Ministers were expected to be inconspicuous dispensers of blessings.

As it turned out, now was actually not the time for me to fully experience this particular monastic discipline. Just three days after I had gotten my first job in a restaurant (as a bus boy), I was given instructions to move to our third center in Virginia City, Nevada, where the Church maintained a press shop dedicated to publishing Gurudeva's books. I was told the reason for my rather abrupt relocation to this desert place was quite practical. I had previous training in the field of graphics and design and was needed on the press team.

So, there I was traveling again. After less than a week in San Francisco, I was now sitting front-seat shotgun in our monastery car, a Citroen, heading for Virginia City with two other monks.

9

As we began our drive, the late October weather was noticeably cool, but not uncomfortable. When we arrived at our destination four and a half hours later, it was excruciatingly cold. Winter had arrived in Virginia City and the winds were fierce.

Our jackets weren't nearly heavy enough to withstand the icy chill that stunned us with a shock as we got out of the car. It was all we could do to grab our sparse luggage and hurry up the cracked wooden stairs of the old town brewery Gurudeva had recently purchased to serve as our Virginia City monastery.

Two hardy monks greeted us at the door. They were the valiant fort holders, waiting for us with big grins, all toasty in their thick, down, winter coats. The electricity was out—temporarily we were told. So our hosts were scrambling to create as much light as they could with flashlights and candles. We stumbled inside, tripping over this and that, who knows what, until we finally found a flat space covered with a rug.

After rolling out my sleeping bag, I discovered a bathroom by the flickering light of a dying flashlight I had just been given. There, I brushed my teeth in water that felt colder than ice. There was no way I was going to take a shower. Was there a shower? I started to ask but figured it would be better to just wait until morning to see for myself.

If ever there was a time to lean on a mystic strength within, this was it. We were hungry, tired, cold and apprehensive about what might happen next. The Virginia City Monastery had a reputation for being a tough place to live, especially during winter. Now I could see how that reputation had been well earned.

Just before sleep, I casually thumbed through my yoga journal to an arbitrary page and beamed my flashlight down on a quote I had scribbled out during one of Gurudeva's Innersearch classes. Wading through my bad handwriting, I managed to read: "Recognizing all experience is but a fading dream, you are closer to a permanence within you that has always been as it is. You can sense this permanence. It is God. It has never changed. And it never will."

As I lay down in my new bed, completely forgetting where I was, bliss was all I could feel. The next thing I knew, it was morning.

Staying Put

I woke up with the rising sun feeling refreshed and renewed, but not fully awake. I was having trouble getting oriented, partially because I was in a new place, yet also because I had slept deeply. Because the warmth of my sleeping bag was providing a welcome haven from the cold, all I wanted to do right then and there was stay put.

As I lay there somewhat zoned, I vaguely heard some hustling and bustling. Slowly, a fundamental truth of life dawned upon me: This was a shared home. If I wanted to use the bathroom any time soon, I'd better move quickly.

In one long, clumsy lunge, I grabbed my toiletries pouch, rolled out of my sleeping bag and stumbled into the hall. Too late. I had to wait. "Damn!" Whoa! Did I say that out loud?

I would come to know this particular scenario—waiting for the facilities—as an important and often-repeated opportunity to develop patience, humility and forbearance in the monastery. Drawing in a long, deep breath, I wrapped up tight in a heavy blanket and stepped outside onto the front porch. The sharp, windy cold at this high altitude was hard to ignore. Yet there I sat, trying to do just that: ignore a windy cold, while watching a blood-red sky turn ice blue in less than two minutes.

As I looked out upon this strangely powerful scene, I was surprised to find myself feeling very much at home. I didn't know why—had no idea. It was a desolate looking place cloaked in the scent of desert sage, set against a distant landscape that looked like a watercolor painting textured with sand—not exactly a wonder-winter-land tourist destination. What was it about this place I loved? Its simplicity? Its physical severity? Its purity? To this day, I can't put my finger on it.

Virginia City is one of the oldest cities in Nevada and one of the most famous boomtowns of the Old West. It appeared virtually overnight as a result of something called the "Comstock Lode Silver Strike," which lasted from 1859 to 1898.

Virginia City was also the place where, in 1863, a reporter for the local Territorial Enterprise newspaper named Samuel Clemens, first used the pen name, Mark Twain. When the three-story building we were now calling our Virginia City monastery was the town bar and brewery, we were told, it was quite often frequented by Mr. Twain.

Now, Virginia City is an idiosyncratic tourist destination, with a

11

wild west back story. For better or worse, she's dead or alive—dead in the winter or alive in the summer.

During summer *and* winter, our monastery schedule was quite rigorous, and subject to change on short notice. For the most part, we were fairly consistent in gathering for meditation and worship observances at 6 am, 12 noon, 6 pm and 12 midnight. The rest of the time, we worked, ate and slept. The liturgy for our ceremonies was conceived and written in a language called *Shum*.

The language of *Shum* was unfolded clairaudiently and clairvoyantly to Gurudeva in Switzerland in 1969. For Gurudeva, the arrival of *Shum* was a long-awaited fulfillment of a long-nurtured desire for a spiritual language.

Back on Kauai, I had asked Gurudeva why he had been so interested in bringing through a special language for meditation. He replied, "English was created for life on the physical plane. So were French, Spanish, German and all the languages of countries. These languages don't have words for inner states of mind. Their words name things, emotions and some thoughts. We need an language for inner life."

"Aren't thoughts and emotions part of inner life?" I asked.

"Certainly they are," said Gurudeva, "but thoughts and emotions are only skin deep."

There was an awkward pause. I was thinking his answer would or should be longer. "So, *Shum* only names states of mind deeper than thoughts and emotions?" I asked.

"*Shum* has words for everything, but the *Shum* perspective is from within the deep inner mind, looking out. As a point of reference, it never becomes externalized into thoughts and emotions. It sees things, thoughts and emotions from a distance, somewhat objectively—or from the inside out, so to speak."

Gurudeva further clarified that *Shum* would be primarily used in meditation and for conversation among mystics. When I asked him how *Shum* might benefit meditation, his answer was unique.

"The mind is like a forest," he said. "When you work your way though a forest and locate a wonderful place, wouldn't it be nice to be able to find your way back there later? In working with the mind, you can do this with a *Shum* meditation map. A map like this can record what you just did, or it can propose what you want to do. You can also chant

12

Shum. *Shum* is a mantra language with a special vibration all of its own. The vibration of *Shum* alone can put you into a state of meditation. Talking and writing in *Shum* can help you live in the external world while maintaining an internalized state of consciousness."

After a short pause, I asked Gurudeva how *Shum* could be used in striving for the ultimate realization of the Self.

"With *Shum* you can draw a map through the mind right up to the brink of the Absolute. There you have to wait patiently. The Self is the one thing you can't *get* like you get other things, for the Self is beyond the mind—beyond getting. Getting occurs only within the mind. Strictly speaking, you don't realize the Self, the Self realizes you, for the Self is God. And the Realization of God happens in God's timing, not yours."

Self

I once overheard a not-so-serious student ask Gurudeva, "What's the big deal about the Self. Why is it so important?"

To this, Gurudeva replied, "The totality of all manifestation—spiritual, mental, emotional and physical—issues forth from the one source and essence of all, which is the Self. Sooner or later, all you're going to want to do is merge with this one source of life. When that time comes, you won't be asking why the Self is important."

Gurudeva would refer to this "totality of manifestation" as "the mind." From Gurudeva's point of view, life was daringly simple: There was Self and there was mind. Even souls were of the mind.

Gurudeva was taught and taught us that souls are created into the mind with an ingrained program to evolve by following desire to experience all the mind has to offer—everything: the good, the bad and the ugly. At the completion of all this total mind experience, with nothing left to desire, these souls then merge with their truest Self.

"Self Realization is the culmination of a soul's journey through all of its lives on earth," Gurudeva would tell us. "Yet only toward the end of this vast journey can a soul be expected to view Self Realization as the primary goal of existence. Up until then, there's just too much desire to do other things instead."

Self Realization, Gurudeva asserted, marks a turning point in the evolution of the soul, a point when the experiences of physical life have

13

been so successfully encountered and resolved, there is no longer any need for the soul to be reborn in a physical body.

The way Gurudeva talked about the concept of karma was as practical as it was unique. "Following each of our actions, we must live through an unavoidable reaction and through that reaction learn a little more about life," Gurudeva explained to his students during the 1970 Innersearch on Kauai. "An important fulfillment of any experience is the understanding that experience yields in its aftermath. All of this takes place in accordance with the law of karma.

"Karma literally means 'action.' But action cannot exist without reaction. So the resolution of any experience occurs when that experience matures full circle into understanding. But this understanding is not intellectual. It's a satisfied feeling, a sense of knowing that arrives when we feel something just no longer needs to be explained. Isn't it true that excessive thought and talk are simply desperate attempts to achieve this kind of understanding that can only really occur through experience?"

Yet words were important to Gurudeva. Otherwise, he would not have been so driven to bring through a language like *Shum*. "We all share a one essence," Gurudeva once said in reference to the creation of the *Shum* language. "The discovery of essence is step-by-step. At each step, we need to know where we are, where we have been and where we are going. This kind of knowing requires thought, then words — preferably words that are meaningful in reference to introspection."

My first day in Virginia City was magical, not because of any particular event that occurred but because of the way I felt inside myself. I was filled and thrilled with a fearlessly exhilarating anticipation of an unpredictable future. What would happen next? Would I be moving again tomorrow or the next day? As it turned out, I stayed right there in that brewery-turned-monastery in those stark mountains of American history for almost two more years.

Will

By the time I finally met Gurudeva in person, I had studied his teachings for about two years. All through that time, I could never quite understand why he placed so much emphasis on the cultivation of willpower. Although he strongly encouraged the development of devotion, love,

14

compassion, service, liberation and a great many other such mystical qualities, it was *willpower* that was pivotal from his perspective.

"Will is the fuel which carries awareness through all areas of the mind," Gurudeva proclaimed. "It is the spiritual quality that can make any inner or outer goal a reality. You need a tremendous, indomitable will to make real the quest of merging with the Self God. Unfoldment doesn't take time. It takes willpower."

From Gurudeva's daringly simple perspective, will provided the means by which awareness could be moved through the complexity of life to the simplicity of Self. "Even the grace of God," he asserted, "comes in response to the will of man."

Living in the Virginia city ashram, I slowly began to understand how Gurudeva's mystical teaching was more about life than yoga. From his perspective, Self Realization was the ultimate goal of yoga because it was the ultimate goal of life, and—as with the pursuit of any life goal—the eventual attainment of this ultimate Realization of Self was most expeditiously accomplished through the cultivation of willpower. I came to this understanding because absolutely everything we did in our mountain desert monastery revolved around the development and use of willpower. And it was in this cultivation of willpower that we all felt the wholesome blossoming of an invincible strength.

Our ashram building was old and in constant need of repairs that we had to make ourselves. It had no central heating or air-conditioning, and its old, crudely boarded walls were so lined with gaping cracks, they couldn't stop a breeze, much less a howling mountain wind. During the summer, we were too hot. During the winter, we were too cold.

In addition to all of this, we were going through the birth pains of learning what Gurudeva called "people skills." After all, we were a group of vital, young men, quite newly acquainted, with very little in common except for our interest in yoga.

Living and working together in tight quarters, we simply had to get along with each other. However each of us preconceived the life of a monk should be, we all had to eventually agree that any life anywhere tends to get bogged down in pettiness, and that dealing with pettiness would somehow have to find a place in our practice of yoga.

Apart from all of this, I have to admit, I kept asking myself "What *is* the yoga we're practicing here?" Slowly, it dawned on me. The

15

development of willpower was our yoga at that point in our training.

We all learned quickly there was simply nothing to be gained by complaining to Gurudeva about circumstances or people. He would just smile and say, "*This* is what you came for. You're here to learn you can do anything. Where there is a will there is a way." It was often during the worst of times, when we were least inspired, that Gurudeva would be most inspired to talk enthusiastically about yoga.

Even for the most perceptive among us, nothing was turning out as anticipated. We had to hear again and again, "change is the only permanent reality" and "fortitude is your strongest ally in maintaining peace of mind." By "fortitude," Gurudeva meant *willpower*.

"Feel the energy in the spine," Gurudeva would tell us when we were tired and wanted to go to bed. "There is no lack of it is there? The more you use, the more you have to use. The power of your spine is the power of your will. Will means this: If you're going to complete something, complete it. Finish what you start. And finish it well, beyond your expectations, no matter how long it takes."

When the intensity eased up and we were just relaxing together, Gurudeva would elaborate on the powerful but usually sparse instructions he shared with us during our more challenging times.

"Work with willpower, awareness and energy as three separate items first," he would say. "Be aware of awareness and discover that. Use willpower and discover that. Feel energy and discover that. Separate these three in your intellectual mind and experiential patterns. After you've done this, you will begin to see inside yourself how these three are one and the same."

Our monastic life was divided into two distinct realms: service and *sadhana* (spiritual practice). Work was our service. Each monk had specific work to do in some area of service. Yoga was our *sadhana*.

My assigned work in our Virginia City monastery was in the prepress department of our print shop. I produced art as needed, helped design our various publications, processed photos to film for printing, stripped up negatives and burned plates for our printing press.

Although each monk's job was different, we all had to learn to be precise, methodical and intelligent in small, practical ways. While maximizing our work efficiency was undoubtedly important to us, being kind and humble enough to live and learn with each other without disturbing

16

the harmony of the monastery eventually became our first priority.

As time passed, we became aware of a certain subtle something occurring in the background of our life. In our own timing, each of us witnessed the other monks becoming better people. This observation was not something we were consciously attempting to achieve. It was simply a natural consequence of our ongoing struggle to meet the everyday challenges of living within monastery restrictions.

Certainly, this process of becoming a better person was quite uncomfortable at times. The lower side of our human nature resisted change and hated trading familiar habits, even if they were negative, for unfamiliar habits, even if they were positive.

"You're learning to have enough faith in yourself to step off into nothing," Gurudeva would often say. "You're perfect. You just don't know it. Your job is to realize your perfection."

Occasionally, we worked 24/7 to finish production on press jobs with stepped-up deadlines, deadlines stepped up by no one but us, I should mention, and often for no good reason, other than to create a stimulating challenge. At these times, we tried to sleep little and work more in a bold move to prove—to ourselves and Gurudeva—we had this valuable thing called *willpower*.

Gurudeva didn't object to these "press pushes," as we called them. He let us figure out for ourselves how such impulsiveness came more from emotion than will—and was almost always counter-productive in the long run. During these press pushes, we made more mistakes than usual.

Mistakes were upsetting—and sometimes costly. When we printed a book with one page upside down and it was determined this catastrophe was my error, I agonized for days before going to Gurudeva to apologize.

By the time I finally got up the courage to go see him, I had worked myself into a state of considerable anxiety. Ready for a good scolding, I listened watery-eyed as he said with the kindest of smiles, "The only mistake is a lesson not learned. Just double-check your work. It won't happen again."

He was right. I never made a mistake like that again. But we still had to reprint that book at considerable expense, and I had to discover that living with a mistake was a tough way to learn.

Gurudeva was amazing in his ability to gently relieve monastery tension just as it was about to turn negative. At such breaking points, he would take us down to Reno for a show, to the Carson City Hot Springs for a soak or to Lake Tahoe for an afternoon of relaxation. This was rare though — about once every two months.

Gurudeva would cycle through his three monasteries as often as he could. We always looked forward to his coming. It meant fun and good times. Around him there was always joy, even during times of trial. Nothing could get him down. He was the one who was forever calm, content, unruffled and happy. His best teaching was his example.

The Warrior
In Virginia City, we had a dog. I'm not sure if he was bought, found or given. He was already there when I arrived. His name was Babashum. In the *Shum* language, *baba* means "dog," and *shum* means "pleasant." Although this dog was certainly a *baba,* he was by no means *shum.* Still, we all loved him, for he was a fearless warrior and a mighty sentinel.

Babashum was not large. In fact, truth be told, he was rather small — especially compared to the other Virginia City canines. He stood 18 inches tall, weighed 20 pounds and was such a mix of breeds not even our veterinarian could accurately identify what he was. When I arrived at the Virginia City ashram, Babashum was ten years of age and had been in so many dogfights he was lucky to be alive.

Babashum looked the life he lived. The tip of his right ear was missing and he was covered with laceration scars, camouflaged only slightly by his long golden brown hair. He walked with a limp one of the monks said he got during a fight with his mother shortly after he was born (I don't believe this). And his neck was locked in one position, which froze his skull rigidly at a slight angle so that, if he wanted to look back to his right or left, he couldn't just turn his head, he had to rotate his entire body. His left back leg was mostly numb. So he sort of dragged it when he walked or ran.

Regardless of all this and despite his age, Babashum never missed an opportunity to gallop crookedly along with us on our daily two-mile jog through the sparse residential outskirts of Virginia City.

On one such occasion, as about six of us were out huffing and puffing toward our second wind, Babashum was hobbling alongside us more vigorously than usual. It was a brisk, clear fall day—not a cloud in the sky. Just as I was thinking to myself, "What could possibly go wrong on a day like this?" something did.

Babashum stopped abruptly. Somewhat perplexed by this most uncharacteristic behavior, we stopped too.

Sniffing the air and darting looks right and left, Babashum hopped over a pile of debris and sniffled his way toward a spot he seemed to think was an important place to be. There, he kicked up a sizable cloud of dry mountain dust and cocked his head like a little lion. To his apparent glee, this move prompted a fierce eruption of snapping and woofing sounds from a group of large, mean-looking mongrels basking in the sun about a thousand yards away. Babashum then raised his right leg and released two or three bullish squirts of urine at which point those dogs crossed that thousand yards in what seemed less than a few seconds.

What happened next was disturbingly traumatic. It was the kind of shocking ordeal that can usually only be grappled with in retrospect, since, as it occurs, perception itself seems paralyzed. For me, in my distress, some sort of psychological mechanism took over to scoot my awareness away, as if forward in time, to witness the violent misfortune taking place like it was a memory of an event that had already happened. From that protected vantage point, I was able to observe the drama with some degree of dispassion.

Later, each of us remembered a different version of what had happened. When we were called upon to describe the event, some of us said there were five dogs. Some said four. But we all agreed on one thing: Babashum saw them coming and didn't flinch.

When it was all over, Babashum was just lying there. He wasn't dead, but he was close. And he was bleeding badly. The worst wounds were on his head, neck and legs. He tried to get up, but couldn't. We started to move him, but didn't.

A woman walked up from a nearby house to offer us what looked like a horse blanket. We covered our wounded warrior with the blanket and thanked the lady graciously. Otherwise, we said nothing.

Two of us stayed with Babashum while the others went back to the monastery for the Citroen. Fifteen minutes later, we were driving to Carson City. One of the monks was holding Babashum, cradled in a

19

towel wet with fresh blood.

The Carson City Vet rolled his eyes and shook his head when he saw Babashum. It was like he had been expecting us and was wondering why we were late. Even his assistants seemed to be just standing there waiting for us. We hadn't called ahead.

The doctor had us lay Babashum on a high table covered with a clean plastic sheet. Without saying a word, he immediately got to work. A lady at the front desk asked one of us to sign some paperwork. As I watched from the side, I noticed a record sheet with Babashum's name listed on it over and over. The girl who had helped us bring Babashum in from the car noticed me looking and said with a smile that Babashum had the longest "rap sheet" of any dog they had ever treated. There was a tinge of pride in her voice. After about fifteen minutes, the doctor came out and told us he would have to keep Babashum for a while. So we drove home to Virginia City.

As we arrived back at the monastery, Gurudeva was preparing to go to the airport. He asked about Babashum. We said he would live. He replied, "Probably not for long."

I remember thinking that Gurudeva seemed remarkably unemotional in a way that seemed somehow appropriate. It was like he cared, but not past a certain point.

When Gurudeva was ready to go, we pulled the car around front for him and loaded three small bags into the trunk. One monk had been chosen to travel with Gurudeva back to Kauai. It was going to be a long flight with a brief stop in San Francisco where some family devotees would be meeting Gurudeva for a quick coffee at the airport. No one ever wanted to miss a chance to talk with Gurudeva.

Just as the car was pulling out, Gurudeva rolled his window down and said, quoting his spiritual teacher, Satguru Yogaswami, "No coming, no going." After a pause, he added, "All is always fine deep within where there is no coming, no going—just stillness. Be still. Be aware. Be the soul you are. The soul is perfect and cannot die, nor can it be harmed. From the perspective of the soul, the external mind looks like the dream that it is."

With that, he slowly and gracefully raised his large right hand in a final good-bye wave as the car drifted off. We stood for a moment, forgetting Babashum's plight, the icy Nevada winds and our own petty difficulties in adjusting to a monastic life of moderate austerity.

As I look back now, I can see what I couldn't see then: Those brief messages of precious insight from Gurudeva during what he called "psychological moments" were important. They helped us stretch our yoga from a periodic practice to an all-encompassing lifestyle.

We bought Babashum back to the monastery two days later. He was all patched up, more or less. The doctor told us to keep him as still as possible—not an easy task. In about ten days, we took him back down to Carson City to have some sixty or seventy stitches taken out.

After that, Babashum didn't run with us any more. Actually, he couldn't run at all. He had to just stay at home.

The Last Stand

Babashum's battles were not over. The local dogs who hated him now sensed his defenselessness and slowly moved in for a kill. Although they were crafty stalkers and scarily quiet, we knew something was about to happen. The nightly barking was no longer as distant and there were new sounds in the sage near the monastery. Sensing danger, we built a doghouse for Babashum's protection.

Finally, one evening around nine o'clock, the hellish sound of attacking dogs broke the night silence like a crack of thunder. We all rushed out the back door of the monastery, screaming at the top of our lungs and flailing flashlights. The intruding dogs bounded off into the night without a fight. Although they had not harmed Babashum, they had gotten dangerously close.

Babashum gave limped chase to the retreating dogs for about 20 or 30 feet. "That's right, you guys," he seemed to be yelping menacingly, all riled for a fight." You want a piece of me? You know where I live. I'll be waiting."

With a little work, we got Babashum inside. One of the monks made a bed for him in the kitchen where it was warm. Slowly, he settled down enough for us to be able to get some sleep. The next day, we built a fence around the doghouse so Babashum could go outside safely. Some time passed without incident. We went on with our life.

About a month later, I woke up around three in the morning for no apparent reason. There was an eerie feeling in the air, as if I had just had a nightmare. But I hadn't. Also there was no wind. Strange. There was always wind on top of our mountain.

I got out of bed, walked around, went to the kitchen and drank some water. Something was wrong. I just knew it. I went into the living room where there was a rug on the floor and plenty of space to do some stretching exercises. After moving through a series of simple hatha yoga positions, I returned to my sleeping mat, thinking I was relaxed enough to get perhaps an hour of sleep before dawn.

Just as I was about to dose off, I thought I caught a glimpse of Babashum to my right. Yet, when I aimed my flashlight in that direction, I saw nothing. Unsettled and fretful, I lay there on my back staring up at the ceiling. The room was now filling with the soft, red/orange glow of sunrise. Impulsively, I decided to take a walk. As I put on my coat, a cloud of depression descended upon me. I wondered why. As I went outside, all was quiet—too quiet.

Babashum wasn't immediately visible, but this wasn't unusual. He was most probably in his little hut, I thought to myself. As I started to walk down the path that led away from the backside of our monastery, I noticed the door to Babashum's fenced-in yard was open. It looked like it had been knocked loose from the inside. I went in to check his hut. It was empty. I looked around briefly. There was no sign of violence.

Just then, another monk appeared in the back door of the ashram. He looked at me with his hands in his pockets and asked, "How's our Babashum?" Before I could reply, he saw in my face that something was not quite right.

After trading worried theories as to what happened, the two of us began a methodical search for Babashum, starting from the monastery and working our way out into the surrounding terrain. As the other monks saw what we were doing, they joined in.

In about twenty minutes, we found Babashum up on a hill some two thousand yards from his fenced-in doghouse. There had been a fight—a bad one. This time, the warrior had not survived.

Although the ground was hard as a rock from the cold, we dug a grave right then and there. It took at least 45 minutes. Because of the frozen earth, it was difficult work. We had to take turns digging.

I found an old wood-burning tool in the mail room and etched "Here lies Babashum, the Warrior" on a small board which we nailed onto the unpointed end of a fence post. Even that post was difficult to hammer into the ground.

Eventually, a friend of ours, who worked for a local cemetery, carved a headstone for us. Its simple wording read: "Babashum, the Great—1961-1971."

Babashum's death cloaked the monastery in a somber pall for about a week. We talked little, joked less and went about our work rather mechanically. It wasn't like we were mourning Babashum's passing. We weren't. We had been taught and we truly believed that the life of that which dies is deathless.

What stunned us about Babashum's savage demise was the raw brutality and apparent mercilessness of his killers. The whole affair had forced us to adopt a rather stoic look at life, a look that did not elicit philosophical reflection. One of the monks said, most unpoetically, "I don't mind dying, I just don't want to see it coming."

When we talked with Gurudeva about all this, he surprised us with one of his typically untypical replies. "Don't you live in an animal body?" he asked. "You have the capacity to understand exactly what those dogs did, for there is only one instinctive nature, which we all share. Haven't you all felt hunger, thirst, greed, hatred, anger, fear, lust and jealousy? Before we realize the Self, we must realize life and all life has to offer.

"Babashum's departure is a lesson offering an understanding of karma. His loss of his body marks a debt paid for deeds done. Now, he's a little wiser. We're always learning from life, even after death."

This prompted some discussion about karma and reincarnation. When one of the monks ramified off track and asked one of those many unanswerable "Why?" questions, Gurudeva responded by answering another question of his own instead. He was good at this.

"How can we purposely resolve karma?" Gurudeva inquired. "Our external, conscious mind has a knack of not being able to learn from the experiences of life, which is why these experiences have to get repeated again and again. By simply not allowing ourselves the luxury of having an emotional reaction to an experience, we provide intuition with a graceful moment of quiet clarity to do what it does best. Then, any lessons we are meant to learn become self-evident, and the experience no longer needs to be repeated. The resolution of all karmas is

23

finalized in intuitive knowing. Intuition does not need much help. It just needs a quiet moment—a chance to get through. Also, intuition does not conflict with reason. It's just a little quicker and a lot simpler."

About three months after Babashum died, we bought an adorable hound dog we named Madika. "Madika" means something in Shum— I've forgotten what. That dog was the sweetest, dopiest thing I had ever seen. We couldn't help but love him. And he was as gentle as a lamb.

Shortly after we purchased Madika, Gurudeva gave him away. When I finally got up the nerve to ask Gruudeva why he did this, his reply was, "Babashum can't be replaced."

The Flip Side of Formal

We all loved how Gurudeva would always let us speak first during almost any conversation we had with him. We also liked how he really listened when we talked. We could tell he listened by the way he responded to us when he finally spoke. What he had to say always came across in a relevant way, forever in context with our concerns rather than his. Over time, we came to realize this sort of friendly interaction was a significant aspect of his unique teaching method. It was the informal flip side of his formal yoga instruction. We called it his "live yoga."

One day, a monk was sitting with Gurudeva talking extensively about the difficulties he was having in controlling emotion. When he finally ran out of words, he asked Gurudeva for some advice.

"Cultivate affectionate detachment," Gurudeva said. "Detachment yields observation. Observation unfolds knowledge. Knowledge motivates right action. Right action doesn't run on emotion. It walks with intelligence."

"But it's so difficult to be detached in the midst of emotion," the monk replied, stating the obvious.

"Practice detachment when you are not emotional," Gurudeva said. "Then, you'll be less inclined to get emotional in the first place. Once you have developed a habit of being detached when it's easy, you'll find yourself more naturally inclined toward being detached when it is difficult. And you'll be able to see emotion coming. This foresight will provide you with the opportunity to choose with insight how to deal with emotion as it arrives—or even before it arrives."

"But what do I do when I am so right in the middle of a powerful emotion I can't even think straight?" the monk asked.

"Just stop. Don't say anything. Don't do anything."

"What if there's something that should be said or done?" the monk asked bluntly.

"Nothing needs to be said or done when you're in the midst of a powerful emotion. Whatever apparently needs to happen at that point can happen later better. By simply stopping yourself, you avoid the creation of what would most certainly be a negative karma. Don't worry. This waiting won't have to last long. Emotions are short-lived. Soon enough, you'll have a clear enough head to say or do the right thing."

"Easier said than done," the monk said, almost without thinking.

"Certainly it is. But self-restraint is an acquired skill you can cultivate by will. The first thing to focus upon developing is willpower, then observation."

"Observation?"

"To observe something, we have to get separate from it. Isn't it true others often see us more clearly than we see ourselves? They can see us like this because they have separation—detachment. If we could see ourselves as others see us, we would have the detachment necessary to be observant, wise, moral and unemotional. Suddenly, a whole slew of fine character traits would just fall into place—all through the cultivation of willpower first, then observation."

Shum

Our monastic day began at six in the morning when we gathered in our meditation hall for *lilisim* (*Shum* chanting).

This meditation hall was the biggest room in the monastery—about forty square feet of mostly Zen-empty space, featuring nothing but an *mdimrehm* hanging on the front wall.

"Mdimrehm" is the *Shum* word for anything round designated as a symbol of the Self within. The *mdimrehm* in our meditation hall was a flat golden disc about four feet in diameter and three inches thick.

The meditation hall was also where we slept. When we woke up in the morning, the first thing we did was store our bedding out of sight so this sacred place would look like the vast inner space it was supposed to exemplify.

Our chanting system was "call and response," meaning a leader would call out a chant and the followers would repeat it back. Because I had previous musical training, I was given the responsibility of leading *lilisim*, even though I was a young monk.

As I chanted, I played a percussion instrument I designed and constructed myself. This instrument—the monks called it "the rack"—consisted of four pieces of bamboo, each approximately three feet in length and two to four inches in diameter, lashed onto a rectangular frame built so that its surface plane faced me at a 45-degree angle. The four legs of this "rack" were cut to a height that would allow me to sit on the floor with my folded legs tucked comfortably underneath the structure as I played. The four pieces of bamboo were positioned horizontally and parallel, about three inches apart, from the bottom of the angled surface plane to the top.

Our *lilisim* chants consisted of simple but meaningful *Shum* sentences with words, called "portraits," that fell together in a pleasing rhythm. A typical chant would look something like this:

> *reh-vum-si-reh-li* • *mim* • *moo-ni-si-a-ka* •
> *ka-li-ba-sa* • *sim-shum-bi-si* • *a-oo-si-si-oom* •

The meaning of this particular chant is: Let go of external concerns step by step (*rehvumsirehli*) as you go within yourself (*mim*) and become immersed in a love for all of mankind (*moonisiaka*) while you control the breath (*kalibasa*) and feel the power of the spine (*simshumbisi*) as well as the primal force of life at the spine's core (*aoosisioom*).

Often after chanting, we would sit for a long time in the power of the residual vibration we had just stimulated. On mornings like this, we might spend two hours in the temple. This would put our breakfast at about eight o'clock, allowing us to start our workday around 8:30.

At 11:00 we would stop work to practice hatha yoga in preparation for *shumnam* (a guided *Shum* meditation), which began at noon. These meditation sessions were usually led by the most senior monk present. His duty was to call out *Shum* portraits artistically rendered in two large meditation maps hung on the front wall of the meditation hall on either side of the *mdimrehm*.

26

One of these meditation maps was called *mamsani*. The other, *mambashum*. There were 12 *mamsani* in all, one for each of the 12 months of the year, and 52 *mambashum*, one for each week of the year. The *mamsani* were changed every month—the *mambashum*, every week. All of these *mamsani* and *mambashum* were composed by Gurudeva as examples of maps we were encouraged to create for ourselves.

Each meditation map included graceful lines, signifying awareness flowing, that connected *Shum* portraits, representing "areas of mind," that were laid out in a sequence designating a step-by-step journey from the outer world of mundane concerns to the inner world of bliss and peace. The idea was for the meditator to follow the lines of flowing awareness from one area to the next until he or she arrived at a final destination. Gurudeva instructed us to meditate on these maps both alone and as a group.

Gurudeva saw great value in group meditation. As he put it, "the group helps the individual and the individual helps the group."

One of my favorite *mambashum* laid out a journey that encouraged awareness to flow from *kalibasa* (breath control) to *karehana* (the power of emotion) to *vumtyeoodi* (the power of thought) to *simshumbisi* (the power of the spine) to *tyebabalingna* (inner bliss) to *oonalisiam* (the totality of all manifestation felt as a oneness) to *kaif* (awareness aware of itself) to *ikaif* (sustained awareness aware of itself) to *imkaif* (the absence of awareness also known as Nirvikalpa Samadhi).

The overall meaning of this meditation map might be expressed in the following way: "Strive to use breath control to flow awareness from emotion to thought, then to the balance of emotion and thought, which can be most easily felt in the center of the spine. From the center of the spine, flow awareness into the bliss of *being*, and from the bliss of *being* into a sense of the oneness of all that exists. In this grand sense of oneness, strive to remain aware of being aware until there is finally a merging with Self."

We learned a lot from Gurudeva and his *Shum*. "Lesson one" was simple: *Spiritual illumination marks the culmination of a long, steady, dedicated and persistent spiritual effort.*

Yes, we all had trouble adjusting to this requirement of patience in spiritual life. Even though, in this adjustment, we found a firm seat in a contemplative nature that wasn't burdened with an ego's insatiable desire for a sense of accomplishment. This contemplative nature, we all eventually discovered, was the thing to "get." It was the getting that made all other getting effortless.

After meditation, we would have lunch, usually a simple meal of soup or stew and salad. Then we would continue working. At 5:30, we would stop to prepare for *lilisim* at six.

Our evening chanting session was not usually as long as the one in the morning, although sometimes we got inspired enough to chant late into the night. We were freer in the evenings. That was when we could compose new chants and experiment with alternative rhythms.

Evening meals were less formal. The food was usually served buffet-style with six or seven raw fruits and vegetables to choose from. Monks could and would get inventive in the preparation of this last meal of the day. Some would fry seeds, slice open an avocado or heat up leftovers from lunch. Others would throw together fruit or vegetable salads. Breads and dairy products were rarely made available.

We were vegetarians following an eating plan we called "Nutrition for Meditation." On this program we tried to eat one-third fruits, one-third vegetables and one-third nuts and seeds. Grains and dairy products were treats. Everything was as organic as possible.

We did a lot of fasting. Water fasts. Juice fasts. Fruit fasts. These fasts lasted for three or nine days—occasionally longer. We didn't eat at all on Fridays, a day considered holy to Hindus. Actually, our Friday fast began on Thursday after lunch and continued on through to six pm on Friday when we enjoyed a feast of edibles not usually available during the week.

This Friday-evening feast, which we all looked forward to with great anticipation, was called the "brother's meeting." Although a great many wonderful discussions occurred during those brother's meetings, what I remember most was the food.

Inner Friends

While I was living in the Virginia City monastery, Gurudeva had a number of clairvoyant visions during which he saw our ashram building burning down. Because these visions were occurring repeatedly, he had us stop sleeping in our upstairs shrine room, which was technically our attic. Although there was never any apparent danger of fire that we could see, we never questioned Gurudeva's judgement. Still, I wondered what all those visions meant. I wondered until about 15 years later when—some two months after we sold our Virginia City property—the building that was our ashram burned to the ground.

Gurudeva was born with psychic abilities. With the auspicious assistance of a number of qualified teachers, he was able to intelligently recognize and wisely develop these abilities early in life.

One of the first principles conveyed to him by one of his first teachers was starkly direct: *You were born on this Earth to realize the Self. Life has no other purpose.* Another fundamental principle he was taught early was that *any psychic skills developed should be applied only in benevolent kindness and for good purpose—but never overtly.*

When new students were just getting to know Gurudeva around the time I was in Virginia City, they would often ask him for occult training. Needless to say, many were disappointed with his reply.

"The first goal of yoga should be the full realization of your truest Self," Gurudeva would say unapologetically. "After that, clairaudience and clairvoyance can come as needed and of their own accord. Until then, they are but side-tracks on the mystic's path."

When clairaudience and clairvoyance arrived in Gurudeva's life "as needed and of their own accord" after he realized the Self, he worked to intentionally develop them. These two skills were not his friends. They were his business partners. And they never hesitated to come looking for him on business.

Even though we fully and happily accepted the pursuit of Self Realization as our first priority in yoga and life, we were thrilled to be present with Gurudeva at a "*deva* reading," a channeling session during which Gurudeva received dictation from non-physical entities.

Witnessing one of these *deva* readings was a mystical experience in itself. Right before a "reading" began, the *devas* who wanted to speak would announce their impending arrival by sending Gurudeva identification codes consisting of specific sounds and colors that had been set up by these *devas* when they first established their working relationship with Gurudeva. A different code, or no code, would expose the presence of an entity or entities with whom Gurudeva had not yet become acquainted.

29

From start to finish, a *deva* reading was *deva* controlled. "These communications are always one-way," Gurudeva explained, "We don't decide when the *devas* will come or what they will talk about. They do. Beware of psychics who claim to be able to arbitrarily turn their inner communication on and off."

Everyone in the room would know when a *deva* transmission was about to occur. The atmosphere would suddenly vibrate with a sense of potency. Yet, there would also be a lighthearted playfulness.

The *devas* dictated their messages in three or four word phrases, separated by two or three seconds of silence. Gurudeva would then say these phrases aloud so a designated person present, acting as a scribe, could write them down. The scribe was usually a monk.

"This system short-circuits the intellect," Gurudeva would tell us. "Otherwise, the message can get distorted by second-guessing."

I was quite often a scribe during these *deva* readings. While they were occurring, I must admit, I did indeed try to mentally assemble the continuity of the broken sentences being transmitted. I can't remember ever having been successful at this. Invariably, when I read back the dictation later, I realized I had not even gotten close to understanding what was actually being said.

To further cloak the essence of messages coming through, the first words spoken were often almost frivolous if not meaningless, as in the affable banter of two friends setting a stage for conversation.

On March 21, 1987, according to my diary, I scribbled down the following beginning of a *deva* reading: "Joy and sorrow ... pleasure and pain ... are happy together ... they are the same ... from a riddle ... in the middle ... of life now ... as well as then ... catch us when ... and if you can ... and ... we start again. The day is done ... you've had your fun ... the night has won ... a new dawn. This year is ... the wake-up. Last year was ... the shake-up."

Once into serious messaging, the *devas* would dictate valuable information on a variety of topics from accounting to construction to monastery management to abstract philosophy. Like Gurudeva's many insights, *deva* readings were always original.

Change

I had the good fortune to meet Gurudeva in person *after* I had absorbed his instruction that a high-minded love of stoic aloneness and a healthy appreciation for self-confidence and fortitude were necessary to practice the type of yoga he taught through commands like, "Lean on your own spine," or "Realize the Self, yourself." By the time I decided to become a monk, I was ready—or at least I thought I was ready—to live in a cave, lean on my spine and realize the Self within.

Yet, in Gurudeva's physical company, I was overwhelmed—as were we all—by the sheer magnitude of his presence. As wonderful as this was, it was also disconcerting. Around him, it was all too easy to lean more on his spine than mine.

This became readily apparent to me when I realized that much of my initial adjustment to monastic life was going to require not getting closer to Gurudeva, but rather getting away from him. I could see I needed to get away from Gurudeva at least enough to separate short-term fascination from long-term motivation.

For me, Virginia City was the perfect place to get this done. It was a supreme testing ground. Because Gurudeva wasn't there much, there was only the yoga and the work—day after day after day.

While I was in Virginia City, five of my monastic brothers left the order. As each one of these fine young men departed, another one came to take his place. And I began to see repeating patterns of adjustment as I watched each newcomer cope with the unyielding protocol of monasticism in the harsh austerity of a cold, winter mountain. Although this necessary adaptation was easier for some than others, it was undeniably difficult for all.

In this monastic scenario, I happened upon a bit of practical and valuable wisdom: The more difficulty I could understand indirectly through an observation of others, the less of that difficulty I would have to deal with directly myself.

Even for those who were able to set their minds in commitment to the monastic life we were living, there were significant challenges. We all learned, for instance, that habit hates change, and living a life so different from the life we had lived before was all about change.

Enduring such change was less noticeable if our infatuation with the new at least slightly outweighed our distaste for modifying the old.

31

Unfortunately, as the novelty of living this life wore off, we all—sooner or later—had to come to grips with the fact that we could not avoid the necessity of stoically adjusting past patterns of living in dedication to *a spirituality not yet realized.*

Finally, for those of us who stayed, there came a moment difficult to pinpoint—like the precise instant a headache goes away—when we realized we were angst-free. When I finally arrived at this blissful place of contentment and adjustment in Virginia City, it was time to move again. This time, it was back to San Francisco, where—just as anywhere—"change was the only permanent reality."

The books we had been printing were not selling as well as we had hoped, and we had over-extended ourselves in marketing expenses. Also the monastic order was growing, we were renting more property in San Francisco, and our new monastery in Hawaii was in much need of expensive building, maintenance and repair. In short, we needed money. Hence, most of the monks in Kauai and all of the monks in Virginia City were moved in mass to San Francisco to work as waiters.

The plan was for us to shut down the Virginia City monastery and press only long enough to build up our other two centers. As it turned out, however, we never again used the Nevada property as a long-term residence for the monks, even though we didn't sell it for another fifteen years. Except for hosting a very occasional Himalayan Academy yoga retreat or seminar, that old building's only function was to represent a long American history that now included us.

Picking Up the Pace

It felt like moving from one extreme to another—this abrupt transition from the barren austerity of the cold Nevada mountains to the bustling vivaciousness of a place known to some as America's hippest city. There I was, back in San Francisco. The two years I had spent in the monastic order seemed like two lifetimes.

Like a mystic sorcerer, Gurudeva was forever blooming something out of nothing. His masterpiece-in-progress was Saiva Siddhanta Church. Not a day went by that he didn't tweak its development in some ingeniously creative fashion.

Soon, like a healthy child swelling into a strong young man, the

32

church was growing up with a life of its own. Its land, buildings and publications formed its body. Its monks were its living blood; and its ancient yoga philosophy was its substance and message.

Because we monks—all of us, young and old—were viewed as representatives of this flourishing church, we had to live with a sense of responsibility that mostly obliterated any potential for the development of petty concerns and personal problems. This was a good thing. Yet, in all of the high-profile activity that got stimulated by all this healthy growth, I couldn't help but wonder, "Where is the time for in-depth meditation in all of this?"

As the years rolled by, those of us who remained in the monastic order learned and re-learned that questions like this were usually asked by monks working to get Gurudeva fitted to their program rather than their program fitted to Gurudeva. Yet still, I must admit in all honesty, I kept wondering, "Where is the time for in-depth meditation in all this?"

In March of 1973, our monastery in San Francisco consisted of three properties. The first of these properties was at 3575 Sacramento Street where the monks who came before me had transformed an old store into a temple.

The second property, purchased a little later, was just around the corner at 436 Locust Street. The apartment building on this property was where the monks lived.

I don't think the third property had an address. It was located at the center of the city block formed at one corner by the crossing of Locust and Sacramento streets. This third property, with its adorably obscure little two-story dwelling that had no street entrance, sat amidst its own garden in a fort-like bubble of protection afforded by buildings tightly surrounding it on all four sides.

This lovable, little hobbit-house was a grand marvel of early San Francisco architecture built more than a hundred years before at some remote location, then moved to this spot before the buildings now around it were constructed. Because it could only be approached from the outside through the two other buildings we owned, it was wonderfully private. We called this secret place our Mamadi Ashram. *Mamadi* is a *Shum* term of endearment meaning "spiritual teacher."

Although Mamadi Ashram was primarily Gurudeva's cozy San Francisco home, it was also our refuge from the world.

Tough Monks

All but a few of the long-time, San Francisco, resident monks had spent most or all of their monastery years working in the city's most famous restaurants. Their reputations preceded them. Aside from being exceptional waiters, they were a tough, no-nonsense crew of durable yogis who could go with little sleep, work long hours and still sit like a rock for a two-hour meditation. Gurudeva referred to them as our "front ranks."

It would not be an exaggeration to say I was intimidated—not only by these resilient city monks but also by the Silent Ministry program itself. The way it was described to the six of us newbie's arriving from Virginia City, the "silent ministry" of waitering sounded like a survival-of-the fittest war of wills.

In the foyer of our 436 Locust Street apartment building, there was this five-foot-square blackboard, crisscrossed with painted white lines forming a vast spreadsheet of rows and columns. All the public names of the Silent Ministry monks were scribbled out in chalk down the left side of this board.

I say "public names" because each of us had two names. One name was for the monastery; the other was for the restaurant. Neither of these names was the one we were given at birth. My legally changed, monastery name was Muni Natarajan and my (fictitious) restaurant or public name was Frank.

The person listed at the top of this silent ministry blackboard was the monk who had earned the most tip money during the previous week. Just under him was the next highest earner. And so on down the board it went to the lowest of the low earners.

The dates of the days of the week were scrawled across the top of the blackboard. Each day, each monk had to tally his tips and write that figure on the blackboard by his name under the appropriate date. The hierarchal list of monks would be rearranged every Sunday, according to each monk's total earnings for the previous week.

It was made abundantly clear to us that a high placement on the blackboard scorecard was important. Such placement, it was strongly implied, indicated an admirable application of will in the performance of duty and a successful dispensation of silent ministry blessings.

I later learned that Gurudeva never sanctioned the strong sense of competition naturally generated by this approach. In fact, as time went on, he would openly condemn competition, in any form it took, as a major deterrent on the spiritual path. But that time was not now.

The monk who was assigned the task of hosting the six of us was the "Silent Ministry Coordinator." As our host, it was his duty to make us as comfortable as possible in the monastery. As our Silent Ministry Coordinator, it was his duty to get us "started" in the restaurants.

With regard to acquiring a job as a waiter, this Silent Ministry Coordinator encouraged us to follow a "sink or swim" approach. As he explained it, we were to walk boldly into a restaurant and ask to speak to the owner or manager. If we were fortunate enough to get an audience with either of these people, we were encouraged to confidently ask for a job while avoiding too much discussion, since the more we talked the more we were likely to reveal our lack of training and experience.

If we got the job, our first night at work would show our bluff, at which point we would either be angrily fired on the spot or compassionately kept on as "a young fellow of sincerity worthy of training." All of this was referred to as "getting over the hump." After getting over this hump, we were to keep moving on to better and better restaurants, one after another, until we hit the best, whatever or wherever that "best" was. Lastly, we were strongly encouraged to remain "incognito," which in this context meant not revealing our identities as monks.

Shellshock

On my first day of job hunting, I was turned down eleven times. On the second day, I got lucky—with a little help from a friend. I was hired at a small place called Dario's Pizza, only because I was recommended to Dario himself by one of the monks who had previously worked there and had done well.

I showed up an hour early for my first dinner shift at Dario's. It was my faint hope that, with a little extra time, I might perhaps be able to put together a working plan that would get me through the night. Dario's wife was trying to be helpful in this regard. Had I been even a slightly experienced waiter, her extensive advice would have been of great benefit. As it was, however, she may as well have been talking another language. After a point, I just couldn't follow her.

"Everything works best with a plan," she was telling me. "It's

35

simple. Gang up your pizza orders, then sort them in the kitchen so you can get—oh, say, for instance—cheese before sausage. That's easier on the cooks. For your faster orders, you've got time to get beer from the bar to the table first thing, but not mixed drinks. You've got to go back for those. With the wine, you are on your own. It's in the back of the kitchen if it's cold. The red's outside on the shelf. If you've got a pasta like spaghetti or linguini, try to time the wine, but only if there's cocktails first. This wine thing works best if the pasta chef is not too busy. Otherwise you just have to play it by ear. If worse comes to worse, the cook will ding. Remember, one ding is for Dario, two is for me and three is for you."

Somewhere back there around getting "beer from the bar to the table" was where I got lost. I did, however, catch the instruction that I was three dings.

Even before the restaurant opened, people were lined up around the block waiting to get in. I had no idea Dario's was so popular.

There was no way I could have been prepared for what took place when those doors to hell opened. From the moment the first herd of hungry people stormed the tables at six pm until the last party was ushered out drunk around midnight, absolutely nothing happened like it was supposed to. It was chaos.

When it was all over, Dario was unbelievably polite as he paid me for the evening and fired me. "You're a nice guy," he said. "But I'll be honest with you. Tonight was really rough and I don't ever want to go through anything like that again."

He wished me well and encouraged me to "drop back by" when I had a little more experience. I looked around for his wife so I could apologize for my countless flounderings. Alas, she was not to be found. Dario smiled and calmly reassured me, "She's back there some place recovering." The main cook nodded his farewell to me through the open kitchen door. He was beaming a big grin, ear to ear, as if he'd just been told a very funny joke.

While I was standing out in the street, waiting for a city bus to haul me back to the monastery, I tried to reflect on what had just taken place. It was difficult. Everything was such a blur. All I could actually recall was hearing those three dings over and over until Dario finally told me, "Just clear the tables." Even as a bus pulled up and I climbed on, I was still in a daze, thinking to myself, "This must be what shellshock is like."

The next day I went downtown to a place called John's Grill and got a job right away. I told the restaurant manager I had absolutely no experience and had just been fired from a pizza place. He looked at me for a moment and smiled. "Are you willing to be trained?" he asked. I said, "Yes." He said, "Okay." And I went to work that afternoon.

I was learning a lot in San Francisco. Like Virginia City, it was a testing ground, but one of a different sort. In Virginia City, we were allowed unlimited access to a contemplative life. In San Francisco, we were provided unprotected exposure to its opposite. The Virginia City test determined the measure of our ability to "detach awareness" in meditation. The San Francisco test revealed our true capacity to remain effectively detached in dealing with the challenges of gut-level life. By this testing of our nature at two extremes, the quality of our character and the degree of our commitment became obvious.

Forced to Pray

It is all too true that, when I arrived in San Francisco, the monks there seemed cold and harsh. Yet as I lived that life for a while and began to develop those qualities myself, I finally had to concede that our tough demeanor was an eccentric's protective shield. Yes, we were eccentric — according to the folks we worked with in the restaurant. Those folks thought that a bunch of guys living together, practicing yoga or what-ever, and trying to keep their life a secret, was at least eccentric.

In this aloneness that we imposed upon ourselves, I eventually managed to discover "affectionate detachment." "Affectionate detach-ment" was a phrase Gurudeva often used to describe a dispassionate objectivity inspired not by disdain but by love and respect. As I began to find this particular objectivity within myself, I was also able to see it more clearly in my brother monks — especially those more senior.

At their best, these seasoned monastics exuded an inspiring sense of unforced calm. Without apparent effort, they carried a certain stillness that in turn carried them. Of these monks, Gurudeva said, "they move in the eye of a hurricane."

Yet, with all this obvious development of affectionate detach-

37

ment and with all of Gurudeva's harping on the fundamental importance of monks being sensitive, refined and humble, there was still a decidedly unmonkly spirit of aggressive competitiveness pervading the monastery that I just could not ignore. To one degree or another, we were all pushing ourselves to get a high placement on that Silent Ministry blackboard. And most of our tactics in this effort were anything but contemplative. Bluffing, bulldogging and even lying our way into waitering jobs was a questionable practice, and hopping from one restaurant to another just for the sake of making more money was at least unethical. Yet we were all learning, learning from our successes *and* our failures.

There were also temptations. Although it would be inappropriate for me to share other monk's close encounters of the enticing kind, I can say something about my own. But only a little.

I was bewitched more than once by the look and allure of some particularly beautiful women and, several times, came close to following my sexual urges—but didn't. I attribute my fortitude in this resistance to the fortunate fact that, during my time as a waiter, I was still under the spell of my original inspiration to be a monk.

Gurudeva was a master of getting out of the way so that life could be our teacher, if such was necessary. The development of the church and the monastery offered infinite possibilities for the monks to work with and learn from Gurudeva in creative efforts that bore the possibility of being mutually beneficial for all involved. As Gurudeva worked with us in this way, he would initiate a creative project in principle, then step back to let us work it out in practice. He gave us opportunities to make mistakes, recover, and in that recovering, grow.

Through all of this, we all spent some time "facing ourselves." Usually, when Gurudeva told a monk he must now "face himself," it came across as a bit of a grim proclamation. "Facing ourselves" most often followed getting ourselves into a situation or a series of situations that demanded our admission and correction of personal weaknesses we were previously unable or unwilling to admit or "face."

For me, my first months in San Francisco stimulated a lot of self facing. I often experienced loneliness, fear, humiliation and depression. Most of this stemmed from a dread of venturing into something new.

To make matters worse, I was also having to admit to myself that I had become at least as competitive as everyone else, if not more so, and that all of my secret criticisms of others were more accurately true about myself. Through all of this, I was uncontrollably coughing up memories of the competitiveness I had felt and acted upon when I was working as a professional musician. I had to see in myself a malicious aggressiveness that wanted to win at all costs. I had to witness in myself my own creation of an ego, hard, cold and proud.

Fortunately, all of this eventually passed. After about six months, I was fully adjusted to our city monastery and was living its life with some degree of balanced contentment.

In Virginia City our daily schedule was pliable. In San Francisco, it was not. In San Francisco, the restaurants ruled our days and nights, and each monk was bound to a different timetable. To find an hour when all of the residents of the monastery could meet together as a group was virtually impossible. This meant any sort of consistent, daily regime of yoga practice had to occur individually.

To accommodate this scheduling challenge, Gurudeva established what he called a "one-hour vigil," which was to be performed once a day, every day, by each monk individually, as his restaurant schedule allowed. This one-hour vigil consisted of twenty minutes of study, ten minutes of *pranayama* or breath control and thirty minutes of meditation. In addition to this vigil, we were also expected to practice at least 30 minutes of hatha yoga and 30 minutes of physical exercise. Each monk also had about an hour's worth of daily monastery chores.

I did my vigil at night, midway through sleep—whenever that sleep occurred. This rather fanatical approach was my attempt to establish some semblance of a consistent meditation routine in a forever fluctuating daily life. Although it was a bit unorthodox, Gurudeva seemed to like it. He even said it showed "good spirit."

During these early years of monastic life, I was performing a lot of extra meditation—not because I loved it, but because, somehow, I felt it was fundamentally necessary. Although I fully trusted that Gurudeva had me well positioned on a spiritual path, some hidden part of me kept throwing up thoughts and feelings I could not understand. Within this private angst, I felt a great need for deep introspection. Unfortunately, I just couldn't seem to introspect enough. "Why can't meditation give me more of what I'm really looking for?" I kept asking myself.

After a while, I decided, if I could not extract some recognizable degree of satisfaction from the *results* of my meditation, I should at least be able to gain some solace from a consistency in my *approach* to meditation. Yet even a regimentation of practice seemed to leave me lacking what I wanted.

The *idea* of regimentation felt great. I just couldn't seem to land on a practice worth regimenting. As my mood changed, so did my yoga routine. As my routine vacillated, so did my faith.

I had this sense of there being a one way—a best way—even if that one, best way should perhaps be different for each person. After relentlessly mulling this over for some time, I was starting to think my dream of a one supreme system was just that, a dream—just another one of my erroneous preconceptions.

During several conversations I had with Gurudeva about this, however, I was assured such was not the case.

"There is a one way for you," Gurudeva said. "Just because you can't define it in a neat, clean set of words doesn't mean it's not there. It's there waiting for you right now. Just be alert and sensitive. You're looking for something that cannot be written in a book."

Although this assurance gave me confidence, it forced me to change my approach to inner life. The only obvious option I could then see as I tried to be "alert and sensitive" was to pray. So, I switched gears. For a while at least, open-minded prayer became my "one way."

Our 3575 Sacramento Street Hindu temple was dedicated to Lord Ganesha. In Hindu mythology, Ganesha is the son of Siva. With His elephant head, full belly and playful manner, this good god of sweet benevolence and grace is the one Hindu deity that is worshipped at all times by all Hindus, regardless of their sect. His many attributes make him exceptionally popular. He is helpful like a father, loving like a mother, kind like a friend and responsible like a brother. Because of his immediate availability and his expertise in solving practical problems, his presence is often sought and easily felt. Who couldn't or wouldn't have faith in a deity like this? The need he helped me satisfy now no longer exists. For this alone, I am forever grateful to Lord Ganesha, "the remover of obstacles."

Yogaswami

According to the New Oxford American Dictionary, *yoga* is "a Hindu spiritual and ascetic discipline, a part of which, including breath control, simple meditation, and the adoption of specific bodily postures, is widely practiced for health and relaxation. The yoga widely known in the West is based on hatha yoga, which forms one aspect of the ancient Hindu system of religious and ascetic observance and meditation, the highest form of which is raja yoga and the ultimate aim of which is spiritual purification and self-understanding leading to Samadhi."

Samadhi is defined in the same dictionary as "a state of intense concentration achieved through meditation. In the yoga of Hinduism, this is regarded as the final stage, where union with the divine is reached."

When Gurudeva was born in 1927 in California, the words "yoga" and "Samadhi" were not even in the dictionary. Yet Gurudeva attained his first yogic Samadhi at the age of 22—without the assistance of a teacher perfected in yoga. This was astounding for at least three reasons: 1. At that time in the West, *yoga* and *Samadhi* were obscure concepts at best. And there was little knowledge of how to follow these concepts into practice. 2. Then, as well as today, in the West and the East, the practice of yoga and the attainment of Samadhi were and are considered major accomplishments for even well-trained aspirants. 3. According to ancient Hindu tradition, a first breakthrough into Samadhi is only possible through the grace of an enlightened preceptor.

When I asked Gurudeva how his Self Realization (Samadhi) could have occurred "against all odds," so to speak, he replied, "I was just picking up where I left off in a past life." This was not a complete answer, but it was the best one I ever got.

Gurudeva was first introduced to the yoga of Hinduism at the age of ten. The fundamental depth of this original Hindu yoga so fascinated him that, at the age of 21, he hitched a ride on a freighter to India in search of his lifetime guru. This quest led him to Sri Lanka where he studied with one teacher after another and another until he finally discovered Yogaswami of Jaffna. By that time, he had already attained spiritual illumination in the nearby caves of Jalani.

For the remainder of his life, Gurudeva embraced Hinduism by trying to live it a little more completely every day. For him, this vast tradition—which he acknowledged could never be understood in all of

41

its fullness by a single person in a single lifetime — was a rich source of hands-on wisdom to be used as needed.

Gurudeva was a cautious follower. He was a strong advocate of faith, but not of the blind kind. He always encouraged us — even in following him — to crosscheck everything we absorbed from the outside with intuition we derived from the inside.

"Learn principle and reflect on principle," he said. "Apply the spirit of principle in action. Grow. Let the testimony of your own life be living proof of the efficacy of your faith."

This was the way he taught us to integrate the physical, mental and spiritual dimensions of Hinduism into a yogic lifestyle that would inspire the essence of this faith to blossom "from the inside out."

When Gurudeva was told again and again, "you have to be born a Hindu to be a Hindu," he asked himself, "Is this true?" Intuitively, he sensed it was not. As he suspected, our extensive research discovered no indication that conversion to Hinduism was not possible.

When he was told, "Only men can realize the Self," he asked himself, "Is this true?" After due consideration, he concluded that no such blanket statement could be made, although many young women might not be inclined to seek illumination if they were immersed in raising a family. Research validated this to be true with strong evidence indicating the history of India is replete with famous stories of both younger and older women who were respected as saints because of their selfless service and spiritual illumination.

The Cellar Below and the Parlor above
Learning from Gurudeva, adjusting to monastic life and working in the restaurants were stretching me. Yet there was never a point when these three apparently disparate aspects of our unique monastic program did not seem mutually beneficial. It had always been unquestionably clear to me that Gurudeva was the spiritual teacher I had been looking for, that the monastery provided a framework for putting what I was learning into practice and that the restaurants offered both a fine test of this practice as well as an excellent opportunity to serve.

I was doing well at John's Grill — I think. The staff there was wonderfully patient with me as I awkwardly bumbled my way into the world of waitering. I was learning that grace doesn't just come from God, it also comes from the sweeter people we live and work with who could make our lives difficult but don't, simply because they are kind.

Although my lack of experience was causing me grief, it seemed to be providing the staff at John's Grill with a wealth of mirth. One of the seasoned waiters there told me I was making him feel young again. He said he hadn't laughed so much in years. With a little bit of work, I took this as a compliment.

Built in 1908, John's Grill is somewhat renowned as a historic San Francisco landmark often frequented by celebrities. Because of its fame as a setting in author Dashiell Hammett's *The Maltese Falcon*, it is commonly referred to as "the home of the Maltese Falcon" and for this reason considered a prestigious place to eat. Even while I was working there, well-known people would come in—or so I was told. Truth be told, I never saw anyone I knew to be famous.

Actually, at John's Grill, there was a good deal of adventure far more exciting than serving famous people I didn't know. On one memorable occasion, I was sent down into the restaurant cellar to bring up some rice and vegetables. Bolting down the stairs, I almost ran into two rather large men lurking in the shadows near the food supplies.

"Who are you?" I asked.

"Uh, we're here ... You're .... We're checking inventory." They stammered.

"What?" was all I could think to blurt out.

In an awkwardness hard to describe, all three of us stood locked in place, staring at each other for much less time than it seemed. One of the men took a step toward me but was pulled back by the other. In a disparate attempt to fix something unfixable, they both spoke at once, sputtering out a jumble of words I couldn't quite decipher. All I could think to do was try to get a clear look at their shadowed faces.

After about three more seconds of fidgeting, the two men backed completely out of sight. Almost immediately, there was a thump and a crash followed by a silence—then the sound of feet scuffling and stumbling. Finally, there was a creak of a door being opened—and light. For a moment, I could see them, but not clearly. As they disappeared out into the street, I tried one final time to catch a clear glimpse of their faces, but couldn't. It all happened so quickly. Before I had a chance to think coherently, they were gone.

When I told the restaurant manager what had happened, he and a few of the other waiters concluded we were being robbed by a couple of guys who had entered the basement through the service entrance, which had been inadvertently left unlocked. My favorite part of their assessment was their determination that the operation had been thwarted by lil' ol' me. That was the day I achieved job security at John's Grill.

Then there were the ladies upstairs—the ladies who worked in the massage parlor above the restaurant. When they called down for lunch for themselves or drinks for their customers, I was given the job of delivering their orders. I am not sure why this duty fell to me. My friendly coworkers said it was for my education, although I suspect it was probably more for their entertainment.

Just prior to my first trip up to the parlor, I was told only, "Take this tray up to the third floor, second door on the right." Only after I got up there did I realize I was serving prostitutes. I guess I was supposed to be surprised. I wasn't. The ladies were very polite and tipped me well. Just before I left, they asked if I would mind taking down the dirty dishes left behind by previous waiters. When I said, "Of course," they seemed surprised and smiled with sweet appreciation. Actually, the dishes weren't dirty at all. They had been meticulously cleaned.

One of those ladies—actually a girl about my age, perhaps 22 or 23—was uncommonly beautiful. As she was loading me up with plates to take downstairs, I couldn't help but ask her, "Why are you doing this?" to which she replied, "Why are you a waiter?" While I was searching for an answer that seemed plausible, she looked down and added softly, "I have no choice." Although I delivered perhaps ten or more orders to that massage parlor over the next two months, I never saw that girl again.

Leaving

I began work at John's Grill in March of 1973. Three months later, I left. Not because I wanted to. I really liked it there. But, as the girl upstairs said, I had no choice—or at least, I thought I didn't.

My exit came suddenly in the first week of June. Immediately after a busy lunch shift, my Silent Ministry Coordinator called me at the restaurant on the front-desk phone. I couldn't believe it. Why was

44

he calling me at work? Couldn't he have waited until I got back to the monastery? I was immediately upset.

"How's it going down there?" he shouted through the receiver in an overly cheerful voice.

"All right, I guess." My reply was muted. I was standing in the most public part of the restaurant, talking on a line that was supposed to be kept open for incoming calls. There were two or three waiters within earshot and the restaurant manager was giving me a stare that meant I should be getting off the phone soon.

"Hey, how was the lunch shift? Busy?" my friendly, fellow monk continued, still conveying an annoying exuberance.

"All right, I guess." I knew I was repeating myself, but I didn't care. He had something to tell me and I just wanted him to get to it.

"Well listen. I got some good news for you. Really good news! Are you up for it?"

"Yeah, sure."

"A job just opened up down on the wharf at Number Nine, and we were thinking you might go for it."

"Ok." I had come to understand that when a monk said "we," he usually meant "I."

"So, how about if you slip on down there on your way home and check it out. You know its prime time on the Wharf. Summer season. Tourists. Money."

"What about my job here?" I asked boldly.

"Well, hold on to it, of course, until you've got something better. Then give notice."

"Just like that?"

"Oh yeah. It's done all the time. Don't worry about it."

I was in no position to discuss this over the phone. The manager was now circling in close to let me know I should really be wrapping it up. So, I said good-bye abruptly, hung up the phone and stepped outside of the restaurant for a quiet moment of thought.

As I stood on the sidewalk, I supposed, probably correctly, I had become "overly attached," as my fellow monks would have put it. Such attachment was a no-no in monk-land—and for good reason, at least in principle. Obviously, *clinging to the world* would hamper the *letting go of the world* so essential in the deeper practices of yoga. Although

45

no monastic would ever deny that striving for detachment should never convey a sense of heartlessness, it all too often did. It was for this very reason that Gurudeva was always telling us we should be *affectionately* detached. Easy to say. Hard to be.

Certainly, I had forged some fine friendships at John's Grill. Whatever I knew about waitering, I had learned from the magnanimous people I worked with there. "How can I leave now?" I thought to myself. "Their investment in me is just beginning to yield its first dividends."

After a few minutes of deliberation, I decided to make a few swift moves to keep with the monastic program. I boarded the Market Street bus for the Wharf, got the job at Number Nine and gave notice at John's Grill just after my dinner shift that night. Not surprisingly, the manager was a bit upset.

"So you came here to get to know the business a little," he said, "and now you're leaving for better money somewhere else. I guess I shouldn't be surprised. I've seen it before."

I tried to stammer out an apology, "Well, I appreciate what ...."

"It's ok," he interrupted. "Forget it. I understand. Good luck."

We agreed I should work out the rest of the week so he would have time to replace me. The next few days were awkward.

At the end of my last shift, the manager handed me a letter of recommendation, which I had not asked for. In part, it read: "This young man is as conscientious, hard-working and as honest as a monk." So much for remaining incognito.

On the Waterfront

What I learned at John's Grill only minimally prepared me for what I encountered at No. 9 Fisherman's Grotto on San Francisco's famous Fishermen's Wharf.

During winter, Fishermen's Wharf is quiet and unassuming—a quaint little waterfront collection of charming restaurants and storybook fishing boats. During summer, it morphs into a mad mishmash of carnival-like sideshows, knickknack stores and sidewalk vendors, infiltrated with tourists enduring California heat and basking in the smell of dead fish. Did I want to be there? No!

My very first day working as a waiter at No. 9, was immediately intimidating. For starters, I was late. Even though I was sure I had left the monastery in plenty of time to arrive early for my lunch shift, all of the tables on my station were completely full of people when I stepped onto the restaurant floor only minutes after I was supposed to be there.

It had taken me half an hour just to plough through the hoards of people packed wall-to-wall two blocks out and around the Wharf. Even inside the restaurant, there were bodies jammed together everywhere: in the kitchen, at the bar, in the dining room—even in the dressing room. It was maddening.

No. 9 was and is a hugely successful fast-food restaurant especially famous for its clam chowder and shellfish. When I was working there, it was also notorious for the quarrelling of its three owners, the Giraldi brothers. I didn't need to be told they lacked brotherly love. On my third day of work, I watched two of them trade blows in the kitchen.

"They're all millionaires," one of the waiters told me in a tired voice. "What's their problem?"

I unenthusiastically muttered something about money not being able to buy happiness, to which he replied, "Yes it can. Are you nuts?" When I said, "Well, I don't think I'm nuts," he replied, "You will be if you work here long enough."

As it turned out, this blithe conversation was the beginning of a long and happy acquaintanceship I would develop with a somewhat unconventional waiter everyone there just called "Joe" because they couldn't pronounce his long Italian name. Joe was at least three times my age, and nearly twice my weight. Because he had worked at No. 9 longer than anyone else, everyone respected him—even the Giraldis. When the Giraldi brothers argued, which was often, Joe was the only one who could jokingly mutter, "Take it outside," and not get fired.

Joe basically said anything he wanted, any time he wanted. And he talked a lot. He generously shared with me a great many more stories than I ever wanted to hear about the Giraldi brothers.

"There they are," he proclaimed, standing in the back of the kitchen with a cigarette in one hand and a cup of coffee in the other. "They got all this money. Yet they're working shoulder to shoulder with the likes of you and me every day, come rain or shine."

"Seems they've been raised with some sort of strong work ethic," I replied timidly.

"They work together here in this same building," he continued, ignoring my comment, "and yet they manage to never even look at each other. If two of them cross paths, they're each looking the other way."

"They come early and stay late," I said.

"Why aren't they out on a yacht sipping martinis?" he muttered under is breath.

"They like working," I said, shrugging my shoulders.

"Yeah right. Well, they can have my job and I can spend their money. Sound good?"

"Sounds good. Shall I tell them you said that?"

"No, I will."

Joe was teaching me the art of talking to release tension. All the waiters did this back there in the rear of the kitchen next to the dishwasher. It was the only available space to do something besides work.

There were two dining rooms at No. 9. The kitchen was adjacent to the one upstairs. I worked in the ground floor dining room with young guys who could run up 18 stairs 100 times a night to the kitchen, and not trip charging down those same stairs with full plates of food. There was also a third dinning room with its own kitchen. It was called No. 10.

There was one other monk working with me at No. 9. He got hired there perhaps six months before I did. He and Joe helped me learn how to work with the Giraldi's. Nino was the Giraldi who hired me. He was the youngest of the brothers—a kind, gentle man who often worked as my busboy.

The Shastras

When I received initiation into the monastic order in 1971, we did not have much money. Gurudeva was just in the process of pulling together his teaching curriculum, as well as his administration plan for Saiva Siddhanta Church, Himalayan Academy and the monastery. The monk's training at that time occurred through the performance of practical tasks associated with the basic work of setting up an organization.

Through our Silent Ministry program, we learned as we earned. With the money we made, we supported ourselves and bought monastery properties. Through our experience as waiters, we developed memory, will, concentration, ingenuity and self-control. As "silent ministers," we tried to take the art of fine waitering a step further by striving to give blessings through a comportment of kindness, maturity and integrity.

When not serving in Silent Ministry, we learned as we worked in monastic teams responsible for our publications, monastery building and maintenance, office administration, food preparation and religious ceremony. At this first stage of our development, there was little talk of theory. All training was "hands on."

The earliest years of church and monastery development were the most challenging. As the sixties mellowed into the seventies, San Francisco was rife with a spirit of abandonment. A lot of young men were freewheeling their way in and out of the monastery, realizing quickly the tight discipline of monastic life was not exactly what they had anticipated. Those who remained shared with Gurudeva the formidable task of establishing and maintaining an atmosphere of peaceful equanimity within the monastic order.

Unfortunately, a handful of the men who stayed were unintentionally disruptive. Their incessant preoccupation with a wide assortment of personal and emotional problems stemming from unapparent sources was forever absorbing Gurudeva's time. In living circumstances that could and should have been ideal for contemplative life, they were continuously stirring up tumultuous clouds of melodramatic trauma. And into these worlds, they beckoned and welcomed Gurudeva as their heaven-sent problem-solver. All of this created a general sense of confusion. Work that should have been easy was difficult, and the development of the monastery was stifled.

As Gurudeva confided to some of the monks later, there came a point during that period of time when he almost disbanded the monastery. In a final moment of crisis, he said, it was the *devas* who saved the monastic order by revealing the *Shastras*.

The *Shastras* was a one long *deva* reading, communicated from the beginning of 1973 to the end of 1974. The first part of this mammoth document explained a long-distant past. The second part predicted an immanent future.

In the first part, the *devas* talked about the discipline and purification of mind, body and emotions that characterized monastic life during some ancient time long before recorded history. In the second part, they spoke hypothetically about the future of Gurudeva's monastic order—

49

how it might look in 1995 if guidelines from the first part were adopted and followed. By intuiting from the *Shastras* a practical understanding of a past and a future, Gurudeva was able to construct a monastic and church program that worked well in the present.

The monks who remained within the order for ten years or more generally fell into two groups: those who came in early—from 1965 to 1973—and those who came in later—from 1990 to 1998. The lives and training of these two groups were as different as night and day. The first group formed the tree trunk of the church—the second, its branches.

By the time the second group of monks started coming into the order after 1990, the church was functioning like a well oiled machine. Gurudeva had instituted a number of important guidelines from the *Shastras*, and a great many lifestyle changes had occurred as a result.

Not surprisingly, those who had the greatest difficulty adjusting to the *Shastras* were those perpetually unhappy monks who had created so much confusion before 1973. When these more troublesome men left, as they all eventually did, they took their problems with them, and life within the monastery became more peaceful, as the Church and its Academy began to flourish in a less hampered way.

Mamadi Ashram

We all loved Mamadi Ashram. It was our haven away from city life, and it was Gurudeva's home in San Francisco. When Gurudeva was there, the very walls of that little storybook cottage seemed permeated with his fun otherworldliness.

The monks stationed in San Francisco used to carefully save up their deepest questions and discussion topics just so they would have lots of reasons to spend lots of time with Gurudeva in Mamadi Ashram when he came to town.

Not surprisingly, Gurudeva's impending visit generated no end of excitement, and his arrival was an event of great celebration. From the time he stepped in the front door of his San Francisco home, the monks gave him no rest. This was not a problem. Gurudeva loved it.

During the day, Gurudeva would sit in the downstairs living room of Mamadi Ashram just to make himself available for casual conversation with the monks. He was wonderfully accessible in this way.

Monks could and would drop in on him freely as they came from and went to their respective restaurant jobs. He was rarely alone, and around him there was always intriguing discussion.

One late afternoon, I breezed into Mamadi Ashram while a young monk named Santosha was awkwardly asking Gurudeva some personal questions. Santosha's privacy ended with my arrival. Although I hesitated at the door, Gurudeva waved to me politely and motioned me into the room.

"Are you going or coming," he asked me.

"Neither?" I asked rhetorically. (Gurudeva's teacher, Yogaswami, often described the mystic state of *being in the moment* as: "No coming, no going.")

"Good answer," said Gurudeva with a gentle laugh. Santosha looked down at the floor with a grimace. He was tolerating the fact that Gurudeva's time now had to be shared.

As soon as I sat down, two more monks came in, followed by another — and five minutes later, three more. This made a crowd.

"Santosha and I were talking about the goal of yoga," Gurudeva said, sculpting the air with his hand in a flowing motion. "Do I have that right, Santosha?"

"Yes, right," Santosha replied with a forced smile.

"And Santosha was wondering how to achieve this goal."

"Flick a switch," said one of the other monks in the room.

"Push a button," said another.

Everyone chuckled courteously. There was a lingering pause.

"We say the Self is the goal of yoga," said Gurudeva, breaking the silence. "Yet the Self isn't a goal like other goals, because the Self is something we already are. What we are seeking is a *realization* of what we already are. So our work is to gradually shift from a false sense of identity to a true sense of identity. In this context, "false" means "unreal" and "true" means "real." So we are moving from the *unreal* to the *real*. Easy to say, hard to do."

"But exactly what is it that we do?" Santosha boldly asked.

"The deeper work of yoga has to do with remolding our outer nature so that it becomes transparent," Gurudeva replied. "Through this transparency, our inner nature becomes apparent."

"And that outer nature is the ego?" asked Santosha.

51

"Yes," Gurudeva said quickly.

"Do we want the ego to be transparent or do we want the ego to just go away?" Santosha looked surprised that he might have asked a really insightful question. The other monks in the room leaned forward with anticipation.

"The ego is the person you must sometimes be," Gurudeva said. "If you aren't that person when you don't need to be, that would be transparency."

"When is it apparent you're not transparent?" Santosha asked.

"When you take things personally and get your feelings hurt."

Santosha's face turned red. Several of the monks looked down.

"In our beginning yoga practice, we work with three identities," Gurudeva continued. "The first of these is our external identity, usually referred to as the "ego." This is our out-front presentation of ourselves, that image of us we want others to see. We consciously construct this identity, this external person, according to our liking and in consideration for our needs and desires.

"Our second identity is subconscious in nature. This second self is not an identity we create consciously. It creates itself behind the scenes. Most of the time this secret self remains hidden beneath the surface of our conscious awareness. But occasionally it slips out. If we have a lot of unresolved subconscious issues, this subconscious identity, this most secret version of ourselves, can be embarrassing to us. This background identity plays a big part in forming our personality, which can be likable or not.

"Our third identity is closer to the real us. This third identity is felt as a deep state of *being*. Residing in *being*, without getting overly distracted into the externalities of the mind, eventually yields a grand illumination, a Realization of our truest Self. This Self is not *personal* at all because it is the one *impersonal* identity of all.

"So what we work for in yoga is to dissolve the ego in devotion, resolve the subconscious through understanding and maintain *being* long enough for identities one and two to settle back into identity number three. When the three become one, there is no difference between the inner and the outer, and the Self becomes apparent as the one and only Absolute Reality. So, dissolve, resolve and *be*. Those are some down-to-earth things you can work on, Santosha. Will that keep you busy?"

Just as Santosha was beginning to reply, the front door opened and two more monks walked in. One was carrying a huge pot of lentil stew. The other was following with a tray of bowls and spoons. Even Santosha lost interest in what he was about to say.

"Food!" said Gurudeva. "Dig in."

Soon enough, the air was filled with light talk, laughter and the sound of slurping.

Because most anyone tends to open up in the friendly ambience of informal chatting, Gurudeva often used casual conversation as a means of working with his monks and students to explore their usually hidden and guarded subconscious issues.

Gurudeva was taught and now taught us that an investigation of the more troubling realms of the subconscious was important because the simple act of honestly facing unfaced memories, especially memories of a painful nature, was the very means by which those memories got resolved in understanding and eliminated as obstacles to a more introspective yoga.

Gurudeva had at least three good reasons why he didn't usually do a lot of talking at the beginning of a casual conversation with monks and students. First, he wanted to have an opportunity to listen so he could get to know the person he was talking with. Second, he wanted to give the person he was talking with an opportunity to trust and like him. Third—and this was of great importance—he wanted to provide that person with an opportunity to empty out his or her issues into words so there would be a vacuum to fill. This vacuum could then pull forth through Gurudeva a wisdom truly and directly relevant to that person's current concerns.

The Life Matures

Gods

During a busy Sunday-afternoon lunch shift about a month after I started working at No. 9, one of my customers "took a hike" without paying his check. When this "dine-and-dash" sort of thing occurs in a restaurant, the waiter serving the "walk-out" is usually expected to cover the loss.

Although No. 9's policy was no different, Nino took pity on me. "I'll give you this one," he said stoically. Thus, by the grace of Nino, I avoided loosing $93.46.

Thirty minutes later, however, when I tallied a check incorrectly and lost another twenty dollars, Nino's benevolence waned. "This one you pay for," he said with a wink. I really felt like a dunce.

Stepping off the city bus in front of our temple around three that afternoon, I was still wallowing in the depressing aftermath of my most unfortunate lunch shift. In two hours, I had earned about $50 in tips—not bad for 1973—but had lost $20 of that on my check mistake. If it hadn't been for Nino stepping in to help me with the walk-out, I would be arriving back at the monastery about $75 in the hole.

"What a nightmare," I was thinking to myself as I opened our temple door and heard Gurudeva's booming voice. Suddenly, I remembered. Today was Sunday. Sunday, was the day Gurudeva gave a public talk in the temple when he was in town.

I stepped inside quickly, shut the door immediately and entered our small main temple chamber as quietly as I could. Gurudeva had just concluded his lecture and was now five or ten minutes into a question-and-answer session with some sixty people packed into about a hundred square feet of space. The atmosphere was thick with a luscious calm. Not surprisingly, my concerns about the wharf vanished like vapor.

As I took my seat, a lady to my right was standing and talking in Gurudeva's direction. She was punctuating her speech with awkward gaps of time, as if she was not talking to Gurudeva as much as she was thinking out loud to herself.

"Hello there," she said. "My name is Nancy. I've been coming here for some time. Although I am a Christian by birth—not a very good one, I should mention—I feel drawn to Hinduism. And I especially like your explanation of Hinduism as it relates to yoga. But, to be honest, when I go looking for information on Hinduism in the library, all I can find are stories about Hindu gods killing each other. What's your take on these stories and do you believe in all these gods?"

"In the mythological stories of Hinduism, Ganesha, the deity of this temple, is one of those gods," Gurudeva explained. "He is also the son of the one God, Siva. Since we are all the children of a one God, that makes Ganesha your older brother."

"That's an answer I didn't expect," Nancy whispered to herself.

"All these mythological stories are supposed to assist us in our understanding of Hinduism," Gurudeva continued. "Actually, I find them confusing. They require more explanation than Hinduism itself."

"Well, I certainly wouldn't mind having an older brother like Ganesha," Nancy said jokingly. "He seems like a nice enough fellow."

"He *is* your older brother, and mine too," Gurudeva said.

"And here I thought I was an only child," Nancy said. As the room filled with friendly laughter, Nancy looked to her left and right as if she was just seeing the people around her for the first time.

"Now, you'll never be lonely," Gurudeva said softly.

Nancy looked down. Gurudeva had hit a sensitive spot. After a nervous moment, Nancy continued dryly, "So, you're making the point here that there is only one God and that the other gods and goddesses are his children. Right?"

"Yes," Gurudeva replied.

"Did this one God you are calling Siva create these many gods and goddesses?" asked Nancy. Before Gurudeva could respond, she added, "For that matter, did He create us? Is the one Hindu God like the one Christian God? Is the God of Hinduism like the God of Christianity in other ways as well?

"That's a lot of questions," Gurudeva replied. "I'll just jump in with one answer. According to one well-accepted school of Hindu thought, Siva is continually creating the world, just as he is continually creating the souls who live in that world. These souls that he creates evolve into maturity like a child grows up into an adult. All souls follow this same pattern. So all souls are equal in that sense. However, because all souls were not created at the same time, some of them are young and some of them are old. The souls we call gods are just older souls. They are on the same path we are. They're just further along."

"If Ganesha is so much like us, why doesn't he have a physical body like we do?" asked Nancy.

"He is beyond reincarnation," said Gurudeva as if he expected the question. "The soul's evolutionary journey is long and arduous. Only part of it occurs on the physical plane."

"But you used the word, 'reincarnation.'"

"Yes?"

"Reincarnation means many lives, right? Why do we have to live many lives? Why not just one?"

"Too much to learn."

"Okay. So where am I in this reincarnation?"

"God only knows." The room exploded with laughter.

"Okay, okay," Nancy said, when everyone settled down. "What do you mean by 'too much to learn?'"

"We are here in a physical body to learn through physical experience," explained Gurudeva. "Through this experience we create karma, which must then be resolved. All of this takes a lot of time—more time than we have in one life."

"So we don't just go around once, huh?"

"No."

"Let's back up for a moment. What does karma mean?"

"Action."

"Action? That's it?"

"Yes, but for every action there is a reaction. You can't make a move without creating karma and every karma you create must be resolved. Action-reaction. Karma is like gravity. What goes up has to come down."

"So, is there a purpose to all of this, or is life just a chain-reaction that we are trapped into playing out?"

"The idea is to experience all the world has to offer through the process of creating and resolving karma. When we've done that completely, we merge with God to realize He was our Self all along."

"So our experience of God occurs through our experience of the world? Is this what you are saying?"

"Doesn't that make sense?"

"Almost. Somewhere back there in one of your lectures you were saying we had to renounce the world to realize God. Now you are telling us to go out and embrace the world to realize God?"

"We renounce toward the end. We can't renounce what we have

not yet embraced. Curiosity will keep us coming back. You've heard the story of the old man on his deathbed who's just about to die when suddenly he hears the creak of a door opening. Even death has to wait on this fellow while he turns his head to see who just came in. Such is the power of curiosity, the instigator of desire."

"So, you leave the world when you're tired of it, when you've seen it all, when its like ...."

"An old pair of shoes."

"Yes, exactly. You're reading my mind."

"Sorry about that."

Although I was the only monk in the room, I did not feel out of place. I felt like a child happy to be alive.

When everyone left, I told Gurudeva what had happened with Nino at the restaurant. He smiled and said, "Ask Nino if he would allow you to pay for that walk-out."

The next day, I followed Gurudeva's instructions, even though I didn't want to. First, Nino just looked at me without much expression. Then he said, "Keep your money. You earned it," and walked away.

When I came in to work the following day, I didn't see my name on the schedule sheet. As I was standing there thinking I might have been fired, one of the waiters came up and said, "Check with Nino. You've been moved up." As it turned out, I had been moved from downstairs No. 9 to upstairs No. 10. In a waiter's world, this was a promotion.

Seeking the Core

Over the next five years, from the first of 1973 through most of 1977, I worked mainly in Wharf restaurants—especially during those long, hot California summers. Toward the end of that time, I had become quite a familiar face down there on the marina—at least enough for the hard workers at the sidewalk crab stands to give me a nod as I passed by.

Of those five years, 1973 was the most significant. It was a year of firsts. During that year, the *Shastras* were revealed; the monastic order was turned upside down and reformed; Saiva Siddhanta Church and Himalayan Academy were completely reorganized; new monastery lands were purchased and developed, and the Virginia City monastery and press shop were closed down. That was also the year I survived my

60

initiation into the San Francisco version of our monastic life.

The longer I stayed in San Francisco, the more I was able to eke out extra time for extended meditations. The more I meditated, the more committed I became to my ever-changing perception of yogic enlightenment. In Gurudeva, I saw what I thought meditation could make of a person. And I wanted to be that person myself.

Although I was quite happy in my chosen life of inner search, I was also discovering something quite sobering about one of its central principles: *The Self is illusive.* This illusiveness of what Gurudeva was calling "the only meaningful goal of life" was not allowing me to enjoy the sense of stability I was led to believe I should be able to expect from a pursuit of this ultimate goal. The most I could see I was getting from my meditative efforts at this point was a mild quelling of angst.

Also, for a reason I have never been able to completely understand, I was driven to devise some sort of system for measuring progress in my yoga practice. The more I worked at this, however, the more I had to concede that measuring such progress was about as reasonable as catching sea breeze in a fishing net.

Of course, I talked about this with Gurudeva—more than once. The first time I broached the subject, I was untactfully blunt: "Am I making any progress?" I blurted out.

"Of course you are," he replied. At the time, we were sitting outside the San Francisco airport terminal, waiting for a taxi to take us into the city. Although Gurudeva had just endured five hours of confinement on a plane from Hawaii, he was looking as fresh and invigorated as a professional model showing up for a springtime photo shoot.

"I don't feel like I'm making progress," I said quietly.

"That's what keeps you striving, isn't it."

"Perhaps, but does it have to be that way?"

"At first."

"When will I stop being a beginner at this?"

"At what?"

"Meditation."

"What you seek is bigger than meditation."

"Transformation." Did I say that?

"Yes!" Gurudeva said, visibly impressed. "See? You're closer than you think."

"I am?"

"Sooner or later, a serious yogi establishes *being* as home base."

"I'm trying."

"Maybe too hard. Don't make it difficult by thinking too much. Try to live your life like nothing is happening. That would be putting your meditation to work for you all day long. When you sit for meditation, enjoy the bliss of *being*. When you get up from meditation and move into your day, take that bliss with you wherever you go. Those around you will feel your bliss as a blessing. They will think you are intentionally blessing them. This is silent ministry. Right now, you think your work as a waiter is an imposition upon your contemplative life. When you see it as an expression of that life, you'll be less frustrated."

"So, the feeling of nothing happening is the feeling of life being easy, right?"

"Right."

"Easy is not so easy between noon and one at No.10 on the Wharf. You don't mean for me to space out do you?"

"Spacing out is a diffusion of energy, not a focusing of it. The bliss you feel during meditation comes from an intensification of energy due to focus. Right?"

"Right."

"So what's the key to maintaining the bliss of a high-powered, morning meditation throughout the day?"

"Focus."

"Right. Now, what was that question you had about progress?"

"Oh, I don't know. At this very moment, asking about progress on the spiritual path seems kind of like posing a question that doesn't really have an answer."

After a moment of pause, Gurudeva said, "If you were learning to play classical piano, how would you gauge your progress?"

"By the amount of time spent in correct practice." I replied.

"Very good," Gurudeva said. "It would be the same in yoga. Formal meditation is like playing the piano. The two are the same in the sense that they both require a habit of focus. Although it sounds like a classical pianist is doing a lot of things when he plays, he's really just doing one thing: focusing. You can work on focus in everything you do. How much time did you spend sitting for meditation today?"

"None, so far," I admitted.

"How about yesterday? He asked quickly.

"About two hours," I said after a moment of calculation.

"What did you do during those two hours?"

"Well, those hours didn't occur all at once. I spent a total of two hours in three meditation sessions. During each session I meditated on my *mambashum*."

"That's a good focus. Did you say *your mambashum*?"

"You encouraged us to make our own."

"Yes, I did. Can you describe yours?"

"I have more than one."

"Did you meditate on more than one yesterday?"

"No, just one."

"Good. Good to focus on one. Which one was that?"

"I think I might have to show it to you."

"Give it to me in a nut shell."

"Well, actually it's pretty simple. It's *rehmtyenali* (forth chakra), flowing to *simvumkami* (fifth chakra), flowing to *tyemavumna* (sixth chakra), flowing to *kamakadiisareh* (seventh chakra), flowing to *imkaif* ('no awareness' or Self Realization)."

"Very ambitious," Gurudeva said.

"Is that a good thing?" I asked.

"Very good," he replied with a kind smile. "Would you consider simplifying? Sometimes if we shoot too high we get discouraged."

"What would you suggest?"

"Perhaps one chakra at a time."

"Back to basics?"

"You never outgrow the basics. Holding awareness focused, which includes gently bringing it back when it becomes unfocused. That is really where it all starts and ends. If you can just keep striving to perfect this one task, you will make quick progress on the spiritual path. You know this because you have already done this, but for some reason you keep forgetting. Keep up the simple practice of focusing awareness in simple ways until this focusing becomes a way of life—a habit, a *good* habit. Just try to remember: attention, concentration, meditation, contemplation, Samadhi. This is the magic sequence that occurs of its own accord if you can just stay focused."

63

I felt like I should not respond with more questions. He was starting to say things he had said many times before. This was not a good sign. Basically, his implied message was: Ask a little less. Listen a little more. I thanked him and changed the subject slightly.

"I'm really enjoying my worship in the temple," I said.

"Doesn't hurt to have friends in high places," Gurudeva said. "Ganesha is a big-hearted being just looking for a chance to help. We serve because we think we should. He serves because he wants to."

"I *do* pray and I *do* feel his assistance," I said.

"That's good. Let that approach become second mature. Even the born Hindus who are not particularly religious worship Ganesha. It's part of their culture."

The next day I worked a "straight eight" at No. 10 from nine in the morning until five in the evening. At about six pm, I was standing in front of our 436 Locust Street monastery apartment building, fumbling around in my pocket for my key and looking at a piece of paper penned crudely to the front door just above eye level. It was flapping in the wind so I slapped down a corner of it with my right hand long enough to decipher its scrawled message. It read: "Yoga talk session for young monks. Mamadi Ashram. 7 pm."

"Fantastic," I thought. "I can make it." I was free that evening and would be able to attend the class. The timing could not have been better. I had an hour to shower and eat before hurrying over to our secret ashram cottage.

By the time I got to Mamadi Ashram, it was just before seven. Gurudeva was talking quietly with a few monastics that had gathered early. The class was supposed to be just for young monks, but everyone was showing up. This was going to be good. I could feel it.

Thought

By six o'clock, at least 20 monks were sitting in the main living room of Mamadi Ashram. All was quiet and still. Gurudeva was savoring the setting sun and obviously in no hurry to get started. We were used to this. It was what we had grown to expect from him. He was our peacekeeper. So, there he was, keeping the peace and teaching us to do the same by his example. Finally, he broke the blissful silence.

"My goodness," he said. "This is good attendance for such short notice on a school night." The room filled with a hesitant laughter. "Are all the restaurants closed?" Each monk looked around as if this question was not directed at him. "Can we have a show of hands from all those who called in sick?" Amidst forced chuckles, a few monks sheepishly raised their arms. Gurudeva beamed his broad smile to let everyone know that all was well and absolutely nothing was out of place. "Ok, let's begin," he said. "Santosha, can you please start us off?"

Santosha sat up as straight as a morning rooster and chanted an ancient Sanskrit *sloka* invoking the blessings of Lord Ganesha.

"Good job, Santosha," Gurudeva said as he lightly applauded the young monk's performance. "Very good job."

Two monks then jumped up quickly to pass out oatmeal cookies. Within five minutes, everyone had eatables and most had proceeded past the loudest of their first munching. Gurudeva looked around, sighed a long out-breath and prepared to speak in his uniquely gracious and most unhurried manner.

"What we want to talk about tonight are the five bodies of man and how they work together in yoga. Please feel free to ask questions as we go along.

"First of all, we don't *have* a soul body. We *are* a soul body. But this pure soul body of light, fresh out of the Self, needs clothes to wear, especially if it's going to live in the cold, hard physical world. So the other four bodies are like clothes for the soul.

"The first body out from the soul is the mental body. In this form we live in the world of thought. We think. We plan. We create. We're hardly aware we have a physical body. We're cool to emotion. It is in this body that we make our first attempts to become consciously aware that we are a spiritual being.

"The next body out is the emotional body. In this body we live in the vast and fluctuating world of interpersonal relationships. We don't think as much as we feel. And we are often impulsive and illogical.

"The mental body begins its development as a vehicle of control for the emotional body, while the emotional body begins its development as the recipient of that control. Because of their close working relationship and interdependence, these two bodies are often lumped together and referred to as the astral body.

"The fourth and fifth bodies out from the soul are the pranic and physical bodies, the former being the life of the latter. When we are primarily conscious in the physical body, we experience the physical world exclusively and live instinctively. We don't think or feel deeply, for we are primarily living an animal's life in an animal's body. Like the mental and emotional bodies, the pranic and physical bodies are often perceived as one, and are usually just referred to as the physical body. Are there any questions so far?

After a short pause, an older monk named Ravi spoke up. "So, in a general sense, there are three bodies and three worlds."

"You could say that," responded Gurudeva. "The five are a more detailed understanding of the three."

"Could we get by without doing that?" asked Ravi.

"Dangerous question," said a monk from the back of the room.

"Doing what?" asked Gurudeva.

"Could we get by without intellectually understanding all these bodies and worlds and still practice yoga?" asked Ravi timidly. "I mean, you have always taught us to not be too intellectual or think too much, and I guess I am just looking for an excuse to not think too much here. Am I getting into trouble?"

"Although thinking too much is not a good thing," Gurudeva said. "Not thinking enough is worse—and far more common."

"I can vouch for that," said Ravi. Everyone laughed.

"Can't we all," said Gurudeva with a smile. "Yes, it's important to be able to think clearly and logically when necessary. Because pure intuition is not always as assessable as we would like it to be, we need logic as a guide we can count on in making the decisions of life. And we are making these life decisions all the time. Good decision-making is quite crucial to a happy, healthy life. How many decisions have we made impulsively or emotionally? And how many times have we mistaken impulse or emotion for intuitive inspiration? Even in asking and answering questions, are we not required to think?"

"And also, when we meditate on something don't we start by thinking?" asked Ravi.

"Absolutely," Gurudeva said. "Especially, in a certain type of meditation, that is true. Solid thought can lead quite naturally toward solid intuition in meditation, because intuition is a natural tweeker of thought. If thought were a writer, intuition could be his editor. But then, of course, some writers don't like to be edited."

"Let me think about that," said Ravi. Gurudeva laughed. Everyone in the room slouched a little and shifted in their seats. The group mood was relaxing.

"With regard to the five bodies," Gurudeva continued, "it's good to think a few ideas through. As souls, we are simple in essence but complex in outward development. What's that famous quote? 'In the beginning there was one, and the one became many.' This principle of life applies to the development of the soul. All the complexity of a soul's manifest existence is crucial to its development and needs to be understood as such so the day-to-day decisions of life can be made with a healthy sense of purpose."

"Are the five bodies real or symbolic?" asked Ravi.

"They are real for sure," replied Gurudeva.

Ravi seemed lost in thought. "So, if we're 'lost in thought,'" he asked, "are we off somewhere in our mental body traveling through the mental world?"

"Absolutely," Gurudeva replied. "Although all these worlds and bodies are accessible at all times, we each choose where to go, what to do and which bodies to use at any given moment. Five different people sitting together in the same room might quite literally be fully absorbed in five different worlds, and therefore be completely unaware of each other. Through conversation, however, they can come together into one world, as we are doing right here tonight. But conversation needs words and words need thought. Here we are, back at thought."

"How does all this varied experience in these five worlds relate to our primary goal of realizing the Self?" asked Ravi.

"As our experience of these worlds develops, so do our bodies," replied Gurudeva. "The goal of yoga is to fully develop all five bodies by fully experiencing all each world has to offer. Self Realization marks the conclusion of that process. It's what's left when everything else has been fully explored."

"So we really do have to work our way through a lot of stuff to get to enlightenment," said Santosha. "Sounds a little like the monkey's forest in the Wizard of Oz."

"Actually, it's very much like that," said Gurudeva. "Perhaps that's why that story is so popular. In my early yoga practice, I remember thinking this search for Realization was like hacking through a tangled jungle. Very good, Santosha. Does anyone else have any questions?"

After a long pause, a monk named Deva asked, "Gurudeva, would you like a cookie?"

"Now that's the best question I've had all night," said Gurudeva as everyone politely chuckled. "Yes, please."

Deva gave Gurudeva a cookie. It was now dark outside, and a gentle rain had begun to fall. Again, there was peace and silence. Finally, Gurudeva spoke.

"Ok," he said. "Let's talk about yoga."

Moderation and Balance

"In our various yoga practices," Gurudeva began, "we follow what my guru referred to as the middle path. 'Middle' here means *moderation* and *balance*. So, we are *moderate* in our pursuit of *balance*.

"Although our ultimate goal is Self Realization, there are some short-range goals along the way. *Balance* is one of those short-range goals. Following logic, it just wouldn't make sense to go to extremes in seeking balance, would it? That would be silly. This is where *moderation* comes in. Therefore, to begin our journey on the middle path, we seek balance through the practice of a few yogas in a schedule that is not so extreme we can't keep it up with consistency for a long time.

"The yogas that are safe to practice during a period of adjustment to a middle path are hatha yoga, bhakti yoga and karma yoga. Hatha yoga releases physical tension and unblocks the flow of energy through the physical body. Bhakti yoga softens emotion into devotion. Karma yoga transmutes selfishness into selflessness.

"Once we are balanced on a middle path in a moderate approach, we can add in the more powerful yogas like japa yoga and raja yoga, which naturally unfold kundalini yoga and jnana yoga. Japa yoga, the yoga of mantra repetition, curbs distraction and stills a ramified intellect. Raja yoga, the yoga of meditation, reveals the bliss of being. Kundalini yoga and jnana yoga occur naturally as a consequence of practicing the other yogas. All of this catalyzes yoga's end in Self Realization.

"So, none of us can complain that we lack tools to work with.

Yet these tools are all means to an end. They are not ends in themselves. They are all preparations for Samadhi. Samadhi is what we are referring to when we say, 'Self Realization.' You are all performing all of these practices right now every day and you know them well. What we are seeking tonight is an overview—a solid perception of how these yogas relate to each other and work together. Any questions?"

"Can you say a little more about balance?" Deva asked.

"The ever-present power of your spine is naturally balanced," Gurudeva replied. "It's just pure life force fully self-contained in a perfect state of desirelessness. But as you live your life, you externalize this central force either passively or aggressively in accordance with your current state of fear and desire. As you become externalized in this way, you throw yourself out of balance. When you rest or sleep, these forces have a chance to rebalance themselves to a certain extent, as they naturally are inclined to do. But through the practice of yoga you can achieve this balance intentionally—and thus more completely."

"So, desire throws us out of balance?" asked Deva.

"Yes, and it makes each of us different," Gurudeva said. "It's our personal state of imbalance that makes each one of us different. When we are in balance, we are internalized and the same. When we are out of balance, we are externalized and different. Outside, there are many. Inside, there is one."

"Sounds pretty simple when you say it," Ravi commented.

"It *is* simple if you are seeing it from the inside out. It's fear and desire that motivate the ego to complicate and confuse life by creating a lot of negative karma. But this can only occur when we are living out of balance. Through our yoga practices, we create minimal karma as we rise above fear, control desire and seek balance on a middle path."

Several monks started to talk at once. Now, an excitement was brewing. Gurudeva motioned to Santosha to speak.

"How do we know which yoga to practice when?" asked the young monk.

"That's a meditation in itself, isn't it?" replied Gurudeva. "Let intuition be your guide. You have already established many of these practices in your daily *sadhana*. Other practices can be applied like medicine as needed. You'll just come to know what you need when."

"So, is desire good or bad?" asked Santosha. Everyone liked it when Santosha spoke up. In his youthful exuberance, he asked those simple questions that weren't cool for the older monks to ask but that nobody got tired of hearing Gurudeva answer.

"Desire is neither good nor bad," replied Gurudeva. "Desire is a primal force that initiates action. Desire propels us through life to experience all life has to offer. The various satisfactions of desire mark our progress on the path of life. Desire must first be satisfied at the instinctive level. Then at the intellectual level. And finally in the realm of spirit. Through this transmutation of desire, we open and use the powers of the chakras, one after another from the bottom to the top. This happens naturally over a long period of time, but can be consciously escalated through the practice of yoga. As we have said many times, there is no good or bad. There is only experience. How we recognize experience — whether we perceive it to be 'good' or 'bad' — is relative to where we are, where we've been and where we are going as we follow desire."

"Can you elaborate on how these different yogas work together?" asked a monk named Eesan. This was a rare moment. Eesan was one of the more senior monks. Of the senior monks, he was deeply respected. Eesan rarely talked.

"All these yogas work well together because they share a common objective, which is to prepare us for Self-Realization," Gurudeva replied, more or less ignoring the question. "Through all of our yogas we call out to God. In that calling out, we show God we are sincere. To this sincerity, He responds. Yet, He responds in His own way and in His own timing, and not according to our preconceptions or the creed of any one religion. So leave a side door open for Him and go on about your business. Leave a side door open so He doesn't have to knock."

The room grew calm as if a storm were brewing. Gurudeva looked briefly to his left and right, then closed his eyes. A minute passed, than another. We were all clutched with anticipation in a stillness that was stone solid and fixed. No one dared move. When Gurudeva finally started talking again, a wave of relief spread through the group.

"There is one very tedious job right in the middle of all this yogic preparation for Self Realization. That job is referred to in two ways: 'clearing the subconscious' and 'resolving karma.' As time goes on, you're going to be hearing me talk a lot about this task — probably much more than you want to. It's the tough part of yoga that nobody wants to discuss. And because it's not discussed, it's not very well understood. So, I would like to discuss karma and the subconscious right now."

"Does this have something to do with the 'garbage' you were talking about earlier?" Santosha asked innocently.

"What?" Eesan asked Santosha.

"Well, I was telling Gurudeva what a great teacher he was and he was saying that, no, he was just a 'garbage collector,'" replied Santosha with a most serious look on his face. Suddenly, the tension in the room eased with some laughter.

"Yes, that's me," replied Gurudeva. "I'm a garbage collector."

"But you want us to collect our own garbage, right?" Santosha asked with a happy grin.

"From the mouths of babes, comes truth unadorned," Gurudeva said quietly, as he looked at Santosha in amused surprise.

"All right," Gurudeva said. "Let's talk about the subconscious."

The Subconscious Mind

"All of this is the *conscious* mind," Gurudeva said as he gracefully waved his arm through the air. "But the *subconscious* is different. This inner part of our mind retains impressions of absolutely everything we experience in our conscious mind. Yet it's far more than just a memory bank. It's an organizer, a secretary, an autopilot, a thought processor, a trauma nurse..." Gurudeva breathed deeply to create an easy pause for reflection, then continued, "a habit maker, a conscience prompter and much more. This incredibly complex computer-like part of us can be put to great use, once we learn how to perceive its contents objectively, impress it advantageously and use its latent powers purposefully.

"Certainly, if a good portion of our various encounters with the subconscious have been unfavorable, we could reasonably be expected to think there's nothing positive about it. Yet nothing could be further from the truth. Even the negative impressions within this mysteriously hidden region of our inner makeup are not binding. Any attitude, any personality conflict or block in the subconscious can be changed. So, Santosha, how do we change the contents of the subconscious mind?"

"Purification?" Santosha asked in a guessing tone.

"Okay, how do we purify? asked Gurudeva.

"Can someone else have a turn?" asked Santosha, looking down.

"By resolving the experiences that created the impressions," Deva said quickly.

"How do we resolve those experiences?" asked Gurudeva. There was a pause.

"Think them through?" Deva replied.

"Ok, what does 'think them through' mean?" Gurudeva replied. There was another pause.

"Analyze them?" Deva asked with a winced look on his face. A quiet groan rolled through the room. Everyone could just feel this was not the right answer.

"If by 'analyze' you mean 'psychoanalyze,' absolutely not. Our job is easier than that, thank God. A resolution of experiences impressed within the subconscious occurs when we simply observe those experiences without reaction. You've heard me say many times, 'face your self.' This is what I mean by that. By simply observing without reacting, we quite naturally arrive at an intuitive understanding of this self we are facing. If we do this repeatedly over a long period of time, the subconscious becomes more and more transparent to the *superconscious* just behind it. When the subconscious becomes transparent, we call it the *subsuperconscious*. This *subsuperconscious* is nothing but a clear window into the *superconscious* mind of the soul. So, to be able to objectively observe the memory of one's own experiences without reaction is a great mystical power."

Gurudeva sat back, sipped some tea and looked around the room. He always let a little pause pass after serious talk, and this was definitely a good time to linger. When he heard monks in the back of the room munching on cookies, he asked: "Any questions?"

"Yes, I have one," Eesan said. "Can you relate this whole task of clearing the subconscious state of mind to the goal of balance you were talking about earlier?"

"Yes Eesan, good question," replied Gurudeva. "First of all, any sort of introspection is going to start pulling up all these subconscious impressions that need resolution. These impressions are just looking for a chance to surface. You might say they are something like constipated memories seeking release. But because this release is almost always painful, people generally work hard to stay externalized and away from introspection so this surfacing and release can't happen.

"When this release occurs, it causes an unsettling of forces manifesting as a physical, emotional or mental disturbance, which then stimulates a scramble for a balance back to "normal life." This is how subconscious clearing and balance work together in the more ordinary circumstances of everyday life.

"If we are practicing yoga, however, *balance* takes on a new meaning as we get further along the path and deeper into ourselves. In the beginning we have to achieve a certain amount of balance just to practice yoga in the first place. Otherwise, we won't be stable enough to continue our practice after the novelty of yoga has worn off. Once we are stable on a middle path and we are committed to continued yoga, we have to keep seeking balance to stay balanced, right? Still later, when we get so good at balancing we start to become almost complacent, we intentionally induce imbalance to keep going. This is when we might purposely dredge up those more deeply imbedded, negative, subconscious impressions to stimulate a more intense inner cleansing.

"The path of yoga is one big balancing act. But all this balancing deepens and strengthens with each return from imbalance until, in the still aftermath of a final return to balance, we find ourselves emerging from somewhere, we know not where. Yet in that emerging we become aware we've been made anew with a new view—of everything."

With this, Gurudeva fluidly opened his hands upward as if he were releasing birds into flight. "Does anyone have any questions?"

"Do we have to completely clear the subconscious before we can meditate at all?" asked a shy monk named Mular. Mular was young like Santosha, but not quite as partial to the limelight.

"Thank you for that wonderful question, Mular. By all means, no. You can and you are meditating beautifully right now. As we move in and out of balance, we move back and forth from the subconscious to the *subsuperconscious*. Your best meditations will occur when you are in a state of balance with full access to the *subsuperconcious*, but your most meaningful and productive meditations will occur when you are out of balance grappling with subconscious issues that will have to be dealt with sooner or later, anyway, so why not now? As your sense of balance strengthens from dealing with these issues, your meditations will deepen accordingly. The depth of your meditations indicates the degree of your success in resolving the subconscious."

"So you are speaking in reference to raja yoga, because you are talking about meditation. Right?" asked Deva.

"Yes," Gurudeva replied.

"How do some of the other yogas deal with this resolution of the subconscious?" Deva continued. "Like hatha yoga, bhakti yoga and karma yoga, for instance."

"The body is a physical representation of the subconscious mind," replied Gurudeva. "This means that chronic physical tensions represent unresolved subconscious issues. When we release these tensions through hatha yoga, we also release those subconscious issues up into our conscious view. This is why we are often besieged by a lot of seemingly meaningless imagery as we move through our hatha yoga asanas (physical postures). These images appear to us as distractions, which are generally not nearly as disconcerting in the physically oriented practice of hatha yoga as they are in the mentally oriented practice of raja yoga, where they can completely disrupt a meditation. Still, the method of dealing with this imagery would be the same in hatha yoga as it is in raja yoga: disregard or observe in detachment.

"Bhakti yoga and karma yoga are calming and soothing. Even though they arouse the subconscious, they tend to work unobtrusively because they de-emphasize the ego. This is significant because all of your subconscious issues are centered around a false sense of self. Also, these two yogas give you a place to put the negative emotions that often accompany the surfacing of subconscious issues. In karma yoga you can throw that emotion into serving others. In bhakti yoga you can offer that emotion up in devotion. As I was told by one of my yoga teachers again and again, 'You can take the hard way or the easy way. Why make it hard on yourself? Just serve and worship.'"

After a respectful pause, Deva asked, "How about some of the other practices like japa yoga?"

"Japa yoga is great tool to use in facing the subconscious. Your mantra gives you something to hang on to while the winds of thought and emotion blow."

A natural silence fell upon the room. Just as I was getting up the nerve to ask Gurudeva how the resolution of the subconscious related to the resolution of karma, Gurudeva said: "Before we close I want to make one important point. Resolving subconscious issues is the inner side of resolving karma. The subconscious issue is the meat of the karma and where the knot of that karma is held. But the complete unraveling of this subconscious knot can only occur when the cycle of the karma has come full circle from action all the way through reaction. This is a subject for another class. For now, we've all had enough. Go to sleep and I'll meet you on the inner planes."

It was full-moon light outside. The sky was clear, drained of rain. I felt calm and empty and couldn't recall anything we had just talked about, although I knew it would all come back later, piece by piece. It always did. The only thing I could think as I lay down to sleep that night was: "All is good."

Showdown

About two weeks after that beautiful evening class with Gurudeva, I was riding home from the Wharf just after midnight on the *1 California* city bus. Had I had left work an hour earlier, following my usual routine, I would have been riding the *55 Sacramento*.

Unlike the newer, slicker, faster buses (like the 55 *Sacramento*), the *1 California* was one of those old clunkers that runs on a track with a rod and wheel attached to a cable above. When it moved, it shook and rattled like a crate of apples dragged backwards in a wheelbarrow. The only folks that ever rode that old vessel of San Francisco history were tourists with no particular destination or locals like me with places to go but no other immediately available means of transportation.

Another monk named Siru boarded the bus about three blocks after I did. This was quite unusual. Monastics rendezvousing late at night on the way home from work almost never happened.

After showing the driver his bus pass, Siru ambled back and sat down beside me. After polite nods, we fell silent. The day was over and we were tired.

Somewhere along the way, about five blocks before California crosses Van Ness, two guys got on the bus, sauntered down the aisle and took a seat near us. They sat sideways in an odd sort of way, looking all around. One kept fidgeting with his coat.

"Why is that guy wearing a coat?" I thought to myself. "It's not cold." The other man was rocking his feet back and forth from toe to heal and heal to toe for no apparent reason. After a minute or two they moved. One sat in the seat in front of us, the other in the seat behind.

Suddenly, the fellow in front turned around and shoved a handgun into my face. The point of the barrel was positioned about three inches from my forehead so that I could see the tips of the bullets in the gun's loading chamber. Nobody in the front of the bus—including the driver—could have been aware of what was going on through the 25 feet of dark, blinking, yellowish, night light that separated the four of us from them. From the driver's perspective, it might have looked like a man had turned in his seat to chat with a friend behind him.

The person holding the gun was talking to me with rubber-faced contortions so as to make himself unrecognizable, I presume, should I have had a later opportunity to pick him out of a line-up or a picture book or some such thing. If it was his intention to intimidate me, which I'm sure it was, he was not succeeding. His facial contortions looked ridiculous—almost humorous. He was telling me to give him my money with such twisted sounds I could barely make out what he was saying. So I just sat there looking at him. I wasn't trying to be brave. Just looking at him seemed to be the right thing to do at the time. Also—and this had nothing to do with the silliness of his appearance—I was overcome with an unexplainable sense of deep calm.

After the gunman repeated his demand for money about three times, Siru stood up to go to the front of the bus. At that point, the man sitting behind us grabbed him around the neck and jerked him back down into his seat. Now the bus driver could see that something was wrong. He stopped the bus.

"Is everything alright back there?" he asked as he looked at us through his rear view mirror.

"Fine," I replied stiffly after a few seconds of awkward silence.

The driver then turned in his seat to look at us directly. At that point, the gunman slipped his weapon into his coat and rotated around to face forward. His accomplice slouched back into his seat behind us.

Then the driver did a smart thing. He pulled the lever that opened the two bus doors—one in the front, one in the back. The man behind stood up, stepped out into the aisle, walked forward a couple of steps and looked down at his friend sternly. After about three seconds, both men scurried together out the open back door to disappear into the night.

The driver then closed the doors, drove a few blocks, stopped the bus, turned in his seat and motioned for us to come to the front. We walked forward. He asked what happened. We explained. He asked if we wanted to report it. We said no. He asked why. We said we didn't think it would do any good. He agreed. And that was it.

Strange as it may seem, Siru and I never once spoke with each other about our experience that night on the *1 California*. Within a few days, however, we each separately reported the event to Gurudeva on the telephone—he was in Hawaii at the time. Over the next few weeks, news of the incident filtered out to the other monks through Gurudeva, as was appropriate. This was in accordance with monastery protocol. Life beyond the monastery walls was supposed to stay there—beyond monastery walls—unless it came up in discussion with Gurudeva.

My first chance to talk in person with Gurudeva about that foiled midnight robbery came approximately three weeks after it occurred. We were in a conveniently private setting—again, just outside the San Francisco airport terminal, waiting for a taxi going into the city. During this appropriate time, Gurudeva asked me to share my version of what had happened. As I talked, he listened carefully. When I was done, he made it very clear to me that I should have given the gunman my money.

At the beginning of our conversation, I assumed he would see my handling of the incident as an act of stoic integrity, perhaps even bravery. I was wrong. He didn't use the word "stupid" in evaluating my conduct, but he might as well have. By the end of our talk, however, he was much kinder to me than I thought he should have been, considering his expressed perception of my action. As always, I was getting to know Gurudeva as I was getting to know myself.

The cab pulled up and we got in. It was a long ride into the city from the airport. For the most part, we sat in silence. Finally, I asked, "Why did this happen to me?"

"You know the answer to that," Gurudeva replied quietly.

"Karma."

"Of course."

"But does it say something about the kind of person I am? This sort of thing isn't happening to the other monks is it?"

"You are who you are. Your karma is a mesh of good, bad and

mixed. And you don't know what's happening with the other monks."

Finally, we arrived at the monastery. After paying the cab driver, we made our way inside. As I set Gurudeva's one suitcase down in the front room of Mamadi Ashram, I was flooded with memories of our last group gathering there in that very room when we had *discussed* karma. Gurudeva caught the drift of my ruminations.

"An ounce of experience is worth a ton of talk," he said.

"Yes, it is," I replied.

Withholding Information

For waiters, Fishermen's Grotto No. 10 was really easy compared to No. 9. There were no stairs. And the kitchen was easily accessible. Joe was there too. Like me, he had been moved to 10 because Nino liked him.

Also, truth be told, Joe was just too old and fat to work 9 any more. At 10, he had the best station in the house and could do no wrong. If he forgot to pick up an order in the kitchen, the chef brought it out to the table for him. If you knew this chef, you would understand how exceptional this was. Joe had no enemies.

At the time of my adventure with the rubber-faced robber, I was still working at No. 10. Terry, the monk who was serving at No. 9 when I was hired there some nine months before, had long since left both the monastic order and the restaurant. Terry and Joe knew each other.

Somehow, Joe had learned of my experience on the *1 California*. Had I mentioned something to him about it? I don't think so. I couldn't remember for sure. Anyway, he knew. I discovered he knew during a conversation back by the dishwasher in the No. 10 kitchen. As in No. 9, the dishwasher was the place for waiters to linger. So there we were— Joe with his cigarette and coffee, me with a toothpick—back by the dishwasher, lingering.

"Best to change your shirt," Joe said, talking to the air.

"Excuse me?" I replied, somewhat offended.

"Not now. When you get ready to go home."

"Why is that?" I asked, puzzled.

"They look for white shirts and black pants."

"Who?"

"Guys with guns."

"How did you find out?"

"A birdie."

"Which birdie?"

"The one that flew away."

Was he was talking about Terry? Did he know that Terry was a monk? For that matter, did he know I was a monk? And how did Terry find out about my experience on the *1 California*. I thought he had left San Francisco long before that happened. This was the one thing I didn't like about Joe. He had a way of riddle talking. Anyhow, that was good advice about the shirt. White shirts and black pants late a night meant waiters just off duty with pockets full of tip cash.

"Who's this flyaway birdie?" I asked, trying to sound casual.

"You remember Terry, don't you?" Joe asked. "I thought he was a friend of yours."

"I know him. That's all. Have you seen him lately?"

"Every day. He's just up the street at Tarantino's, making more money than us."

"Oh yeah?"

"If I were younger, I'd get a job there." Joe said, tactfully changing the subject. "How about you?" he asked, as he looked over at me for the first time in our conversation. "What's holding you here?"

"Nino's been good to me," I replied.

"He'd understand. Waiters are a dime a dozen. He'd just go in the back and open another can."

"Another can of waiters?"

"Right—dime a dozen."

Suddenly, talk-time was over. A tour bus had just pulled up and the restaurant was flooding with people. That was the way it was on the Wharf. We were either insanely busy or just standing around. Right now, even Joe couldn't talk. We had to huff and puff.

Over the next few weeks, I came to understand that our monastic identities in the restaurants were not really secret at all. The people we worked with were just politely humoring us by pretending they couldn't see we were about as transparent as a brick wall.

And Terry? Indeed, he was working at Tarantino's and making a lot of money. I took note of this for future reference. (I *did* eventually work at Tarantino's.) Terry had heard about my *1 California* adventure because he was still in communication with some of the monks. This was not as it should have been. He was supposed to have broken off all contact with us when he left the order.

Actually, this information about Terry turned out to be much more important than I thought. When I mentioned it casually to our Silent Ministry Coordinator, he told me to tell Gurudeva right away. Conveniently, Gurudeva was there in San Francisco at the time. So I went to see him immediately.

As I walked into the front room of Mamadi ashram, Gurudeva was talking to a monk. Their conversation stopped abruptly as I entered. The monk was looking down.

"Yes?" Gurudeva asked sternly in my direction.

"I'm sorry. I can come back," I replied, feeling awkward.

"What do you have?"

"I just need to share something with you, but it can wait."

"What is it?"

"Terry."

"What about Terry?"

"I think he's still around and talking to some of the monks."

"I see." Gurudeva said, "Mark here is thinking about leaving." Mark's monastic name was Suriya. Gurudeva was referring to him by his restaurant name. "He's upset."

"Gurudeva, I think I will excuse myself if you don't mind," I said. I really wanted to get out of there. "I just thought I should share that small bit of information about Terry."

"Good. Thanks. I'll see you a little later."

As I was leaving Mamadi Ashram, one of the monks told me that Gurudeva already knew about Terry talking to some of the monks, that one of those monks was Mark, and that I was really smart to have passed on to Gurudeva what I had learned about Terry—not because Gurudeva needed to be informed about what he already knew, but simply because my sharing of that information cleared me of withholding it.

This was all starting to look like a soap opera to me—and a complicated one at that. I was starting to think to myself, "Where's the yoga in all of this?"

It was about dinner time, so I stepped into the monastery kitchen to make myself a salad, plus a little extra for Gurudeva, if he wanted it. By the time I got over to Mamadi ashram with a full meal on a tray, Mark had left and Gurudeva was alone.

"How does fresh spinach, ginger, onions and tomatoes, covered with a creamy-style, oil-and-vinegar dressing sound?" I asked Gurudeva from the ashram doorway.

"Sounds wonderful," he responded.

I had expected to find him in a rather serious mood, but he was actually quite jovial. In fact, he was so jovial, it looked like I might be able to pose some daring questions.

"Are you concerned about losing monks?" I asked as I grappled with wooden tongs to transfer my salad into a large, special dish I had brought just for Gurudeva.

"Not at all. Some young men need to get lost," he said with a smile, "so they can find out for themselves where they stand in the over-all scheme of things. Things will be a lot easier now."

"Do you think Terry will be a problem?" I asked.

"Temporary drama. This is all part of a healthy transition. The men that should stay will stay. The men that should go will go." He took a big bite of spinach and munched enough to swallow. "Everything is exactly as it should be. Not one thing is out of place. All is well and couldn't be otherwise."

"But what about things that go wrong and have to get fixed?"

"Something is always going wrong and something is always having to get fixed," he said with a twinkle in his eye. "Life is sort of like a soap opera."

A Ledger of Life

My yoga journal was such a hodgepodge of disassociated notes I often thought of throwing it away. Yet I just couldn't. Even though it served no apparent purpose, I just couldn't be without it.

This thing I was calling a "journal"—for lack of a better term— vacillated between being a meditation notebook and a daily diary of monastic life. It was the latter only as a chronology of the former. Yet it could never really develop with any sort of continuity, because, as soon as I learned something new or perceived something differently, all I had written up to that point would seem to be either wrong or irrelevant, and

81

therefore obsolete. So, this growing tome—for all the effort I was putting into it—wasn't really much more than a grand exercise in rewriting. As a coherent document, it was completely indiscernible—even though, in some odd way, it made perfect sense to me.

I'm sure my fellow monks wondered why I couldn't go a day without scrawling away in this thing. I just couldn't help it. It was my one-page book, driven by angst and weighed down by an ever-growing mountain of crossed-out notes. I honestly thought, as I wrote—and this is what kept me positive—I would eventually arrive at a perfect page, a page that wouldn't have to be rewritten.

As might be expected, in going back over what was left of this text years later, the most interesting stuff was what almost got trashed. Much of that has been reworked and incorporated into this book, but here following is an example of one page, raw as it was, straight out of my original journal.

January 6, 1974, one day after Gurudeva's birthday:

"Self Realization is the goal of yoga and life." Do I believe this? If so, what is the source of my belief? Faith? Faith in what? Knowledge? Where is the knowledge? Memory? Thought? Intuition?

Imbalance makes intuition unavailable. Balancing mind, body and emotion brings stillness. In stillness, clarity. In clarity, intuition.

Faith—difficult to understand. Like love. Feeling is key.

Ups and downs. Dangerous. On a good day, intuition is easy, faith is unnecessary. On a normal day, intuition comes and goes, faith is necessary but tenuous. On a bad day, no intuition, no faith. Doubt.

Question for Gurudeva:

If yoga is the stilling of mind, body and emotions, and what we are calling Self Realization is the ultimate aim of yoga, what is the one best way to still mind, body and emotions?

"So you want a one way," Gurudeva said, after hearing me read him my journal question.

"Sorry to be simplistic," I replied. My journal was open in my lap.

"May I have a look at your notes?" he asked.

I handed my journal to him. After carefully reading my January 6 entry, he casually thumbed back through the rest of the journal.

"This is quite a work," he said. "The last page is good."

"A work in progress just between me and me," I replied. "Can you read my handwriting?"

"Oh yes," he said with a peaceful smile. "Maybe some day you'll write a book."

I laughed.

After a short but calm and blissful pause, Gurudeva began to address my request for a "one way."

"Why not just take a chance?" he asked. "Sit still with nothing and pull on the inner sky for what you want. Be humble. Mentally hold up an empty bowl. In the last second of the last minute of your waiting you'll receive what you seek. And in that receiving you'll have greater faith for the next time you strive to do that same thing all over again. Stillness is the key — more than a one method. You have written this to yourself. It's right there in your notes. If it helps, call stillness a method. "

"And balance?"

"Same thing. The very idea of balance comes up when there has been an imbalance. When we have balanced an imbalance of forces, we have stillness. Stillness is not possible when the physical, emotional or mental forces are out of balance."

Gurudeva looked at me to see if I understood his answer. I did.

"May I ask you a question about something completely different?" I inquired hesitantly.

"Sure."

"Snitching."

"This is in reference to what?"

"Terry."

"Oh yes, Terry."

"I felt like I was snitching on him and you were encouraging it."

"Absolutely."

There was a pause. "Is that really necessary?"

"Absolutely."

Another pause. "Why?"

"There is a time to withhold and there is a time to share. Need is the key. With regard to any information in any given situation, we must ask, 'What is the need here? Do we need to give this information out or do we need to hold it back?' An employee probably wouldn't be inclined to talk about his family with his boss. Nor would he be inclined to talk about his boss with his family—unless there was a need. In addition to need, there must also be honesty. Honesty is purifying."

"Yes, that makes sense when it's about me. I can see the relevance of need and honesty in talking with you about myself. But other people?"

"The monks are not 'other people.' We are a family. And a family with secrets is a family with problems. In the purity of honesty, lines of communication are straight, open and clear. When there is deception of any sort, those lines get crossed and blocked. Communication breaks down. How can we successfully work together as a family without clear lines of communication?

"Although Terry is no longer a monk, he is affecting the lives of monks who are still here, and he is putting those monks into a position of having to choose whether or not to keep secrets from me. This is not good for the monastic order. And because it is not good for the order, I need to know about it. If any monk should choose to not tell me something I need to know about Terry just because of a friendship they have with him, that's not doing anybody any good, especially Terry."

"So, it's not really snitching at all."

"No it's not. In 'snitching' there is ill intent. In making a decision whether or not to withhold information, consider motive. Even a bad decision can be canceled out by a good intention."

"Life can get complicated, can't it?"

"Like a soap opera." Gurudeva said with a smile. "But it can be a little less complicated if there aren't too many secrets."

"K-I-S-S"

"Right. As we always say, *Keep It Simple, Stupid.*"

"No secrets."

"Here in this place." Gurudeva pointed to the ground. "No secrets."

The East and the West
Now seems a good time to share a handful of Hindu philosophy-and-lifestyle fundamentals, as I was taught these by Gurudeva. If you have investigated Hinduism and have come to a different understanding of that which I am about to share, I would not be surprised, for it has been

said there is a greater diversity of religious opinion within Hinduism than there is outside Hinduism among all the religions of the world. Generally speaking, however, it may also be said with some degree of certainty that a great many Hindu scholars would consider Gurudeva's well-schooled interpretation of Hinduism to be highly respected.

In most Western religious thought, evil is perceived to be intrinsically separate from righteousness—something like the bad nature of Satan irrevocably distinct from and opposed to the good nature of God.

To be sure, Hindus believe that evil does exist as a powerful, worldly force, and that there is nothing good about it. They also believe, as would most any sane person, that any immoral thought, word or deed causing harm, pain or misery would have to be considered evil. But they do *not* believe that evil emerges from a source separate from God.

While Hindus believe evil is simply the flip side of good in a one world that is unavoidably duel by nature, they also believe man's deepest nature transcends all opposites, including good and evil.

Hindus hold the view that the consequences of all actions, negative and positive, are determined by the law of karma. When man commits evil deeds, they believe, he accrues negative karma, which he must then resolve. In the resolution of this negative karma, he comes to a full understanding of his evil deeds by personally experiencing their effect. This is God's tough love, His flawless system of justice and education programmed right into life at its root level. No one is exempt from this primal law. Its crux is threefold: 1. Evil is not intrinsic. 2. Evil is not permanent. 3. Evil deeds can be resolved.

A sin, according to Hindu thought, is an evil deed committed intentionally. This is not to say bad deeds committed unintentionally don't accrue negative karma. They do—but not as much. Hindus would not view a sin as a crime against God. They would see it as an affront to dharma, the inherent order and nature of the universe. Hell only exists, they believe, within the mind of those who sin; and hell, like evil, is not permanent.

Like Jains, Sikhs and Buddhists (as well as Christians before the advent of the Nicene Council in 787), Hindus believe in reincarnation, the return of souls to physical life. Through this process of reincarnation, they believe, each soul has ample opportunity to experience all of life's manifestation through the creation of literally every conceivable karma.

85

Once a demon, later a saint, each soul works its way back to its origin in God. In the end, if such a point can be said to exist in a circle, the soul fully merges with God as its Self.

Somewhere in the middle of this long process—right within these many lives we live—an internal war is waged between the forces of good and evil. As we become consumed in these inner battles, we sense there is some sort of death hanging in the balance. Yet, at some point, through all of our blundering in trial and error, we realize nothing can die into absolute oblivion.

After this important revelation, we begin to live above fear in the higher realms of mind from which vantage point we have a tighter, more efficient control over the resolution of our past and the creation of our future during a careful and deliberate life lived in the present. In the clarity of this living we move quickly away from bad toward good and beyond—in, up and out of the world of apparent reality.

All of this is some of what Gurudeva taught us about the ancient Hindu view of good, bad, evil, sin and the evolution of the soul.

As Gurudeva mellowed in age, his clairaudient and clairvoyant powers became stronger and stronger. As this occurred, he lived more and more deeply within himself. This mystical metamorphosis was hard to ignore. The euphoria of his effulgent inner life was more than evident in the ethereal radiance we continually felt around him.

It was inspiring when he shared with us even a little of his inner life. Just his mention of it was transporting. The people he met on the inside, the experiences he had—it was all quite magical. Interestingly, out of the richness of his uniquely diversified and fascinating inner life, actually because of it, he was encouraged to guide us into the lap of traditional Hinduism.

In Hinduism, which is so ancient its true beginning is unknown, Gurudeva found a validation of his own mystical experience. In his own mystical experience, he found a validation of Hinduism.

Especially after the scribing of the *Shastras,* Gurudeva strongly encouraged us all to follow a Hindu way of life. From a utilitarian point of view, incorporating a Hindu lifestyle made Gurudeva's life easier. Within the study of Hinduism and the practice of its worship, we each discovered a means of solving our own personal problems without having to download them onto Gurudeva.

The practice of Hindu worship made us humble and gave us a place to put our emotion. The study of Hindu philosophy provided us with a solid conceptual basis for our yoga practice and gave us a place to put our thought.

So, along with our restaurant work, monastic duties and daily vigil, we worshipped and studied—a lot. And we were most rigorously tested. Gurudeva had the senior monks devise a well-researched course of study on Hinduism that included a final examination composed mostly of essay questions requiring in-depth responses. We all had to take this examination—even those of us who helped Gurudeva create it.

The scope of this study program was enormous. It included quite a detailed investigation of how Hindus perceive God, gods, goddesses, guru, soul, service, inner life, outer life, family life, monastic life, home and temple worship, yoga, culture, scripture, ethics and more. It also incorporated a very extensive study of other religions.

Although Gurudeva was strict with us, he was also sweet. This was something he couldn't help. It was so much in his nature to be kind, he found it very difficult to be otherwise for any reason. As hard as he tried, he could not be too tough for too long. For every stern instruction or reprimand he issued, he gave some loving comment to compensate.

Cross Country

In early 1975, Gurudeva announced that all monks and members of Saiva Siddhanta Church would have to formally convert to Hinduism. His reasoning for this was pragmatic: Since yoga was conceived in a Hindu context, it could best be practiced in a Hindu lifestyle.

Some monks balked. A few church families resisted. Nevertheless, Gurudeva was persistent. Being something of a purist, he sought for all of us only what he had always asserted was of primary importance in life: authentic spiritual transformation. As he worked to move us toward this ultimate goal of existence, all we had to do, if we could manage it, was cooperate.

Such cooperation was easier for those who were nimble enough to intuit Gurudeva's intent. These observant ones could see that a persistent unsettling of a false sense of identity was the kingpin of Gurudeva's basic approach to spiritual life. For those who couldn't line up with this approach, all that Gurudeva said and did came across as an imposition.

"Change is the only constant," he would reiterate, time and time again. We each had to catch the drift of what he meant by this in our own way in accordance with our own karmas, which were all quite different. Yet, we were all united in our attempt to follow Gurudeva with full faith in our pursuit of yogic illumination.

"My job is to push you to do what you won't do by yourself," Gurudeva told the monks more than once. "In your quest for the *Self*, you must change your *self*. Even your own parents should not be able to recognize you. When they visit, they should say, 'Who is this wonderful person? Do I know him?'"

With regard to religious conversion, Gurudeva was told one must be born a Hindu to be a Hindu, and that conversion into Hinduism from outside a Hindu bloodline was not possible. Gurudeva was certain this was not true. With a little research, substantiated by confirmation from a number of respected Hindu priests and scholars, he discovered that conversion to Hinduism *was* possible and *could* occur through the performance of a temple sacrament called the *Namakarana Samskara*, or name-giving ceremony. So, Gurudeva instructed each of us to work toward having this particular Hindu sacrament performed.

Gurudeva was quite thorough in setting up his requirements for our accomplishment of this task. We all had to choose a Hindu first and last name and get our born names legally changed. Those of us who had any sort of previous religious affiliation—which was just about all of us—had to return to our family homes to officially sever those early ties at the place where those ties were originally established.

This meant we had to go to the minister or priest of the church we attended during our youth to personally ask for an official letter of dismissal or excommunication. Also, while we were doing this, we were to compose in writing what Gurudeva referred to as a "religious point-counterpoint." In this document, we were to compare the beliefs and attitudes of our former religion with the beliefs and attitudes of Hinduism. The entirety of this process was supposed to catalyze an intense self-reflection. I know for a fact that, for those of us who endured the program from start to finish, this was exactly what happened.

It was too expensive for all of the monks to go home at the same time for this religious severance. If a monk was gone for four months, which was about the amount of time this severance process most usually required, it could mean a loss of at least ten thousand dollars in Silent Ministry income. Also leaving the restaurants for an extended period of time generally required quitting, which meant having to find new jobs with perhaps less pay upon returning to San Francisco. Because this process of severance was a risk and a burden from a monetary point of view, the monks only traveled home one or two at a time.

My turn came in early February of 1975. At that time, I was also beginning a long period of training in preparation for taking lifetime monastic vows.

There are two levels of commitment to monastic life in Saiva Siddhanta Church. At one level, monks take vows for only two years at a time so that, every two years, they have an opportunity to reevaluate how they feel about monastic life and decide whether or not they want to continue living as a monk. At the other more committed level, monks take vows for life.

Gurudeva's initiation of a man into a lifetime of monasticism includes taking a vow of renunciation, which requires releasing past attachments, including ties with family and commitments to previous life goals. The ceremony of initiation into Gurudeva's renunciate order of monks is called the *Antyeshti Samskara*, the Hindu funeral ceremony. After this ceremony, a newly ordained, renunciate monk is expected to see himself as having died in one life to take birth in another.

Thus, my trip home was meant to accomplish two objectives: sever my ties with the Presbyterian Church, and—this, as it turned out, was the toughest part—sever my ties with family.

In preparation for my journey, I quit my job at No. 10 and said goodbye to Joe.

"You'll be back or I'll see you around, which ever comes first," Joe said casually.

Back at the monastery, just before making final arrangements for my departure—like buying plane tickets and such—I went to see Gurudeva in the temple. This turned out to be a most unusual meeting.

Although, as I understood it, we were supposed to discuss matters of practical concern like travel arrangements and such, we didn't.

Since I was going home both to sever previous religious ties (in preparation for becoming a Hindu) and family ties (in preparation for becoming a renunciate monk), Gurudeva was more concerned about making sure I fully understood what I was doing rather than how I was going to do it. This I could see. What I couldn't see and therefore didn't anticipate was the heavy tenor the talk would take.

For a reason not completely apparent to me at the time, he was choosing this particular moment to remind me of all my personal weaknesses, which, after he had been talking for a while, began to sound like all the weaknesses any person could possibly have.

All I can remember of that experience is a hot rush of emotions. Almost immediately, I stopped hearing what he was saying. It was too much. All I could do was feel it. And it didn't feel good. When he was finished, I thanked him, stood up, made my way out the front door of the temple, turned right and started walking toward Knoxville, Tennessee, 2,500 miles away. This was an impulsive move to be sure.

I later learned Gurudeva had this same tough talk, naming all the same "personal weaknesses," with all the monks right before they went home for their religious conversion. I also learned later, much later, Gurudeva's intention in talking straight like this was to give us a dose of our future's down side: the tough side of character building and a necessary aspect of serious monastic life.

It took me a little less than an hour to hike, without hitching, straight down Sacramento Street to Van Ness where I turned right to walk all the way across town to the ramp entrance onto Central Freeway extending across Oakland Bay Bridge.

There at that ramp, I stuck out my thumb for the first time. By then, I was plenty ready to hitch. But it was not meant to be—at least not right away.

I could not have chosen a worse place to catch a ride. There at that freeway entrance, drivers were forced to focus forward in a horde of cars that were speeding up like a herd of buffalo stampeding through a mountain pass.

I moved back a few blocks. Still, it was bad. It was about one in the afternoon and I was tired from walking. Now I was waiting. Five minutes. Ten minutes. Fifteen. Twenty. I could feel a heavy cloud of despondency moving in.

Standing there pointing at Tennessee with my thumb, it slowly began to dawn on me what I had gotten myself into. I had no money, no

90

warm clothes and no plan. Plus I had never hitchhiked in my life.

After about a half hour, a small beat-up Honda stopped in front of me. By then, I was more relieved to be rescued from my own thoughts than I was happy to finally be getting a ride.

As I hustled to jump into the car, I didn't even try to get a good look at its driver, although I could sense, vaguely, it was a *he* that was *big*. I was more aware of all the honking coming from the cars blocked behind the stopped Honda.

Imagine my surprise when—after I finally got settled into my seat—I turned to see the driver of the car was Joe. Yes, Joe, the waiter.

"Hey Joe," I exclaimed with genuine astonishment. "You're the last guy I expected to run into out here."

"Likewise," Joe replied. "I knew you were heading cross country, but I didn't know you'd be walking."

"I didn't either, to tell you the truth. Where are you going?"

"Oakland."

"How come?"

"Relatives."

It was a bit odd to see Joe out of uniform. Suddenly, I realized I really didn't know him at all, even though I had worked with him for a year. "Joe has a family," I thought to myself, "—in Oakland. Cool."

I turned to look at Joe, as if for the first time. He was way too large for this little car he was driving. And he was busting out of a tight set of clothes that revealed he hadn't always been as fat as he was when I met him. Still, his hair was slicked back and he had a fresh pack of smokes in his left shirt pocket—just like in the restaurant.

Although I was slightly concerned that he was weaving through heavy, fast-moving traffic with only one hand on the steering wheel, I felt somehow honored to be in his presence, almost as if he was some kind of huge, comic angel come to send me on my way with a blessing. "No," I thought to myself. "That's nonsense. This is just Joe, heading home to see to his family in Oakland."

A Rough Ride

Joe got me across the bridge. That was about it. As he pulled over to let me out near a freeway entrance onto I-580, he started to ask me if I needed some money, then stopped right after, "Do you ...." I could see him thinking he'd be wise not complete the question. Instead, he just said, "Travel safely," to which I replied, "Will do, Joe. Have a good time with your family."

He smiled, waved good-bye and was gone.

So, there I was. Alone—again. I looked at my watch. It was two o'clock. I looked up. Not a cloud in the sky—and the sun was shining brightly. Good. Not too cold. I looked left and right, trying to get my bearings. As soon as I figured out I was stationed in the right place to catch a ride going in the right direction on I-580, I stuck out my thumb. I must have looked bewildered.

"Lost?" I heard someone say.

"Sort'a," I said, before I could figure out which direction the question was coming from. Oh, there he was. A kid about my age in a pickup truck.

"Where ya goin'?" he asked.

"Tennessee."

He laughed. "You jokin'?"

"No."

"Well, I can get you to Livermore if you want."

Livermore was okay. Although it was only about 50 miles away, it was at least a step in the right direction. Having learned to appreciate just getting a ride, I hopped into his truck and we took off.

The kid didn't turn out to be much of a talker, but he did tell me his name. It was John. As John explained, he was named John after his dad who was named John after his dad. That was the totality of our conversation—until just after we took the Livermore exit off the Interstate where he stopped to let me out.

"Where's all your gear?" he asked as I was stepping down.

"I'm traveling light," I replied.

"You don't even have any food."

"I'll probably eat down the road a bit," I didn't want to tell him I didn't have any money.

"Down the road?" he parroted me. "Will you be getting on I-5?"

"Yep."

"There's no place to eat 'down the road' on I-5. You gonna keep on goin' all night?"

This was a lot of talking for John.

"Well, yeah, I guess I'll keep going," I said.

"In that little jacket?"

"I'll be alright."

"So, I guess after Bakersfield, you'll be getting' on I-40 going through the mountains into Arizona."

"I guess." By this time I was outside the truck, talking through the window.

"You know it's supposed to snow six to eight inches through those mountains tonight."

"I didn't know that." I really didn't. This was alarming news.

"And you're not going to put up somewhere?"

"No plans to."

"So you must not have any money."

He had me. I couldn't lie. "Nope. No money."

"Ok, get back in. Let me at least get you some food."

John turned out to be a really nice guy. He just honestly wanted to help. I couldn't believe it.

It was about a ten-minute drive from the Interstate to John's home. He lived on a farm with his parents and a lot of extended family.

It took fifteen minutes just to get walked around and introduced to everyone. Besides a mom and a dad, John had four brothers. Two of these four were married with three kids apiece. By my rough calculations, this added up to fifteen people—all living under one big roof. I was told this count could easily double when relatives came visiting for Thanksgivings, Christmases, marriages, funerals and the like.

I guess John told his mom I wasn't staying, because, by the time I was invited for coffee in the living room, she had assembled a huge bag of food and placed it by the front door. This was embarrassing. I thanked her as she scurried in and out of the room, trying unsuccessfully to remain unnoticed. Now, I was starting to feel guilty for imposing upon this kind family. John could see I was getting antsy.

"You're welcome to stay the night if you like." he said.

"No, no, I couldn't do that," I replied, as I stood up to leave. "I really have to be going. You have all been so nice to me, but I have...."

"Miles to go before you sleep," John said, gracefully finishing my canned reply.

In the truck on the way to the freeway, John explained to me how his dad, with only twenty dollars in his pocket during the "great depression" fifty years before, had hitched from New York to California where he eventually purchased and cultivated the farm they now owned. John was trying to help me feel good about accepting his family's hospitality. It worked.

Within thirty minutes, I was on I-580 turning onto I-5 heading south toward Bakersfield. I had gotten a ride quickly. This time it was with two guys in a VW van.

It was now close to six o'clock in the evening and the sky was just starting to yield its nighttime colors. Although it was beautiful, I just couldn't get myself in a mood to enjoy it. Something was up. Something wasn't right. For one thing, I had been invited to sit in the front seat of the van. Why was that? Why wasn't the other guy in front with me in the back? I was the last man in.

"I'm buzzin' on Ginseng," the driver gleefully exclaimed. The guy in the back cringed with disgust as he squinted out the window.

"Will that stuff keep you awake for driving?" I asked, just trying to keep the conversation going.

"Ginseng ain't stuff," replied the driver. "Ginseng's a food. I'm flying high on a good food." He craned his head up so he could peer into the back seat through the rear view mirror. "Right Mike?"

Mike, the guy in the back, just kept squinting out the window.

After we talked for a while, it became clear that Doug, the owner and driver of the van, was sort of a clueless hippie wannabe, virtuously naive in his own way, but a little slow; and Mike—another pick-up like me—was ... well, Mike was different.

Doug, who had picked up Mike about an hour before me, was just driving home to Bakersfield, where he lived with his folks. From the few words Mike spoke, I was able to put it together that he, Mike, was going to Albuquerque. Because Mike was not in the habit of talking in complete sentences, the content of his communication was somewhat difficult to solidify.

Although Mike and Doug were about the same age, that was

94

about all they had in common. Doug's skin was a soft, rosy pink. His recently-washed hair looked blown-dry. And he was a bit plump. Mike, on the other hand, was bone thin with skin that was more like hide, hair that was oily black and a face that was pasty white and covered with a three-day matt of thick, course beard. His clothes weren't old but they were wrinkled and unwashed. And his black, leather, zip-up boots with one-inch heels looked way too slick and polished for his otherwise crumpled look. Together, Doug and Mike made an odd couple to say the least. And now there I was, forming a trio that was odder still.

Doug was doing all the driving. I offered to spell him, but he said, no, he liked to zone out on the broken white lines down the center of the road. This worried me a little, so I kept talking to him. At about 6:30, Doug pulled off into an interstate "rest stop," parked the van and announced he had to take a leak.

While he was outside, Mike leaned forward from his slouched position in the back and suddenly got talkative. "Are the keys there?" he asked me in a low, gravelly voice.

"What?" I asked, completely surprised. Looking at the ignition, I replied, "No, they're not."

Mike let out a long, exasperated sigh and sank back into his seat, then abruptly leaned forward again, as if he had just decided to tell me something really important. "I know a guy with a chop shop in Albuquerque" he growled. "He'll give me a thousand bucks for this thing. We can split it fifty-fifty."

As I turned around to look at Mike in utter disbelief, Doug was just climbing back into the van.

"Whew," Doug sang out loudly. "Now I'm running on empty. That's a feeling I like." After a pause he added, as he started the van and looked at the gas gauge. "Actually, *we're* running on empty. We got to find us a gas station—and soon. Keep your eyes peeled, guys."

And off we went into a black, moonless night. We were about 150 miles from Bakersfield, traveling through what appeared to be fairly uninhabited wilderness. I was getting cold and thinking hard about what to do next.

Finally, we saw one of those blue Interstate "gas-food-lodging" signs and Doug took the next exit. I started getting a funny feeling in my stomach. Soon, it would be time to do something about Mike. Monks are not supposed to hate anything. But I hated this. I hated being in this most difficult situation.

We pulled into a gas station that was combined with a Food Mart and stopped in front of a self-serve pump. As Doug got out to get gas, Mike stayed put. Not good. I needed to talk with Doug alone. When Doug headed for the Food Mart to pay for the gas, I followed. So did Mike. Not good.

But just as Doug opened the door to go into the store, Mike veered off to the left toward the bathroom. Good. However, instead of paying for the gas right away, Doug got sidetracked at the candy rack.

"Doug, we have to get out of here now," I said sternly, as I grabbed his arm. "Pay for the gas, and let's go. NOW."

Doug pulled his arm away and looked at me wide-eyed. He seemed sort of shocked, concerned and bewildered, all at once. I waited a few moments, then said again, "Let's go NOW. You're in trouble!"

"Why?" he asked innocently.

"I can explain later. Let's go. NOW."

Finally, he caught the feeling of my urgency and quickly stepped up to the cashier.

When I saw him fumbling for his credit card, I asked, "Do you have cash? Can you please pay cash. It's quicker."

Now, he was starting to panic. He pulled out two twenties, gave them to the cashier and waited nervously for his change. His fingers were trembling a little.

"Is this about Mike?" he asked, as we got into the van.

"Yes! Just go. I'll explain in a minute. Go."

Doug started to buckle his seat belt. I looked over my shoulder toward the rest room. Sure enough, Mike was walking toward the van. He was perhaps thirty feet away.

"Never mind the seat belt," I said. "GO."

Doug started the van, rammed the gas, popped the clutch and lurched forward with a screech, almost slamming into a car just pulling into the station. Somebody yelled.

"Never mind," I said. "Just go."

As Doug pulled out into the highway heading toward the inter-state, I looked back one last time. There was Mike, standing at the pump, looking at us—just looking.

A Timely Blessing

It only took about three minutes to get back on the Interstate. Doug focused on driving. I stared forward. Neither one of us felt like talking right away. We both needed to settle down. After a few minutes, when Doug started repeatedly humming a song-fragment from a TV commercial, I figured it was the right time to say something.

I told him about Mike's plan to steal his van and how I learned about that plan at our road-side rest stop. Just to hammer my story home, I made it clear that, if he hadn't taken his keys with him when he stepped out of the van to take a leak, and if I had stepped out with him, we both might now be standing by the road with our thumbs sticking out. Then I apologized for being somewhat tense in rushing him along at the gas station without fully explaining what was going on.

Since that was about all I could say without repeating myself, I stopped talking and waited for Doug to respond, realizing all to well he could be wondering if perhaps I was the bad guy who had just managed to get Mike out of the picture so I could steal the van myself.

"You know what I've learned from this whole thing?" Doug asked as his eyes twinkled and his mouth melted into an impish grin. This was a Doug I had not yet met.

"The meaning of life is obscure?" I replied with a smile.

"No." He said as he paused for effect and finally looked at me. "Don't pick up hitchhikers."

We both laughed. Whatever tension there had been was now nicely broken. I could tell he was okay with my explanation.

"You know, we could run into Mike later," I said. "He's going to Albuquerque and will be coming this way."

"What do you mean 'we'? I'm getting off this road pretty soon."

"Good point."

Doug was doing a good job of keeping the mood light, even though both of us were understandably concerned about Mike.

"You know something?" Doug said after a few moments. "I stopped for you because I knew Mike was bad news. I thought maybe I would need some back-up in dealing with him. He already tried to steal my keys once. Somehow, he snatched them when we stopped for snacks. When I caught him on a fluke, he said I had dropped them. I knew I hadn't dropped those keys. That's when I realized he was up to something. And that's why I picked you up—besides the fact you really looked like you needed a ride, of course."

And there I was thinking Doug was slow. Suddenly, I was feeling like the slow one. "Hey Doug," I said. "Can I give you some advice?"

"Yeah."

"Don't pick up hitchhikers."

"That's for *damn* sure."

Right before Bakersfield, we worked our way through a complicated maze of route changes that I was happy I did not have to maneuver by myself. Being a local resident, Doug breezed right through all the twists and turns like they were nothing.

When we finally got into Bakersfield and arrived at the turn-off Doug had to take to get to his home, we stopped at a coffee shop. As we settled into the welcome warmth of the restaurant and the fine smell of cooking food, Doug offered to buy me anything on the menu.

At first, I shook my head.

In a smooth anticipation of this refusal, Doug made it clear he was offering me food for three reasons: one, he knew I was broke; two, he had helped me munch on the goodies in my brown paper bag; and three, I had helped him in dealing with Mike.

Without waiting for response from me, Mike ordered salad, toast and coffee for both of us. Did he know I was vegetarian? Probably. As I had recently discovered, Doug was not slow.

As we waited for our food, I felt exposed—like a convict on the run. The restaurant seemed way too lit up. My mind kept throwing up images of Mike perched in a tree across the street with a high-powered rifle pointed at my head through the restaurant window. Doug must have been feeling the same way. He was looking around nervously.

I was more tired than hungry. Yet my tiredness was welcome. It left me less inclined toward anxious anticipation. I was also feeling like I should call Gurudeva—especially now after this recent adventure with Mike. I looked at my watch. It was ten o'clock. Was it too late? No, I decided, but I'd better call soon. I borrowed a quarter from Doug for a collect call and strolled over to a nearby pay phone.

I was lucky. I got hold of Gurudeva right away.

As we started talking, I expected him to reprimand me for my impulsiveness in deciding to hitchhike, but he didn't. He just asked how

I was doing and did I have any money. When I answered, "fine" and "no," he told me not to worry, all would be well from this point on and all of my needs would be met. He said there was a flood of *devas* traveling with me who would protect and assist me. Then, he asked for a quick summary of what had happened thus far.

Just when I was starting to feel like I was talking too much, he stepped in. As I listened to his voice, I felt my entire nervous system relax. Never had I been so aware of the power his rich, resonant speech had to soothe and comfort.

"Remember," he said quietly, "you have chosen to live as a monk and practice yoga diligently. Because of this, your life will intensify in every way. You will be facing karmas you would not ordinarily have to deal with in this life."

"Any advice?" I asked.

"Take responsibility for everything you do. Own the life you live. Know that everything now apparently being done to you, you once did to someone else. You have learned this in your head. Now learn it in life. This is a great opportunity. If you can take this adventure as a blessing, you will glide right through it. If you can't, you'll still learn. Either way you're okay. You can't loose. Take heart. Keep your chin up. Try to stay positive. Life is meant to be lived joyously."

"Just to be safe, I think this is a good time to pray."

"To Ganesha."

"Yes, to Ganesha."

"But Ganesha helps best those who help themselves. Pray to Lord Ganesha often, but don't expect everything to fall into your lap just because of those prayers. God and the gods work *with* you, not *for* you. When you have gone as far as you can go, they can take you a little further. Just remember, you have the power to control your life. All you need is a little faith. And right here, right now, is the perfect time to develop faith. Just lean your creative thoughts and feelings in a certain direction, and discover for yourself just how quickly your life circumstances will gravitate that way. You have a great opportunity here. Take advantage of it. I know you will do wonderfully well. Call again when you get home."

When the phone call was over, I felt like I could fly. Anything seemed possible, and all of my current problems seemed insignificant.

More out of inspiration than need, I prayed to Lord Ganesha.

"Aum Ganesha," I said in my head. "Thank you for all you have always done for me, and forgive me for my endless lack of appreciation. Although I could never say I *don't* need your help, I especially *do* need it now. I'm not asking for a miracle, just clarity and insight when I have to make decisions. As always, I stand ever ready to serve you, just as you have always served me. Thank you, Ganesha."

Someone was sitting with Doug at our table when I returned from the pay phone. No, it wasn't Mike. It was a person named Luke, a friend of Doug's. Luke had been eating dinner in the restaurant as we entered. While I was making my phone call, he had come over to visit Doug who, when I returned from the phone, was telling Luke all about Mike. They were both laughing.

"Yeah, very funny," I said, trying to slip into the conversation.

"Funny now. But not then. Right?" said Luke. We all nodded. After Doug formally introduced us, Luke said to me, "Doug says you're traveling east on I-40."

"That would be right," I replied.

"Well, I'm driving all night to Flagstaff and could use someone to spell me at the wheel. You want to come along?"

Luke could see from the look on my face that he had a rider and a driver. A lift to Flagstaff would put me 500 miles—about seven hours of driving time—closer to home. I could not believe my ears. I had just finished trying to make it clear to Ganesha that I didn't need a miracle. Now here he was giving me one. That's a friend.

Our food came. While Doug and I ate, Doug and Luke talked—mostly about some good old days that meant nothing to me. Luke and Doug were happy to be catching up on old times. I was happy to be eating. When we were done being happy, Doug dove his last few miles home as Luke and I headed for Flagstaff.

Happy Juice
We got where we were going at six o'clock the next morning. I had truly enjoyed our trouble-free ride from Bakersfield. Luke and I had shifted driving duties through the night and hadn't talked much more than was necessary to keep each other awake. Now at first light, we were taking

a break at a roadside diner.

Not wanting Luke to know I didn't have money, I told him it was not my habit to eat breakfast. He nodded and ordered bacon, eggs, toast and two coffees. When the food came, he pushed one of the coffees and all of the toast across the table to me. From the first moment of this cross-country excursion, my poverty was my worst kept secret.

Luke's journey with me had now come to an end. All through the night he had been careful not to reveal anything about his personal life—what he did for a living, his hobbies and the like—and I had been just as careful not to ask of such things. Nor had he made any personal inquires of me. I liked that. It made our association clean and clear-cut.

When we parted ways outside the diner, Luke asked if I needed money. I shook my head and said, "No, but thanks." He smiled and stuffed a twenty in my shirt pocket. When I tried to give it back, he said, "That's for driving." That was it. End of negotiation.

I was learning a lot from all these people I was being forced by circumstance to meet in such a short period of time. Believe it or not, it was only just now occurring to me that the image of myself I only occasionally saw in the mirror—when I shaved, brushed my teeth and such—was the "me" other people saw all the time. This got me thinking how foolish I must sometimes look to others as I try to hide what must be as obvious to them as the nose on my face. In this small awakening of sorts, I found some relief in a release of unnecessary self-consciousness. This was nice. I could see this trip was freeing me up a bit.

Also, there was a kindness, a kindness that seemed to be everywhere and in everyone. Through all of the muddle and confusion of all I had been through thus far on this journey, I was discovering a subtle but ever-present compassion forever wanting and waiting to be expressed.

As these thoughts were wandering through my head, I was standing at the entrance onto I-40 East with my thumb pointing more or less toward Tennessee.

I got my next ride in about five minutes. This one was strange—or, I should say, stranger than most of my rides thus far. It was two ladies in a brand new, bright blue car. I think it was a Ford Elite.

"Where ya goin'?" yelled the lady riding shotgun.

"Tennessee," I yelled back.

"What the hell's in Tennessee?"

I shrugged my shoulders.

"Would you settle for Albuquerque?"

"Sure. It's part way there."

Once we got on the Interstate, the ladies seemed to have forgotten I was in the back seat. They were talking a mile a minute—and laughing too. Too much, it seemed to me. "Are these ladies drunk?" I thought to myself.

After a while, Shotgun turned around and gave me a good long look. "My God, you're a cute thang," she said. The driver cackled. "What chu doin' out hyer without cher mamma?" Now, they were both howling with laughter as the car swerved a little.

"My God," I thought to myself. "They *are* drunk."

It was just after eight o'clock in the morning, and these ladies were hammered. So I got busy trying to figure out exactly *how* hammered they were and whether or not I should ask if I could either drive or get out of the car. As it turned out, Shotgun—who identified herself as Sarah—was much further gone than Susan, the driver, so I decided to hold off on saying anything. Besides, I was tired. I had been up most of the night before and just wanted to sleep.

"Hey, honey," said Sarah, wheeling around in her seat holding up a thermos. "You wana little coffee with happy juice?"

"No thanks," I said. "I think I'll just rest for few minutes if you don't mind. I've been up pretty much all night."

"Absolutely, honey. You jes yell if you want a back rub." Again, they both cackled a laugh.

As I quickly faded off to sleep, I could hear Susan and Sarah quipping fat jokes back and forth. They were both in their forties and a little on the hefty side. Somehow, as wild as they seemed to be, I felt safe in their company.

The next thing I knew, I was slowly surfacing into a waking consciousness out of a deep, dead sleep. First, I realized I was in a car. "How did I get into this car?" I thought. Then I heard snoring. As I sat up, it all came back to me—where I was and what was going on.

Our car was positioned slightly cockeyed in the parking lot of an I-40 rest area near Winslow, a small town about 60 miles out of Flagstaff. I looked at my watch. It was just after noon. The ladies were fast asleep in the front seat. As I figured the time of day against the distance we had come from where I got picked up, it looked to me like we had been in the parking lot about three hours.

For a moment, I sat there wondering what to do. Quickly enough, I decided to do what had to be done—use the rest room. As I opened the car door to get out, Sarah woke up.

"Oh shit, look what time it is," she said, looking at her wrist watch and smacking Susan's right arm with the back of her left hand.

When Susan had become sufficiently oriented, the two of them got out of the car to follow me into a nearby building where there were bathroom facilities, vending machines and an information center that doubled as a small convenience store. The ladies asked me if I had money. I nodded my head as I flashed my twenty. It was so nice to be flush with cash. Inside, I made my first and last trip purchase. I bought a packet of sunflower seeds, a bag of dispensable razor blades, a toothbrush, some toothpaste and a bar of soap.

Within twenty minutes—about one o'clock in the afternoon—all our business was done and we were back on the road. I was assuming we would be driving the 250 miles to Albuquerque more or less nonstop, which would put us there around dusk. I was wrong.

Susan and Sarah were *shoppers*. Yes, it would seem these two freewheeling party girls were also mad bargain-hunters. Worse, they were bargain-hunters *on vacation*.

To make matters even more troubling, it was snowing. Actually, snow had been hounding me since Barstow, a small town about 120 miles east of Bakersfield. So far, this had not been a problem. Now the temperature was dropping and wet snow was packing into ice as more new snow fell.

With a leisureliness that was driving me crazy, we finally made it to Albuquerque about ten o'clock at night. As we entered town, Sarah and Susan were talking about being four hours late for a rendezvous with relatives and friends. To avoid unnecessary complications, I paved my way toward a hasty retreat by telling the ladies I had previously made arrangements for spending the night in Albuquerque and required no further assistance from them.

After we cordially parted ways at a gas station, I found my way into a nearby 7-Eleven store just to stay warm for a few minutes and think about what to do next. There, I wandered the aisles long enough

103

for the cashier to become suspicious of what I might be up to. When he asked if he could help me, it dawned on me that perhaps he could.

I shook his hand and introduced myself as Frank (my restaurant name). He said he was Rodrigo. I summarized my current predicament, telling him I was hitching to Tennessee, had little money and no place to stay. He listened carefully. When I was done, he smiled.

Without saying anything, he left the counter and cash register where he had been standing, walked about ten feet to his left and opened a door marked "Private." Leaning out of sight for a moment, he softly spoke a few sentences in Spanish and returned to the register, followed by an older lady carrying a man's heavy coat. After quickly arranging some receipts lying on the counter in front of him, he turned to the lady and took the coat she was carrying. As he moved around the counter toward me, the lady took his seat at the register.

Hoisting on his coat, he headed toward the front door of the store, motioning for me to come along. Together, we left the store, walked three or four blocks—left, then right, then left again. It was noticeably colder now. Finally, we arrived at a door half way down the dark side of a nondescript building. Rodrigo knocked. Within seconds, the door opened and I was welcomed inside. Rodrigo stayed outside. Just before the door closed, Rodrigo shook my hand and said, "Good luck."

I was then led down a long, dark hall into a large room with perhaps fifteen beds. Although the room was mostly dark, there was enough ambient light for walking. As soon as my host got me settled on a bed, he said softly, "The bathroom is through that door over there." In the dim light, I could see he was pointing toward a corner of the room we were in. "Sleep well."

As my host walked away, I breathed a long sigh. The room was toasty warm. So was my bed. It had two pillows, two blankets and two freshly washed sheets. How could this be? Twenty minutes before, I had no idea how I was going to get through the night.

As I lay back to sleep I could barely make out a huge sign on the wall. If I really squinted, I could read it. Its large block letters spelled out "Albuquerque Rescue Mission." There I was again, amidst all this abundant kindness, everywhere waiting to be expressed.

The Dream

That night I had a lucid dream.

In lucid dreams, the dreamer is consciously awake in a non-physical world as vivid as physical life itself, yet free of restrictions imposed by physical time and space.

In my lucid dream, I was flying with Gurudeva in a black night sky filled with a unique sort of music.

I say "I was flying with Gurudeva," but actually that's not quite what was happening. It was more like we were being flown—flown by this special music that could gracefully sweep and swirl us like wind blows leaves. Although we could have navigated by will, we didn't. All we did—all we wanted to do—was ride and glide.

And this music was quite blissful. As we were lifted up, the bliss intensified and coalesced. As we were released down, it relaxed and dispersed. Yet the ups and downs were forever in forward motion so there was always this sense of constant purposeful movement, as in a well-choreographed dance.

The cadence and tempo of the music was paced in slow, three-beat measures, like a grand ballroom waltz. Its feeling was Debussy-like—elegantly peaceful, yet dramatically uplifting.

While, at best, even great earthly music would be considered but a creation of man, this celestial music seemed more like a grand, living, breathing force emanating directly from God. It was a music that was gloriously full, complete and perfect within itself—unimprovable.

Although all of the events of this dream took place at night, there was no lack of light anywhere. Actually, light itself seemed to work quite differently in this other world. It seemed to exist everywhere as an integral part of everything. There were no artificial lights installed for the sole purpose of creating visibility. Such devices were not needed, because each and every object emanated its own light.

And there was color—color like I had never seen on earth. This color was crisply bright without be gaudy, and sharply distinct, as if it was forever being viewed with better-than-perfect vision.

We were flying over a busy little harbor with sailing ships of all shapes and sizes hustling and bustling about. All the sails of all these ships were fully billowed. Yet there was no wind—just music. Shops, restaurants and homes dotted the shore, and there were people everywhere, happily going about their business.

Actually, the most distinctive quality of this dream was not its color or light, but its optimal purity. Even its sharp clarity was due to this perfect sterility. It was as if an ideal version of each created thing had been stored away and catalogued here in this taintless world just in case its imperfect counterpart on Earth somehow got destroyed.

Out in the water of the harbor, there were small islands covered with vividly sparkling, white sand. At one point, Gurudeva broke away from our flow with the music to descend onto one of these islands. Suddenly, there he was, sitting on a white chair at a white table on one of those white sand islands. And there beside him was a chair for me.

"Would you like a coffee?" Gurudeva asked.

"Sure," I said, still up in the air.

Just as I started to ask, "Where's the coffee?" I looked at the table and saw two cups of steaming cappuccino sitting there, waiting.

I started to descend onto the island but stopped about a foot above the sand.

"Coffee's getting cold," Gurudeva said with a chuckle. He knew I was having trouble. "What's keeping you?" He asked.

"I can't touch the sand," I said. "My feet are dirty."

"No they're not. Look down."

I looked down and saw I was now wearing white silk slippers literally radiating an immaculate glow. Looking at the cappuccino with great anticipation, I carefully placed one foot onto the sand. Yet, just as I touched my second foot down, I woke up.

It was five in the morning and still dark out. Although I was fully awake, the dream was still with me. Even as a memory, it was so strong I couldn't shake it. I really wanted that coffee. I could taste it. And I could still see Gurudeva sitting there. Slowly, against my will, I came to terms with the fact the dream had ended and I was now back in the physical world, a guest at the Albuquerque Rescue Mission.

Two hours after that, I was shaved, showered and sitting in the Mission dining room drinking coffee. It wasn't dreamland cappuccino, but it was good. I was also eating oatmeal and toast, free of charge, kind compliments of the Mission.

Just as I was finishing, a thin fellow with bright eyes and a baseball cap sauntered over and sat down. He told me his name was Simon and asked me how I had slept. From the sound of his voice, I could tell he was the man who had greeted me at the door the night before. Now, in the light of day, I was seeing his face for the first time.

"Vegetarian?" he asked, looking at a nearby plate of bacon I had not touched.

"Yes," I answered.

"You look like you're goin' home," he said.

"Right again," I replied. This man was good at reading signs. "How can you tell?"

"Well, I'm thinking you're clothes are fairly new. So you probably don't live out there." He was pointing toward the street. "You don't have a pack or a heavy coat so you're obviously not used to hitching this time of year, probably not ever. And you look like a guy with a nice mom and dad. So I suspect you're going home."

As I soon learned, this very insightful and unassuming fellow named Simon was in charge of the Albuquerque Rescue Mission. He knew everyone staying there—perhaps 40 men, women and children— all by their first names. I'm not sure when he slept. Aside from being the Mission's 24-hour host, he was also its cook, counselor, repairman and minister.

Before I left, Simon asked me if I would like to attend a short Christian prayer meeting. I could not say no, nor did I want to. The meeting was nice. Nothing about Jesus. Just brotherly love and people helping people. I'll never forget Simon.

By ten o'clock, I was standing back out on the road. It had stopped snowing. The sun was out. The temperature was just a little above freezing. And snow was melting into slosh. This was good for driving a car, but not so good for standing by the road. I was working hard to dodge cold-water splashes.

Suddenly, I thought of Mike. Oh my God. Albuquerque was where he was headed. Somewhere around here was his friend with the chop shop. Just for an instant, I felt conspicuous. Just for an instant. Then, there was my next ride. No, it wasn't Mike.

Family

The last events of my cross-country journey do not stand out strongly in my mind. Although this is partially due to the fact it's not all that easy to recollect thirty years back, it's mostly because my Albuquerque dream had at least temporarily lifted me out of a close association with the detail of external life. In the aftermath of that dream, I found myself watching myself from a distance as if I were someone else moving from car to car. Leftover dream bliss and unemotional objectivity are what I remember most about the last two days of my hitch-hiking adventure.

My first short-range destination out of Albuquerque was Oklahoma City, 550 miles away. I estimated this would take about eight hours in one straight ride. It took ten in three.

The first two of these three rides were short and nondescript. The third, with a trucker hauling dog food—I remember a picture of a dog with a bone on the side of his truck—was especially appreciated. It not only got me through another night, it also got me through Oklahoma City all the way to Little Rock, Arkansas, another 330 miles further along I-40. Now I was only about 500 miles from home.

The twelve hours it took to travel from Little Rock through Memphis to Knoxville passed by without incident, I think. I can't really say for sure. I slept through most of it. My clearest memory of the entire last day of my journey—actually just about my only memory of it—was walking through the front door of my parent's home at about seven in the evening.

It had been more than six years since my last visit. Some things had changed a lot. Some, not at all. My three younger brothers looked quite a bit different. They were growing up fast. Mom and dad were mom and dad—same as always. When I arrived, dad was reading the evening paper. Mom was putting out supper.

Although I had not given anyone in my family any warning of my impending arrival, they were more happy than surprised to see me. Dad pulled out his homemade wine, and we all sat around for a while, talking and sipping. We didn't get around to eating dinner until about nine o'clock.

Later that night, I called Gurudeva to let him know I had gotten home safely, and to tell him about the Albuquerque dream. It was a short call. He was happy to hear my news and asked me to keep calling.

Over the next few days, I talked at great length with my parents about Gurudeva's particular version of monastery life. These conversations were more difficult than I thought they would be. When I finally got around to broaching the subject of taking vows of renunciation, which entailed relinquishing family ties, they flinched.

"There is always the possibility of loosing momentum in a long-term practice of yoga," I was saying, feeling around for a way to begin discussing what I could feel was going to be a delicate subject. "To maintain this momentum it's advantageous for a serious yoga aspirant to withdraw from those interactions with the world that might pull him back into the way he was before he started practicing yoga."

"What's wrong with the way you were?" mom asked, looking at me sternly. "What are you trying to change into."

There was a pause. I had not mentally rehearsed this conversation as it was now unfolding. "Am I not different now as compared with the way I was six years ago?" I asked.

"To a certain extent."

"Would that be a positive change?"

"For the most part, I guess."

Uh-oh. I was expecting a resounding "yes."

"What do you see that's negative?" I asked.

"Well, you seem a little hoity-toity—like you're the 'chosen one' or something."

Leave it to mom to talk straight. Dad had just been listening up to this point. Now he was glaring at mom as if to say, "don't do this." Again there was a pause.

"Mom," I said carefully and cautiously, "the idea here is that a Hindu renunciate is the homeless one who strives in his practice of yoga to remain detached from all forms of involvement with friends, family, personal ambition ..."

"You're not homeless," mom interrupted, waving her arm around the room. Now a fire was coming into her eyes. She was a very smart lady who did not like being patronized. I was in trouble.

"I was hoping you would back me up on this," I said quietly.

"We will," dad said with a smile, looking at mom. Those were his two words for this conversation. And they were enough to stop mom in her tracks—at least for the time being.

109

I was quickly coming to grips with a fundamental reality: As I was talking to my parents, I was also talking to myself. If I sensed validity in what I heard myself saying as I was saying it, they would too. If I didn't, they wouldn't either. They were mirrors, unembellished reflections of my current state of mind.

I was also discovering that a lot of my explanations for what might be referred to as the mystical side of my new life consisted of neat, clean sentences I had memorized but hadn't really fully understood—sentences like "God is both immanent love and transcendent Reality."

When I would cough up these convenient packages of prefab wisdom as final conclusions, my parents would challenge me by asking for something a little less rehearsed. This caught me off guard and forced me to really reflect. Ever so slowly, I came to realize all of this was precisely what Gurudeva had sent me home to experience.

As I talked more and more with my parents, we got closer in our thinking regarding renunciate monastic life. For my part, I discovered I did a lot better with mom if I listened at least as much as I talked. In the end, interestingly enough, it was mom who led the way in extolling the merits of reclusive monasticism. When she heard we earned money as waiters to build the church and dedicated a lot of our time to service and worship, she said, "That sounds like the Trappist monks." Soon enough, *she* was the one telling *me* to break away from the family if I really wanted to make this thing work.

Dad said precious little, as usual. He seemed content once he got convinced I was not trying to shirk work or escape the world.

My other job at home was to cut my ties with the Presbyterian Church. Mom and dad didn't object to this at all—nor did the Presbyterian minister of the church my family attended. In fact, that minister was so fascinated with my descriptions of Hindu monastic life, he couldn't hear enough. Not only did he give me the letter of dismissal I requested, he also helped me write my Hindu-Presbyterian point-counterpoint.

After my fourth week at home, I was ready to return to monastic life. What was supposed to take four months had taken only one.

Gurudeva offered to send a plane ticket for my trip back. To save money, I opted to ride a bus instead. Soon enough, there I was. Stretched out in an upper-level front seat of a double-decker Greyhound enjoying a picture-window panorama of America's Midwest melting like an ice cube from winter into spring. In less than half the time it took me to hitch home, I was back in San Francisco, rested and ready to go.

A Shaven Head

I worked in the San Francisco restaurants for three more years. Even though I changed jobs frequently, I spent most of my time in only two places that were not on the wharf — North Beach Restaurant on Stockton Street right next to Washington Square, and Julius' Castle on Telegraph Hill just below Coit Tower.

I never went back to Fishermen's Grotto No. 9 or 10, although I did see Joe again. Somehow, I kept running into Joe.

I had just gotten back from Tennessee and was looking for work. Just as I was walking in the front door of the North Beach Restaurant, Joe was walking out.

"Joe," I exclaimed with surprise. "What are you doing here?"

He was also astonished to see me. "I was just on my way up to Chinatown and stopped in for a second. A friend of mine works here. You looking for a job?"

"Yes I am. Right here at North Beach. You still at 10?"

"Yeah." He paused for a moment as he stepped back to size me up. "So you survived your trip back East."

"Barely."

"Good. I was worried about you. You young guys are nuts. You drive your folks crazy. What did your mom think when she saw you? Never mind, don't answer that. By the way, I wanted to tell you something. You know, after I let you off over there across the bridge, I thought to myself, 'Being a waiter in a restaurant is like being a fly on a wall. You're a nobody with a thousand stories to tell.' So I'm thinking to myself, a smart, young guy like you? You *gotta'* have a lota' stories. Why don't you write a book?"

"Hey Joe," I said. "Why don't *you* write a book? You're the one with all the stories."

"Naw," he replied. "I can barely write my name. All I'm saying is, just take notes. Some day you're going to look back on all this and kick yourself in the butt thinking, 'Why didn't I take notes?'"

Now, here I am, 30 years later, writing a book, remembering Joe,

111

and wishing I had taken his advice. Joe was an interesting fellow. I wondered then as I'm wondering now: Why did I keep bumping into Joe?

Anyway, off Joe went to Chinatown and in I went to North Beach Restaurant, where I got the job I was looking for immediately.

North Beach was a tough place to work if you weren't Italian. Bruno, its head chef and half owner, spoke no English and was volatile. Lorenzo, the restaurant manager and other half owner, was also volatile and tough on waiters—yet sweet as a teddy bear in his own unique way, especially if he liked you. And liked me, he did—luckily.

About three months after I started working at the North Beach Restaurant, those of us who were preparing for initiation into *sannyas*, Hindu renunciate monasticism, shaved our heads. This meant we had to wear wigs in the restaurants.

When Lorenzo first saw me with my wig—a nice, wavy, Italian-looking thing, which he called a "rug"—he was disgusted. But it was the beginning of a Saturday evening dinner shift, and he couldn't just send me home right then and there. He needed all his waiters on deck. At that point, all he could manage to say was, "If you come back here tomorrow with that thing on your head, you're fired."

"Can I work like this?" I asked him as I pulled off my wig to reveal my shaven head.

"What's wrong with that?" he said with a big grin.

So, that night I worked with a shaven head.

To my surprise, I got fewer laughs and more respect from the other waiters when I *didn't* wear the wig. They said the wig made me look gay, which most of them thought was hilarious. With a shaven head, they all just thought I looked mean.

When I stepped up to a table to take my first food order with my new don't-mess-with-me look, Lorenzo waddled up to join me. The party of twelve that we were preparing to address was one big happy family with an age-range spanning four generations. Lorenzo was the first to speak.

"This is Frank," he said. "He'll be your waiter tonight. We're trying out something new here with Frank. Frank just got released from San Quentin and is here with us on a rehabilitation program that we're just now experimenting with for the first time. Frank's never worked as a waiter. So go easy on him. Be patient. He's had some problems, but

112

that's all in the past. Right, Frank?"

As Lorenzo looked at me like a proud father, I was looking at him in bewildered astonishment—as were all the people sitting at the table. There they were, all those nice people, just gaping, wide-eyed.

After a long five seconds, a sweet, blue-haired lady spoke up in a strained voice with a forced courtesy. "Well, congratulations, Frank, on your ah … your release," she said timidly. "You look like such a nice young man."

"Well, let's hope so," Lorenzo interjected quickly. "He was in the pen for armed robbery and second-degree murder." Suddenly, Lorenzo swung around to look behind him as if someone had called out his name. As he turned back toward the table, he exclaimed with glee, "So, now I'm off. I'll leave you with Frank. Remember. Be kind. Be gentle. We don't want Frank flying off the handle."

With that, Lorenzo made his exit, leaving me standing there quite awkwardly, looking like I had just swallowed a tomato whole. By the time I got myself ready to explain it was all a joke, the man at the head of the table chuckled and said, "That wasn't for real, was it?"

"No," I said. "It wasn't."

Just then, Lorenzo returned with a carafe of red wine.

"Vino anyone?" he asked. Several of the men nodded. "On the house," Lorenzo said, as he began to pour. "Not for you, bambino," he whispered to a small child who could not have been more than five years old. Just as he was pouring out the last of the wine, he said softly, "Frank is actually fairly harmless."

"He's not from San Quentin?" asked the lady with the blue hair.

"No madam. He's not," replied Lorenzo with a teasing smile.

"Oh dear," she said, feigning great surprise and looking at me with a sweet smile. "What a relief."

Thirty years after working for Lorenzo and about a year before writing this book, I had dinner at North Beach with my beautiful, new wife. Lorenzo looked good. His hair had grayed a little, and he was a few pounds *lighter*, which meant he was now only about 25 pounds overweight. His restaurant was packed to the brim. Obviously, he was enjoying a growing success.

After a bit of conversation, Lorenzo remembered me. I gave him a picture I had painted. He was genuinely touched.

113

Earlier that evening around sunset, we had hiked up Telegraph Hill to Julius' Castle, just to see it. Although all the people I had worked with there 30 years before were now dead or gone, the place itself had been recently remodeled and looked better than ever.

The view through the windows of Julius' Castle was superb. As I looked out over the wharf to the island of Alcatraz dotting the middle of the water that was visible before us, I winced as I recalled accidentally spilling warm olive oil down the back of a lady's elegant evening gown when I was working as a waiter there at "the Castle" some 30 years before. As horribly uncomfortable as that event was then (especially for that poor lady), it was but a slightly painful memory now.

As we left Julius' Castle, the words, "*summa iru*," popped into my head. In Tamil, *summa iru* means, "Be still." This phrase had often rung true for me from various points of view throughout my time in the monastery. In meditation, it was a command to go within. In restless anxiety, it was a command to calm down. In worship, it was a command to be as God is. Now in this moment, it was a command to see all the comings and goings of life from within the stillness of *now*.

"Life's ultimate purpose?" Surely, thought will conjure up what it needs to satisfy itself on that score, since even the concept of purpose lives and dies only in the world of thought. According to my way of thinking thirty years before, my *purpose* was *the purpose* of all souls as I had been taught to understand that purpose in the monastery: *To realize life's fullest potential by merging with life's ultimate essence.*

After leaving Julius' Castle, I worked a little longer on the wharf at Castagnola's, Scoma's, the Franciscan and Tarantino's—in that order. Although a book could be written about that time and those adventures, the San Francisco portion of this story is now done. Except, perhaps, for the Joe part.

The Life Deepens

The Fast, Beginning

I had always wanted to do a long fast for spiritual reasons. Somehow, I had gotten it into my head that such an austerity would summon grand visions, great powers, extraordinary insights and the sweet visitation of angels—perhaps even the elusive Self Realization we monks had all dedicated our lives to attain.

Again and again, I asked Gurudeva to let me do this long fast. He never said no, but he never said yes. His response was always, "Let's wait for the right timing." Whenever we ventured into a discussion about this fast, Gurudeva would make two points: 1. I was not yet ready. 2. The experience would not be as I expected.

Finally, toward the end of my silent ministry in San Francisco, I received a scribbled message sent through the mail from Gurudeva, who was then in Hawaii. The message read: "Arrangements have been made for you to fly over to Kauai to perform a long fast under monastic supervision." I was excited and could not wait to get started.

As I learned over the next few days, it was to be a 41-day water fast, preceded and followed by carefully designed transitional diets. The eating regimen going into the fast was to be one week of fruit followed by one week of fruit juice. Coming out of the fast, it was to be one week of fruit juice, one week of fruit and one week of vegetable soups and rice. From start to finish, there were to be no dairy products or breads.

Forty one days of fasting plus thirty five days of transitional dieting totaled out to more than two and a half months of time. So I made arrangements to be away from San Francisco for three months.

At this point in the development of the monastic order, Gurudeva was beginning to withdraw monks from the Silent Ministry. Although he was doing this primarily because we were finally becoming financially stable, he also wanted the monks to experience the deeper yoga a more cloistered environment could foster.

When I came to Kauai, five other monks came with me. Ravi, Deva and Eesan were the more senior of the group. Santosha, Mular and I were the younger. At that time, there were only six monks in permanent residence at our Hawaii ashram. This meant the six of us moving in from San Francisco would double that population. I was the only one scheduled to return to Silent Ministry.

As soon as we arrived, I began my fasting regime. A senior monk

117

named Kandiah had been charged with overseeing this 76-day event. Kandiah was, I was assured, working closely with Gurudeva.

Eating only fruit during the first week was pleasant enough. I was used to that. But as the first week unfolded into the second and I shifted from fruit to fruit juice, I began to feel a little antsy. Kandiah was controlling the amounts of juice I was drinking. This I didn't like.

On the morning of the second day of my juice-drinking week, Kandiah gave me one small glass of papaya/pineapple juice, which I drank down in about four gulps. When I asked for more, he politely smiled and shook his head.

I could see that expressing objection would be useless. Obviously, I thought to myself, Gurudeva had instructed him to be firm.

As Kandiah walked away with my empty glass, I was feeling like a doggy on a leash, thinking, "If I guzzled fruit juice all day every day for all these seven days, what's the big deal? The fast hasn't even started yet." As soon as I caught myself in this mental space, I knew Gurudeva was right. Already, this whole ordeal was not what I had expected.

For better or worse, my juice week came to an end and the 41-day water fast began—officially. I tried not to think ahead. Such mental wandering brought moods of gloom that settled down around me like buzzards of prey.

I knew a little from past experience what it felt like to gear up for fasting. Up in the mountains of Nevada at our Virginia City ashram, we had performed three and nine-day fasts of various sorts: on water, lemon juice or fruit. But this 41-day water fast was different—very.

In Virginia City, we dealt with the tedium of relatively shorter fasts by taking one day at a time. Each day was a separate project, and its end brought a glorious victory of sorts. No such games worked for me during my 41-day fast. The end was too far off. I could find no mental trick to assist me in successfully ignoring two hard, cold facts: I wanted to eat and was depressed that I couldn't.

With breath control, meditation and the repetition of mantras, I tried to withdraw from the discomfort of it all. Although this worked to a certain extent, misery was my base camp, and no amount of yogic effort was effective in changing this fundamental condition for significantly long periods of time.

Because Gurudeva thought a fast should be a solitary retreat, he left me alone for the most part. Still, he paid me a visit at least once a day. I found this to be extremely helpful. During one of his visits, he explained to me, as sweetly as any man could, I was now performing my first *tapas*.

Tapas is a Sanskrit word which literally means "fire." In a yogic context, the *practice of tapas* means the *performance of severe austerity, penance or sacrifice*. So, this fast was definitely *tapas*. Certainly, it was not what I had expected.

The first nine days were by far the most difficult. Like a man imprisoned for a crime he didn't know he had committed, my desire to eat was howling with screams of indignation. When my practice of yoga wasn't effective, which was most of the time during the beginning of the fast, I tried to use distraction to ignore despair.

For a while, I attended monastery events to be in the presence of other monks. Soon enough, however, being around my brothers was the one thing I could not tolerate, especially when they were eating. Everything got on my nerves. I could find no peace anywhere. Where were the angels? Where was the divine light? Where was the bliss?

After about two weeks, I got sick. Believe it or not, this was a relief. In some strange way, sickness brought solace and calm. During this time, even my desire seemed to just give up and let things be.

I was coached to perceive the sickness I was experiencing as simply the unavoidable consequence of toxins being released and eliminated from my body. This helped — a little.

As I lay there disinclined to move during the third week of my fast, I discovered my mind was fine. Better than fine, actually. Consumed in itself and enjoying the absence of bodily demands, my mind was dancing with delight. "Wow," I thought to myself, "This is great."

However, when all of this mental activity started to become my only world, I knew I was losing an important balance. I knew I was getting far too "lost in thought." It was at this point during my fast that I made a significant discovery: *Food grounds mind in body*.

After about 25 days, I stopped sleeping more than two or three hours at a time. I wasn't trying to sleep less. I wanted to sleep more. I just couldn't. And when I did fall off to sleep, it was strange.

In the heavy beginning of the fast, sleep provided an escape. As the fast continued, however, sleep stopped being a refuge. Waking and sleeping began to merge. The thin veil separating the astral and the physical worlds began to fade. This was not a wondrous experience by any means. It was spooky.

On one occasion, I *thought* I was dreaming that I was myself as a child sleeping in my grandmother's home in Knoxville, Tennessee. As I was waking up in this dream, I could see all of the furniture in my grandmother's bedroom as well as her various paintings and photographs on the wall. I could even smell the room and feel its warmth. Yet just as I was sitting up in that room and becoming fully awake in that dream, a door opened and in walked Gurudeva.

Gurudeva's entrance was not part of the dream. It was a physical event. As I became aware of Gurudeva's presence, my grandmother's dream room morphed into the physical monastery room I was living in during my fast. And I realized I had not been dreaming in a normal sense at all, but had been, instead, sitting all the while on a monastery tatami mat steeped in what I can only describe as a vivid astral trance. *That* was spooky.

This kind of thing was happening all the time. It was like I didn't have to sleep to dream. Thoughts became magnified and absorbing. And so did emotions. These thoughts and emotions were dreamlike because they completely took me over and swept me away to some ungrounded, nonphysical place.

As you read these words you might be thinking, "That sounds wonderful, I would like to have that kind of experience." But please believe me when I tell you, "It wasn't and you wouldn't."

If my thoughts and emotions were positive, I could enjoy sweet moments of rapture here and there. Yet, as pleasing as these isolated episodes of delight could be, even they were permeated with a feeling of being helplessly uncontrolled. And this was most disconcerting.

Thus, I can say with full assurance that, although my physical condition during the fast made it easier for me to discover altered states of consciousness, the experiences I had in those states, even if they were positive, were not nearly as enjoyable as they could have been had I achieved them during meditation minus fasting.

As my awareness floated along uncontrolled, I would find myself arriving at one obscure destination after another, always somewhere beyond the boundaries of my familiar domain of consciousness. And I was forever loosing continuity—forgetting where I was last, wondering what was going to happen next. In all of this drift, there was no sense of center or balance or stability.

Out of all this, I was able to add a little substance to my earlier revelation about food grounding thought: *A controlled focus of awareness is the essential factor separating deep meditation from psychosis.*

The Fast, Middle

Oddly, the last ten days of the fast were the easiest. Who would have guessed? By day 31, my sickness had vanished and I was bursting with an exhilarating feeling of positive energy flooding my entire nervous system, right into my fingers and toes. As this powerful force flowed through my body, it seemed to light up each body part, tricking me into thinking I was feeling that body part, when actually I wasn't.

What I was feeling was the energy flowing through a portion of the body, filling it with a discernible bliss. I was becoming aware of the physical body through the nonphysical energy that kept it alive. More then this, I was realizing energy as consciousness.

When I tried to move, however, I quickly came to understand that all of this "electricity" I was inwardly experiencing could not be enjoyed as usable physical strength. Although I felt like I could run a mile, I could barely walk across of the room. Nevertheless, I wanted to do something. I couldn't just sit around. So, after spending most of the middle of my fast in seclusion, I decided to attend one of Gurudeva's ongoing evening philosophical discussions.

These evening gatherings were not classes. They were more like casual chats. Gurudeva never had an agenda. He just conversed with the monks as the moment inspired.

We met in a large upstairs room of the monastery called the Sun Palace. During the day, this room was enchanting. But as we gathered there in the evenings, it came alive with a unique effulgence, a dynamic energy charged with a feeling of spirit building and *devas* gathering. During these magical times, just after day merged with night, the monks had their best chance of drawing Gurudeva out into mystical talk.

The evening I attended was special. It was May 29, the birthday of Yogaswami, Gurudeva's spiritual teacher. When I arrived, the monks had just finished off a large carob cake and were now listening most attentively as Gurudeva answered a collection of philosophical questions that had been saved for this special evening. I was glad I'd been late for watching monks eat cake but sorry I'd missed the beginning of Gurudeva's replies.

No one had expected to see me. I was presumed temporarily dead, I suppose. Gurudeva beamed a big smile when he saw me and ceremoniously waved me over to a seat on his right.

I must have not looked so great. Everyone was peering at me sideways as if to say, "Nice to see you but ahhh . . . . Are you okay?" After a few moments of hearing me talk, it became apparent that I was fine enough for the evening to proceed as if I weren't there, which was exactly what I wanted.

Santosha was asking Gurudeva about our study guidelines. His dilemma was this: On one hand, we were being encouraged to "learn from within ourselves" through the practice of yoga and *not* through reading books. Yet, on the other hand, in our formal study of Hinduism, we *were* being encouraged to read books—a *lot* of them.

"Books on any subject—yoga, Hinduism, carpentry, candle-making, gardening—should be read with purpose," said Gurudeva. "What you read should only be news you can use. Excess intellectual knowledge of any sort simply registers in the subconscious as extra baggage. With regard to the investigation of mysticism and yoga, it gets a little trickier. Here, we should only seek out information about what we are actually ready to experience."

"How do we get ready for a deep practice of yoga?" Santosha asked. "And once we're ready, how do we know we're ready?"

"A genuine desire for the practice of yoga is the first and most important sign of readiness," replied Gurudeva. "Beyond that, being ready depends on the clarity of the subconscious, and that clarity varies from person to person."

"Is unfoldment simply a clear subconscious?"

"A clear subconscious allows unfoldment. Karma develops in cycles. We each have our moments of clarity in accordance with the creation and resolution of our personal karma. The subconscious of an unfolded person never gets too cluttered, because an unfolded person *got* unfolded by keeping the subconscious clear. By keeping our subconscious clear, we allow our nature to be transformed from the inside out as the seat of our consciousness rises. A person's state of unfoldment has to do with his seat, where he spends most of his time. If a man spends a lot of time in anger, anger is his seat. We would not be inclined to think of an angry man as being unfolded, nor would we ever expect him to have much subconscious clarity, even in his most lucid moments."

"So, who is it that reads the books on yoga, the unfolded or the folded?" Santosha asked, looking around the room with a smile.

"Unfoldment is not a prerequisite for the practice of yoga. It's a consequence," Gurudeva replied. "Those who are ready should read. Then, from what they read, they should take the best and leave the rest. Practicing this kind of discrimination is a great yoga in itself, is it not? For all people in all walks of life at any stage of development, discrimination offers an accessible approach to wisdom."

Now there was a pause. Gurudeva turned to look at me. "How are you doing?" he asked in a soft voice. I nodded a smile. There was another pause.

"Can you talk a little about detachment?" Mular asked, breaking the silence.

"In detachment we are not.blinded by emotion—or even thought stimulated by emotion," Gurudeva said. "From within detachment, we can see more clearly."

"Do you mean, '*Think* more clearly?'" asked Santosha.

"Clear thinking is good, but clear seeing is better," Gurudeva continued. "Careful thinking is a safe thing to do if you don't trust your seeing. Seeing is a function of the soul. But even the soul can't see through a wall. So here we are again back at a cluttered subconscious. A cluttered subconscious is like a wall. When that wall of the subconscious becomes a window, the soul can see right through it. The practice of detachment summons seeing. Seeing is a stepping back for a better view. If it's a wall we see when we step back to look, seeing that wall for what it is begins its dissolution simply because the darkness that is confusion can't endure the light of pure awareness. When the subconscious mind is clear and the conscious mind is balanced, our seeing is superconscious. In superconsciousness, we unfold."

"This sounds wonderful," said Mular. "But I'm wondering if I will ever be able to see like a seer. It's starting to sound like we have to be saints *before* we unfold."

"Isn't it true that things always get complicated when we talk about them?" Gurudeva asked. "You're all doing all these things we're discussing right now.

"As we mentioned before, we each have our own moments of clarity. If you continue your yoga practice, the number of those moments will increase until they start stringing themselves together in continuity. This is the unfoldment that occurs quite naturally as a consequence of practicing yoga with consistency and applying what we learn from that practice in life."

After a polite space of time, Santosha asked, "If I had a practical problem I wanted to solve, how would I meditate to solve it?"

"Here's where skillful thinking can come in handy as a starter kit. Summarize your problem into three thoughts. Summarize each of those three thoughts into one sentence. Concentrate on each of those sentences individually, and then meditate upon them together. This will unfold hidden knowledge. This is an ancient and deep yoga practice."

"What if nothing happens?" asked Mular.

"Have faith. Remember, you are not doing anything. You're just holding a window open. Give it time. You are working with forces more powerful than you know. Stay with it. Each little success will bring more faith. More faith will inspire more practice. More practice will bring more faith. Faith is your greatest ally."

"This seems almost like a dumb question," said Santosha, "but what does an enlightened person know that others don't?"

"That's not a dumb question, Santosha, but I think you know the answer. What is it that an enlightened person knows?" Gurudeva asked, looking right at Santosha.

With a little hesitation, Santosha replied, "Well, I would say that an enlightened person is more used to working with intuition, for one thing. That much is for sure. Soooooo ... he might not know everything all the time but, at the very least, he would know ahhhhh ... what he needs to know right now."

Obviously very pleased, Gurudeva leaned back and clapped his hands to generate a room full of hearty applause. "There you have it," he said with genuine mirth. "A fine example of intuition well applied. Very good, Santosha. Very good. Just to add a little to that, a person who has become accustomed to living in superconsciousness does not always reside in that state. However, the more he becomes familiar with living there, the freer he is to flow through lower states of mind without getting stuck or attached."

Again there was a pause, allowing for a change of subject. After a respectful wait, Eesan spoke up: "You have mentioned several times how the culture of the East is more mystical than the culture of the West. Can you elaborate on that?"

"Would-be mystics of the West are too often overly intellectual," Gurudeva replied. "With this dependence upon the intellect, they carve out a more difficult and complicated path to the superconscious realms. In the East, because an easy pursuit of well-defined spiritual goals is so ingrained within the culture, mystics can go in and up more efficiently, without getting distracted into extraneous thought.

"By the way, in the East, the kind of discussion we are having here tonight would not be likely to occur. The disciple would not ask and the guru would not answer philosophical questions. The guru would talk. And the disciples would listen. The guru would give instructions and the disciples would obey them. Within this simple relationship, the disciple would be forced to learn through experience without a lot of intellectuallizing up front.

"I am not trying to throw a damper on what we are doing tonight. Most of us here were raised in the West. So naturally, we are going to expect to be allowed to discuss philosophy and will feel slighted if we don't or can't. Any more questions?" There was a pause. After a minute or so, Gurudeva looked at his watch. "Ok, I'll take that as a sign we should end," he said. "It's also almost nine o'clock. Time for bed."

Nine o'clock was lights-out at Kauai monastery. Because our mandatory wake-up time was 4:30 am, no one had a problem with going to bed at nine.

Because my fast had temporally exempted me from the relentless rigor of our monastery schedule, I casually wandered back to my room. There was a full moon out that night—not a cloud in the sky. Feeling no hurry, I sat down in the tall grass of the lawn outside the small building where I was staying. I was so happy I had spent the evening in the Sun Palace with Gurudeva and the monks. It had shaken me out of my weird no-man's-land of foodlessness.

As I sat there in a tranquil zone, I assumed the tropical breezes I was enjoying would ward off Kauai's famously enormous mosquitoes. I was wrong. Now, those little winged beasts were moving in on me like Pacific sharks circling prey in open water. Suddenly, I was banished from my calm by siren-like buzzing sounds and intense itching. Much to my regret, it was time to attempt sleep.

The Fast, End
Amazingly, I slept like a baby that night—at least seven hours straight. The next morning, with only nine days left to go on my fast, I felt like I could go without food for another 40 days. Renewed with a flush of good-feeling energy, and completely inspired by the previous evening with Gurudeva and the monks, I couldn't wait to practice some serious yoga. Now was the time. I just knew it. Now was the time to give yoga some dedicated focus.

Having failed in gaining solace from meditative practices in the beginning of the fast and having endured the crumbling of my various preconceptions as to what meditation would be like during a fast, I had not been inclined to disappoint myself further by continuing any sort of a yoga regime past my first floundering. Now, I was happily reversing my thinking and preparing to leap wholeheartedly into a full day of yoga, highly motivated to strive in every way possible.

Taking a methodical approach, I started off with some hatha yoga postures coupled with some breathing practices. It was surprisingly easy to get into even the more difficult positions, and any form of breath control brought a tremendous influx of blissful vigor. To my delight, the tensions and blocks these yogas were designed to relax and release melted like butter in sun. I became extremely sensitive to what we monks were used to referring to as "subtle energies." Now, I was realizing through this sensitivity that these energies were actually not subtle at all. They were overwhelmingly intense. They just seemed subtle when they were only slightly experienced.

My meditation was freewheeling. Fascinating distractions came fast and furious. I was forever being enticed away by colors, shapes, energies and feelings so magnetically attractive I not only forgot what I was meditating on, I forgot I was meditating. If I allowed myself to flow with these distractions, I had a great time. Yet as I wandered in this strange wonderland of inner sights and sounds, there was a dog of a thought that kept forever nipping at my heels, yelping, "don't do this." In this thought, I was at the mercy of a gnawing notion: Gurudeva would not have been pleased with what I was allowing to happen in the name of meditation.

On the positive side, all of these auxiliary experiences were high, light and uplifting. What was missing, however, was a sense of going deeper and deeper into the solid inner stability of simple *being*. The very absence of this methodical deepening was significant since a controlled penetration of *being* was the crux of a meditation practice aimed at Self Realization. So, even though I was enjoying my inner experiences, I was not benefiting from them—I thought. I was—I thought—allowing myself to remain overly involved with outer stuff.

In a fit of conscience, I decided to throw down an anchor of stability. I decided to write. Meditate—write—meditate—write. This was my new strategy for enticing discipline back into my yoga. And it worked. It worked marvelously.

My strategy was to fill my last days of fasting with my personal version of yoga circuit training, consisting of a three-hour yoga workout repeated two times a day. During this self-imposed program, I moved in sequence through 20 minutes of hatha yoga, 20 minutes of mantra yoga, 20 minutes of breath control, one hour of meditation and one hour of writing. During the writing part of this routine, I found that prose pulled me out while poetry pulled me in. Fortunately, the "in" of my poetry was deep enough to embrace and organize my fragmented insights.

And so it was that I focused upon writing poetry. And in this easy focus, I discovered a friendly collection of words I didn't forever feel I needed to change later. Finally, I was creating text I could read the next day and not throw away. I was happy. I felt like I was really on to something good. There I was, 32 days into a 41-day water fast, riding a lyric yoga, and loving every minute of it.

After a few days, I started editing my poetry into fixed meter. Writing in this way seemed appropriate. It forced a pull on intuition—brought insights down to earth. Here below are some of the verses I composed during the final days of my fast.

Keeping questions open while
The mind frees up its ties
Gives breath control in yogic style
Good purpose for its tries.

Quick breath, in and out, then glide,
Reflection in-between.
This poking stick finds things that hide.
No shield can intervene.

Stretch and move the body first
To stimulate the breath.
Then measure in and out. Immerse,
Till calm falls still like death.

Though varied methods spur a thrill,
There's one that's best of all.
It's breath made slow and finally still.
It's God's great distant call.

Breath is fundamental. Yes.
We know this to be true.
Breath stirs life; it can't do less.
Yet could do much more too.

Two mountains rise from will and bliss.
They both stand bold and tall.
To leap their peaks might risk a miss,
Resulting in a fall.

Yet finally we decide to cross
From one point to the next,
We leave behind a world of loss,
Grey-clouded and perplexed.

Doubt can rise at times like these
To simulate a war

We pray within "God help me please!"
We seek within our core.

Our will is wild when first we try
To wield it like a knife.
We want what's "bad" to fall and die.
We want the "good" of life.

Soon we find that will works well
With wisdom in the wings
Assisting winds of change to quell
The harsher force it brings.

Roaring rapture made us wild,
Surprised us with a thrust.
Yet just as quickly, it went mild,
Laid bare our soul to trust.

We crossed that bridge from peak to peak.
In search of life to be.
Yet then we saw much more to seek
And sought much more to see.

The path goes on and in and up.
Its end is hard to find.
Pure gold within a loving cup
Looks missing to the blind.

We touch into it now and then,
This end that we do seek,
But not enough for soul to win
A solid mountain peak.

Yet touching in does goad us on
To hold the seeking strong.
For touching in, itself, does don
A peace spread wide and long.

Those agile souls, who leap a peak
While clinging to the sky,
Get given what the demons seek,
Yet drop it as they fly.

They will not chance a downward fall
While clinging to a lie,
Nor will they chance a risk of all
By fearing they might die.

What dies in this world to the next
Is loss made into gain
Like lessons learned in life's context
Yield truths born out of pain.

Two mountains rise from will and bliss.
They both stand bold and tall.
To leap their peaks might mean a miss
That's worth the risk of all.

The Missing Seven

During the last nine days of my fast, I attended five more of those fine evening sessions in the Sun Palace with Gurudeva and the monks. Of those five, one was especially inspiring. It was the night everyone was trying to get Gurudeva to talk about his "missing seven years."

What we had been told of Gurudeva's life from 1950 to 1957 was next to nothing. We knew he practiced raja yoga intensely during that time. And we knew he composed a collection of yoga aphorisms with commentary, which would later be published as a powerful book entitled *Cognizantability*. But this was about all we knew.

Gurudeva's seven-year yoga retreat followed a life-changing, three-year pilgrimage he took through India and Sri Lanka. During those three years abroad, he studied with a number of mystics, achieved his enlightenment and met his spiritual guru, Yogaswami. Yogaswami initiated him as a disciple and sent him back to America to "roar like a lion," as Gurudeva put it.

Yet upon his immediate return to the States, Gurudeva didn't roar at all. He retreated into seclusion. In India and Sri Lanka—and even long before that in America—Gurudeva had absorbed a great deal of esoteric training rapidly. It would not be unreasonable to assume he needed time to absorb and digest all of that input. To our best understanding, what we commonly referred to as his "missing seven years" *was* the time he took to assimilate what he had been taught up to that point.

On that evening up in the Sun Palace, we were not able to get Gurudeva talking about what he *did* during those seven years. He was, however, willing to share what he *learned* during that time, especially with regard to detachment, faith, grace, devotion and desire.

"Attachment is a creation of the thinking mind," he said. "The thinking mind must be consoled with some sort of understanding before it can willingly release attachments. Those who aren't so caught up in thinking have a certain advantage here. They are more inclined to be detached in faith."

"Faith in what?" Eesan asked.

"Faith in yourself. Faith in others. Faith in God, gods and the natural order of things. Faith is faith. So often, when we talk about using willpower in the practice of yoga, we imply we don't need any help. Yet, nothing could be further from the truth. We must always remember that spiritual illumination occurs by the grace of God. This means we would be well advised to prostrate in complete abandon before the one God above so we can merge with that same one God within. Yoga requires an abundance of internalized devotion. First we learn to worship in the temple of stone. Then we learn to worship in the temple of soul. There is a secret here. Outer worship leads to inner worship. In meditation, the two become one, just as in creation the one becomes two."

Gurudeva had been talking in a resonate voice that was slowly deepening. "Now we are going to jump subjects a little," he said. "We've talked a lot about desire. And we have established a couple of important principles: One—Desire is a propelling force in life; and two—Desire doesn't need to be eradicated, just transmuted. Yet, we have also talked about desirelessness. So, what do we mean by desirelessness?"

"Transmuted desire?" Santosha asked.

"Yes, but desire is desire. And even high desire is after something. It's on the prowl."

"Satisfied desire?" Santosha asked again.

"Excellent. That's good, but let's broaden that a little bit. Let's call it 'desire, temporarily inactive.' Desire can be rendered temporarily inactive, and therefore desireless, in conditions like satisfaction, bliss, contentment and balance. Yet none of these states is permanent. At any given point, desire can be stimulated out of dormancy into activity as it moves from *being* out into *doing*. This is the way we live our lives, continually vacillating between *being* and *doing*, motivated by desire. Knowing this, yogis strive to take control of this vacillation. They practice yoga to purposely increase a sense of *being* and decrease a sense of *doing*. They do this because they know Self Realization can only occur in a state of desirelessness, temporary as that state may be.

"I am always being asked to give a one single yogic method for realizing the Self. Unfortunately, such a one method doesn't exist. Self is realized through the transmutation of desire, but this transmutation is not something you can choose to do or not.

"Every soul on the planet is continually transmuting desire. We want something; we get it; we don't want it any more. We want something else instead; we get that; we don't want that any more. And so we go from one desire to the next, always forward and upward. Every time we manage to satisfy a curiosity, we transmute desire a little bit.

"What yogis do that others don't is escalate the process. They speed up transmutation by working to generate and satisfy desires on the mental rather than the physical plane. This is more efficient because mental experiences occur more quickly than physical experiences, and mental karmas are far more refined than physical karmas.

"One last word with regard to desirelessness as it relates to Self Realization: Desire is bound up in ego. With the death of ego comes the death of desire in Self Realization. Only in Self is desire completely absent. Any questions?"

There were none. At that point, a question would have looked too much like an unfulfilled desire. So everyone one was just sitting still trying to look desireless.

After a moment, Gurudeva got up, raised his hands, palms flat together in a gesture of prayer, and strolled gracefully some thirty feet to the door of his personal living quarters. We all rose quietly. As a monk opened his door for him, Gurudeva turned like a dancer, faced the monks with a broad smile and waved good night as he backed into the dark out of sight.

Three days later, my fast officially ended. Although my spirits were high, my vitality was low.

When I started my fast, I stood a muscular six-feet-three-inches and weighed 180 pounds. Now I was down to 140 pounds and no longer looked or felt athletic. The weight I had lost had come from muscle as well as fat. I was appalled when I looked in the mirror to see how thin my arms and legs had become.

My last journal entry on the last day of my fast read:

Breath is life. The dead will say
That this is surely true.
"Life is strife," some living pray,
"God, help me see this through."

Desire determines yoga's flight
Or grounded destinies.
Desire will have its way in spite
Of book-read guarantees.

This is true, so say those souls
Who tried before their time
To slip/slide through dead-end loopholes
To circumvent a climb.

Lessons learned in random flight
Could birth a budding sage
Whose will and breath match well his might
Should wanting set his stage

This is to say that breath locks mind
If locked, mind wants to be.
Otherwise such mind will find
It's first good chance to flee.

The Fast, Aftermath

My first taste of liquid food—eight ounces of lemon and pineapple juice—gave me goose bumps. Although its spread through my body was as smooth and cool as menthol, it hit my sensitive nervous system like an amphetamine. My fingers and toes tingled; my taste buds puckered; and my head pulsated like a thumping heart. Within five minutes, I was sweating and trembling. Tried to stand up—had to sit down. Then I was fine. Really fine. In fact, I was feeling so fine, I went looking for Kandiah. Couldn't find him though. Where did he go? All I wanted was a little more lemon and pineapple juice.

An hour later, he found me. This time he had eight ounces of blended papaya nectar. An hour after that, he was back again with yet another glass of the original lemon-pineapple mix. Ok, Kandiah was doing fine. Just fine.

Now, I was fully back. I took another look at myself in the mirror and was amazed. Although my body had not changed one little bit since the day before, it now suddenly looked good to me. In fact, the more juice I drank, the better it looked. "Perception is such a fickled thing," I thought to myself, "and so subjective."

About this time, Gurudeva paid me a visit. He seemed happier than I was that my fast was over.

"How do you feel?" he asked.

"Fantastic," I answered enthusiastically. "Never better."

Monks rather quickly learned to maintain a certain level of positivity around Gurudeva. In the world of yoga, mood vacillation was a mark of self-centered immaturity. None of us wanted that.

"Are you sure?" he asked. Before I had a chance to answer, he continued, "Well, for better or worse, it's not quite over yet. Now is the time to be really careful. We have been advised by experts that coming off a long fast can be dangerous. But we have a good plan. So promise me you'll work with Kandiah on this."

"Oh yes. I will. I promise."

"Remember, he's just doing what I tell him."

"Right. I understand." Just then, Kandiah walked up with another glass of papaya juice. "That's it?" I asked with mock sarcasm. Both Gurudeva and Kandiah chuckled, but not before throwing me a quick glance of deep concern. In that moment, I saw how seriously they were taking my transition off the fast. And I was touched.

During the following week of juice drinking, my appetite came back with a vengeance. I had been warned, and even knew from my own past experience, a *desire* for food far outweighs a *need* for food immediately following a fast. Unfortunately, such knowing was of little consequence when the urge to eat hit and I felt like an animal in the heat of hunting.

At this point in time, it was food that I wanted—not juice. Wet nursing me with juice was like feeding blood to a lion.

I was a good boy though. I managed to get through the week without being "intransparent." And it *did* get easier. With some experimentation, I discovered a couple of valuable tricks. Drinking a great deal of water with the juices kept me bloated in a false sense of gratification. And becoming absorbed in mind-consuming projects helped deflect my awareness from a sense of time passing. Although I was weak, I could work—and was quite happy to do so.

Seven days after my fast, I began eating what I had been drinking. Although one might think there shouldn't be that much difference between eating a fruit and swallowing its juice, there was for me. When I began eating fruit, the amount of food I was given *decreased*. An eight-ounce glass of three papayas pureed became two papayas on a plate with a lemon wedge. Did Kandiah think I wouldn't notice?

"Should I make an issue of this?" I thought to myself. "No, it's only for a week. You may gain a papaya but you'll loose your dignity. Drink more water."

We called the third week after the fast "the last lap." By this time, Kandiah had let up and I was left on my own to serve myself food. My only instructions for these last seven days were to continue eating fruit and begin consuming soups and vegetables cooked lightly; and to avoid white sugar, starch, complicated proteins and processed foods. All went well. The week passed swiftly. Finally, it was over. I was done.

Everyone wanted to throw me a party with a big fat feast, but Gurudeva—rightly thinking such a celebration might be counterproductive—suggested, "How about a smoothie and a movie instead?" And so it was. Out we went to a movie with a smoothie attached.

When I left California to perform my fast in Hawaii, the plan was for me to return to San Francisco to work another year or so in the

135

Silent Ministry. As it turned out, this was not to be.

Gurudeva's gale-force winds of change were now blowing strongly. This meant lots of plans were percolating for a wide variety of projects: temple construction, monastery renovation, book printing, bee keeping and last but not least: a complete overhaul of our monastic lifestyle. To accomplish all of this, we were all needed in Kauai.

During this time, there was so much going on the only workable approach any of us could take to a day was something like: "Okay, I'm awake. What's next?"

We were in the beginning stages of building two temples. While Kadavul Hindu Temple was being assembled onto the front of the main monastery building, elaborate plans were being drawn up for the construction of Iraivan Temple on a portion of our forty acres of heavily wooded land behind the monastery down by the river.

Although both these temples were dedicated to Lord Siva, each was to feature a different central icon. In Kadaval, the main image of worship was to be a six-foot-tall, 200-year-old copper and bronze casting of Siva Nataraja, the Lord of dance. In Iraivan, the main image was to be a 700-pound, three-foot-tall, naturally formed crystal Sivalingam, representing Lord Siva as the Self beyond time, form and space. Each of these temples was inspired by a vision Gurudeva had in meditation.

The first vision came in 1973. In that vision, Lord Muruga, one of Lord Siva's two sons, majestically pounded the ground three times with his divine scepter to indicate where he wanted the image of his father, Lord Siva Nataraja, to be placed in Kadavul Temple. Because the construction of Kadavul had not yet begun at the time of this vision, that which Muruga pounded with his scepter was the front step of the entrance to the monastery—what would become the floor of the main sanctum of Kadavul Temple.

The second vision came in 1975. In this longer vision, Lord Siva Himself appeared before Gurudeva; first, at a distance, walking with a small group of devotees in a valley; then, up close so the intermingling filaments of white light that made up the surface of His androgynous face could be studied carefully; and finally, sitting on a large rock, with Gurudeva to his left. In this last phase of the dream, Lord Siva reached back, lifted His thick, matted locks up from the nape of His neck and said to Gurudeva, "This is the source of my power."

136

Later, Gurudeva searched the monastery property, found the rock that Siva was sitting on and established the area surrounding that rock as the future site of Iraivan Temple.

The construction of Kadavul Temple was begun in 1973 and completed in 1980. Now, as I sit here at my computer keyboard, slowly pecking out this story in 2011, the construction of Iraivan, which was initiated in 1975, is still underway.

Iraivan is rising slowly for good reason. Because it is being hand carved out of granite in India and shipped stone by stone to Hawaii, its construction is unprecedented. As we were told by temple craftsmen in India, no one hand-carves granite any more. Even in India, this kind of work is now being done with machines. But to hand-carve a granite temple in one country, then move that temple stone by stone to another country is virtually unheard of.

Kadavul was different from Iraivan in a number of ways. For one thing, it was primarily a monk's project. By this I mean the monks were the ones out there pouring cement and laying block. Also, unlike Iraivan, Kadavul was made to look Hawaiian. With its three-feet-thick, lava rock walls, it certainly did.

While we were working on Kadavul, we were also doing a lot of renovation work in the main ashram building. Having originally been constructed as a fine hotel, this building was not poorly made. For this reason, our renovation efforts had more to do with creative preference than structural necessity.

Although our construction projects were a primary focus for us, they accounted for only a small percentage of the new activity being initiated in the monastery.

"Change is the only constant," Gurudeva would sing out again and again. To him, change meant leaping into a yogi's blissful freedom. To us, it meant setting aside doubt and trying to keep up.

On the day I was scheduled to return to San Francisco but didn't, I wrote in my yoga journal:

Nothing can be just what it seems
To those who seek a door
That opens on to quantum dreams
They never knew before.

137

Plan Bee

At the beginning of the summer of 1978, five busy years had passed since Gurudeva had closed down the Virginia City press shop. Now, he was sensing the time was right to print again. But reviving printing required considering some rather expensive options.

First, with all of our press equipment still in Virginia City, we had to decide whether we wanted to bring that equipment to Hawaii so the monks could print here (Plan A), or send monks to Virginia City so they could print there (Plan B).

For reasons I could never completely understand, we opted to do neither. Instead, we decided to start over in Kauai with the purchase of a small Ryobi offset printing press, an Itek photo typesetting computer and a process camera with an internal film-and-paper developing unit.

After a couple of months of working long hours to produce only mediocre results with this homespun setup, it became obvious that we should adopt a modified version of Plan B, which would be to bring over from Nevada, not all of the press equipment, but just our high-powered, Heidelberg, KORD, printing press. No less than five minutes after we arrived at this decision, we were on the phone making arrangements to ship the press from Nevada to Hawaii.

With great anticipation, we rearranged our offices so that one entire building could be transformed into a press shop. By the time our three-ton, German masterpiece of printing technology arrived and was set in place, we were ready to produce our first job. Training? Never mind that. We just dove in and knocked about until something better than what we got off the Ryobi started coming out the other end of our newly installed Heidelberg.

At the time, I was the only monk on Kauai who had served on the original Virginia City press team. But my experience in Nevada had only been in pre-press work. I had no idea how to run the KORD—nor did anyone else. We all had to learn. And the way we learned was the hard way—through trial and error.

This freewheeling, on-the-job approach to getting educated was our standard method of becoming efficient in most all of our areas of service. Although occasionally painful, it seemed to work out fairly well for the most part. How well? Who can say for sure?

Isn't it true that most training usually happens this way anyway?

Aren't we all amazed at how much more we learn on a job *after* we have been trained to do that job?

Even as we were wading through the first currents of learning about printing, we were also busy with bees. Actually, our first taste of the sweet world of honey and the insects that make it, occurred back in 1972 when Kandiah investigated beekeeping just for fun.

When Gurudeva was told that Aristotle was an avid beekeeper and that beekeeping had been developed and practiced by monks since the days of dynastic Egypt, he started thinking it might be a good practice for us—a practice that could provide us with a monastic discipline as well as a source of income.

So, the monks ordered bee suits, helmets, veils, smokers and wooden hive boxes from a Sears & Roebuck catalogue and got all set to go out beekeeping. As in printing, we sought no training.

We kept bees from 1972 to 1979. During the first five of those seven years, there were not enough monks in Kauai to do much more than maintain a few hives. Our most dedicated and profitable work in raising bees for honey and money occurred from the end of 1977 to the end of 1979 when our monastic population was larger. It was during those same two years that we were re-initiating our printing efforts.

Certainly, a lot was going on. In our youthful impulsiveness, the only thing we did better than finish projects was start them. Although we were constantly creating just a little more work than we could ever possibly do, there were now more monks to help in the doing. Now, nearly a year after I had come to Kauai to begin my long fast, our home-base Hawaii center had almost tripled in size. The few monks that were left in California were no longer serving in the Silent Ministry. Their only purpose was to manage the San Francisco monastery and temple.

By1977, Kandiah and a few others had become so experienced in working with bees they couldn't wait to go professional. As soon as there was enough manpower on Kauai for us to create an apiary team, we got into the honey business—big time.

By splitting and doubling the hives we already had and buying queen bees from other beekeepers, we expanded our operation from 30 hives scattered around our own property to 3,000 hives in 100 "bee yards" strategically established on farms and in gardens all over Kauai. Because bees pollinate, local farmers and gardeners were more than willing to host our bees for free.

For the monks, beekeeping was not just a curiosity that ended up making us money. It was a discipline—a discipline most of us did *not* enjoy at first. For one thing, beekeeping was strenuous and often uncomfortable if not painful work.

During a normal day of summer honey harvesting—which would begin at four in the morning and end after dark around eight o'clock— we wore thick, hot bee suits in 90-degree heat while lifting hundred-pound honey boxes off hives onto trucks and off trucks into our "honey house," getting stung by angry bees in the process. What was to like about this?

As it turned out, however, the more intriguing question we ended up asking ourselves was: How did we end up loving this job so much? How was it we could spend 17 hours with the bees, then crawl into bed looking forward to getting up the next morning to do the same thing all over again? Yet we did. We all did. Sooner or later, we all came around to loving the bees.

Some monks tried to put a reason on it. But nothing anyone ever came up with ever made much sense to me. No one could really fathom the magic of the bees or explain their beguiling ability to capture our hearts. What I came to was this: *Bees are extraordinary beings.*

In this perception, there was an appreciation of bees as grand exemplars of selfless service and sacrifice. After all, when they stung us, we hurt a little, but they died—just to save their queen and protect their honey.

The Kauai bees kept by the monks came from DNA stock that was predominately aggressive. Even professional beekeepers from the mainland told us they would demand double money as hazard pay if they took a job working bees like ours.

Some of the monks were proud of having done battle with our special breed of warrior bees. They wore their stings like badges of cour-age and saw their days in the field as dramatic tests of valor. Yet, sooner or later, this thespian swagger lost its sparkle. In the monastery—where no adulation of self can last for long—such strut too soon started look-ing too much like what it was.

We sold the bees at the end of 1979. With the money from that sale plus the money we had saved from Silent Ministry, we created an endowment for the monks. The interest from this endowment—along with tithing from church members—provided plenty of capital to fulfill our simple daily needs. This allowed us to invest profits from service-oriented programs, like printing religious literature, back into service, rather than into monastic care. That Gurudeva was a grand mystic was common knowledge. That he was an extraordinary businessman was a fact lesser known.

All through this time, I was forever trying to reconcile all of this externalized activity with our more internalized yogic pursuits. My journal entries during these days indicated my inner grappling.

For lack of better aim and name
We'll make a pointed bet
That all we see comes from the same
And all is solid-set.

Yet all of this can stimulate
Then frustrate preconceptions.
From this we learn it's not too late
To make select corrections.

Saddle cattle, swim on land
Start a heart anew.
Seize a mortal's contraband.
Trade it for a view.

The new in you and free in me
Are ranged within a score
Of fine love flown too high to see
Yet felt as bliss and more.

We look upon the bright and tall
Through nights that come and go.
We seek the measure of them all,
Yet little do we know.

The gods arrange a thing or two
With arms flung far and wide.
Like birds, they feather wings anew
To gild a regal ride.

Looking by the leaving way
For change to make a mark,
We want to go but have to stay.
We stumble on a spark.

Busting a Myth

The New Oxford American Dictionary is sometimes a scary place. It defines religion as a "belief in and worship of a superhuman controlling power," and Hinduism as "a diverse family of devotional and ascetic cults and philosophical schools, all sharing a belief in reincarnation and involving the worship of one or more of a large pantheon of gods and Goddesses." Had these two words been defined for me in only these terms forty years ago, I would never have become religious or Hindu. Nor would I be telling this story.

Gurudeva's first yoga teachers were serious mystics who got him off to a good start. Right away, they let him know in no uncertain terms that Nirvikalpa Samadhi, the Realization of the Self God within, was the principle aim of a serious yoga practice, and that simplicity, purity and discipline comprised a substantial portion of the means by which that end might be attained. These first instructions coupled with his own intense drive propelled Gurudeva quickly toward his first Samadhi.

Although Gurudeva was a serious yogi, he might never have been a yoga teacher had he not met Yogaswami. It was Yogaswami who initiated him into Hinduism in Sri Lanka in 1950 and gave him instructions to "roar like a lion" in the West. Gurudeva had no personal desire to be a teacher. All he wanted to do was go on living his life, deepening his own meditations.

Even when people started asking him to teach yoga in San Francisco seven years after he had been initiated, he was hesitant. His first sessions with students were simple and unassuming. He taught only the basics of hatha yoga, pranayama and meditation. Yet, he always stressed that Nirvikalpa Samadhi was yoga's ultimate goal.

Because his students could sense he was a living example of what he taught, his teachings were generally well-accepted right from the start. As a result of this, he began to develop a following without making special efforts to do so.

Yet the more he taught and the more he discovered through his own yoga practice, the more he realized accessing the unique power of the Yogaswami lineage—an accumulating spiritual force that gets passed from one guru to the next—meant getting closer to Yogaswami. Obviously, he couldn't do that physically. He was in San Francisco and Yogaswami was in Sri Lanka. For him, getting closer to Yogaswami meant "finding Yogaswami on the inside," as Gurudeva would later put it. Finding Yogaswami on the inside, Gurudeva came to understand, meant living as Yogaswami lived. The first step toward living in this way meant getting a better grip on the Hindu philosophy. "This should be simple enough," he thought. Actually, it wasn't.

Hinduism has no central authority or fundamental doctrine. And, as many scholars have corroborated, it is far too complex to be cohesively defined in any one document. Additionally, some of what has been published about Hinduism is blatantly wrong. Add to this the fact that much of Hinduism's deepest mysticism has never been written down.

With some investigation, Gurudeva and his monks arrived at a happy discovery: There was a good amount of quality literature written about Hinduism. It just wasn't well organized and readily available.

For the most part, finding this obscure literature meant wading through a certain amount of confusion left in the wake of India's somewhat complicated political, social and religious history.

All through this period of research, Gurudeva was quite happily fulfilled in his own yoga practice. Nothing he learned through external study could invalidate what he had already discovered within himself. It was, in fact, his beautiful inner life that fortified and motivated him in his quest for a solid documentation of a Hindu spirituality. It could even be said it was his own mystical experience that set the benchmark by which we all assessed the value of what our research revealed.

Much of the most important literature we sought had not been translated into English. Interestingly, Western scholars' dissertations for doctorates or research studies for grants contained some of the most easily readable modern-day English writing on the subject. Although much of this work was rife with criticism born of religious bias and intellectual arrogance, it was a start. At the very least, it was a factually informative skeleton of information upon which we could build.

It would be wrong for me to leave the impression here that we were finding little insightful writing in the West about or in reference to Eastern mysticism. The famous American Transcendentalists Ralph Waldo Emerson and Henry David Thoreau were decidedly influenced by the yoga philosophy of Hinduism—as was Walt Whitman. Other deep thinkers like the W. B. Yeats, Carl G. Jung, Alan Watts, Aldous Huxley and Christopher Isherwood were also looking to the East for wisdom and were writing about what they found.

Of the ultimate goal of yoga, German Indologist Heinrich Zimmer, a colleague of Carl Yung and a teacher of Joseph Campbell, wrote, "Nirvikalpa Samadhi is absorption without self-consciousness, a mergence of the mental activity in the Self, to such a degree, or in such a way, that the distinction of knower, act of knowing and object known become dissolved as waves vanish in water, and as foam vanishes into the sea." (*Philosophies of India*, Princeton University Press.)

The questions that many of Gurudeva's expanding group of yoga students kept asking further encouraged us to deepen our study of Hindu philosophy. This settling into time-tested knowledge was of great practical value. It allowed Gurudeva to respond to "Why?" inquiries with replies like, "because the ancient sages of Hinduism have said so, and Hinduism has withstood the test of time."

Although a teacher of any philosophy that has been accepted as credible by many is at least partially absolved of a responsibility to justify why he (or she) accepts every detail of that philosophy, he (or she) cannot escape the necessity of being well informed about its source of authenticity. So there it was, yet another reason to delve even more deeply into the more essential teachings of traditional Hinduism.

From 1957 to 1977, Gurudeva's monks worked first to synopsize a general overview of Hinduism, then to break that overview down into detail. With regard to Hinduism in general, here is a loose summary of what we discovered:

Hinduism is the world's most ancient religion and the only one not inspired by a one person. Sometimes referred to by its more ancient names of Sanatana Dharma, "the eternal faith," and Vaidika Dharma, "the way of the *Vedas*," it includes a spectrum of theologies that are variously monistic, dualistic and pluralistic.

There are three main devotional sects within Hinduism. Saivism is the worship of Siva. Vaishnavism is the worship of Vishnu. And Saktism is the worship of Sakti.

A non-sectarian form of religious observance, generally known as Smartism, is often considered a fourth Sect. This Smarta sect is more liberal than the other three. It grew out of a tradition guided from the 9th century onward by the teachings of a famous Indian religious and political reformist named Adi Sankara. The Smartas, as they are often called today, adhere to Sankara's view that all the many gods are but various representations of the one God. Hence, the worship practices of the Smartas are eclectic.

Hinduism in general is a religion of tolerance. Asserting the popular aphorism, "Truth is one, paths are many," most Hindus understand, accept and respect the right of others to believe, meditate and worship as they please. They also feel that religious differences should never be cause for conflict.

That Hinduism is exclusively polytheistic is a popular misconception. In truth, few Hindus do not believe in a one supreme God. Most of the many gods and goddesses in the Hindu pantheon—33 million by someone's count—are symbolic representations of the one God, as the Smartas would say. Those that are not are indeed living entities—living, but not embodied. These beings are considered divine because of their higher evolution. In acknowledgment of their evolutionary distinction, they are often referred to as *mahadevas*, "great beings of light."

All Hindus believe in *karma* and *reincarnation*. But their more detailed understanding of these two principles is relative to their chosen perception of God, soul and world. Because all Hindus don't agree upon the specific nature of this trinity, a deeper grasp of the Hindu perception of karma and reincarnation can really only come through a deeper study of the various Hindu schools of thought.

Once Gurudeva felt we had assimilated a suitably comprehensive overview of Hinduism in general, he had us focus upon the specific teachings of his guru, Yogaswami.

Yogaswami was a follower of Saiva Siddhanta, a sub-sect of

Saivite Hinduism. One easily understood technical name for this mind-stretching theology is *monistic theism.* In this theology, which combines the principles of monism and theism and is also sometimes referred to as *panentheism,* God is perceived as both manifest and un-manifest, dual and non-dual, within us and outside of us.

Monism, the opposite of dualism, is a doctrine stating that reality is a one entirety without independent parts. Theism is a belief in a one God who creates the world and maintains a personal relationship with all that exists within that world. Together, monism and theism form a theology Gurudeva liked to summarize in one sentence: "God is Love, both immanent and transcendent."

Gurudeva's published description of Lord Siva from the perspective of Saiva Siddhanta is as follows:

"Lord Siva is Absolute Reality, Pure Consciousness and the Primal Soul. As Absolute Reality, Siva is unmanifest, unchanging and transcendent, the Self God, timeless, formless and spaceless. As Pure Consciousness, He is the manifest primal substance, pure love and light flowing through all form, existing everywhere in time and space as infinite intelligence and power. As the Primal Soul and our personal Lord, He is the five-fold manifestation: Brahma, the creator; Vishnu, the preserver; Rudra, the destroyer; Maheshvara, the veiling Lord, and Sada-Siva, the revealer." (*Dancing with Siva,* Himalayan Academy.)

In Saiva Siddhanta, God is neither male nor female, even though language requires us to specify gender in addressing Him/Her.

In Saiva Siddhanta, a soul is perceived as an immortal body of light created by God. This soul, which is also neither male nor female, reincarnates again and again, creating and resolving karmas, until it has fully experienced all of the adventures available in the manifest world and is no longer held there by desire. At this point, its essential unity with God is fully realized.

Saiva Siddhantists make a distinction between a *soul body* and a *soul essence.*

According to Saiva Siddhanta, each of us is individual and unique as a *soul body.* This means we are each a self-effulgent being of light that matures through an evolutionary process. This soul body is of the nature of God, but is different from God in that it is less resplendent than God is and still evolving. While God is unevolutionary perfection,

146

we evolving souls are not. Even after Self Realization is fully attained in Nirvikalpa Samadhi, the soul body continues to evolve in this and other worlds until it merges with God, or to put it another way, until it becomes not unlike God in every respect.

As a *soul essence*, we are *satchidananda*—existence, consciousness, bliss. At the core of that, we are the transcendent Self beyond time, form and space. In this essence of our soul, there exists no separateness. All is one. Thus, deep within the core of the soul body, we are what we seek right now.

In Saiva Siddhanta, the physical world (*pasam*) is perceived as a stage upon which the soul (*pasu*), acting through an off-center sense of self (*anava*), plays out roles of its own choosing in dramas it produces and directs itself as it deals with the reactions to its actions (*karma)* in a world (*pasam*) of its own making that is actually an illusion (*maya*). In the final act of its final drama, it dies as *its self,* dissolves into *the Self* and achieves liberation from reincarnation on the physical plane.

Our study of Saiva Siddhanta was painstaking for a number of reasons. As a philosophy, it is both ancient and obscure. To further complicate matters, there are two very contradictory versions of the Saiva Siddhanta philosophy, the deeper of which is briefly described in the paragraphs above.

Also the practice of Saiva Siddhanta includes living a lifestyle followed almost exclusively by the Tamils of South India and Sri Lanka. This makes Saiva Siddhanta a race/religion. Quite often, we were told we had to be born a Tamil to even understand Saiva Siddhanta.

With heartfelt sincerity and an honest desire to catch the true spirit of this cultural religion, we spent a significant amount of time traveling through and living in South India and Sri Lanka.

Even though it was difficult, we tried our best to put what we learned about Saiva Siddhanta into practice. We were glad we did, for this was where we found some of the real spiritual abundance we were looking for—in the practice.

One of the most attractive features of Saiva Siddhanta is its amalgamation of worship with yoga. It was this very blending of two into one that attracted Gurudeva to Saiva Siddhanta in the first place.

Even with all of our ardent dedication to learning and application, I didn't really catch the full spirit of Saiva Siddhanta until I had heard and read about Gurudeva's teacher, Yogaswami.

Yogaswami lived in Sri Lanka and wrote a lot of songs in the Tamil language—all of them full of his love for Siva, his joy in humbly serving Siva, his transformation through Siva's grace and his ultimate merging with Siva as Self. Here is a translation of one verse from one of his many songs:

We are the servants of Siva. No harm will befall us, if we but meditate without forgetting on the holy mantra that proclaims there is neither beginning nor end, birth nor death, day nor night, happiness nor sorrow. Yes, we are the servitors of Siva. Rejoice!

Yogaswami was quite famous for his no-nonsense spirituality. People would come from all over Sri Lanka and around the world just to be in his presence and receive his spiritual advice. This advice quite often seemed contradictory because it was conveyed *in context* and therefore relevant only to the needs of the person with whom he was currently speaking.

To one man he would say, "You don't need to see God. You must feel God. God is you. Just be that. Be the witness. Watch. Be and watch. There is a sentence without subject, without object and without predicate. Find that."

To another he would say, "Pray for his grace. This is all you can do. Pray: 'Oh Lord, I know nothing. Thy will be done. Please give me thy Grace. Without thy grace, I am nothing.'"

A Long Walk Begins

Around sunset one evening in the summer of 1979, I was striding briskly along a narrow path through a more densely jungled portion of our back property. Because I was almost jogging in the fast fading visibility of twilight, I had to tunnel my vision on the placement of each next step just to keep my balance. Suddenly, I felt a gentle swoosh.

I stopped. Turned. Looked back. There was Gurudeva. He had been walking toward me on the path. Because I had not seen him, he had been forced to slip sideways to avoid a head-on collision with me.

"Sorry, Gurudeva," I said. "Thanks for being graceful. I'm walking quickly for exercise. Too quickly, I guess."

"No problem," Gurudeva replied with a laugh.

"May I walk with you?" I asked, grateful for this unexpected but most auspicious encounter.

"Please do. I'm headed toward Orchid Mandapam."

Our Orchid Mandapam was a simple wooden structure we had built high on a rocky cliff at the edge of our property. The view from that spot was spectacular, especially now around sunset. *Mandapam* is a Tamil word that means "festival pavilion."

With some difficulty, we waded through about 50 feet of wet, congested jungle and started uphill. Just after we had used our hands to spider-walk up a small embankment of stones onto a discernible path, Gurudeva asked, "Anything on your mind?"

For days, I had been wanting to talk with Gurudeva privately and waiting for a chance. Now, here it was.

"Well, actually, I do have something I would like to ask you," I said in carefully measured words.

We walked a little further in quiet silence. A monk's personal conversations with Gurudeva always got off to an awkward start. This was because such conversations were too often misused by monastics who saw talking with Gurudeva as an opportunity to register petty and personal complaints. Since the questions I intended to ask were about meditation, I thought I had a good chance of being well-received.

"I'm wondering if my inner life here is just sort of standing still," I finally asked timidly.

"Still is good," replied Gurudeva. "Can you be more specific?"

"There's no problem. Just something I don't quite understand. Can't quite put my finger on it."

"Take your time"

"I'm trying to catch the overview."

"Okay."

"There is something I don't quite get about the general structure of our life here."

"About the life of a monk?"

"Well, yes, I guess."

"Are you thinking about leaving?"

"Oh no, no, no."

"It's okay to think about leaving. How else could you be sure you want to stay? It all comes down to what you want. And that's always changing. What do you want right now?"

"More meditation time?" I asked abruptly. I was not prepared for coming to the point so quickly.

Gurudeva laughed. "I'll give you all the meditation time you want," he said with great sincerity, "if that's what you really want. Is that what you're really after? Meditation time?"

I had to take a minute to think. Somehow, I was surprised—I don't know why. I was surprised that I was being called upon to steer this conversation. What I had really wanted was for Gurudeva to just drop some sort of magic pill of a comment that would just set everything straight in my head and leave me feeling stupefied in some kind of nice sublimity. Obviously, that was not going to happen.

Now we came to another hill and had to climb for a while without talking. As soon as we reached level ground, we stopped to rest.

"So, what do you really want right now?" Gurudeva asked me again after we caught our breath.

"I want enlightenment," I said boldly.

"Wonderful," he replied.

I waited for him to say more. When it became obvious more was not forthcoming, I continued. "So that's why I was requesting additional meditation time. I guess you could say all the monks want enlightenment, and if I should be given extra meditation time, so should they."

"No. Actually, I wouldn't say that at all. Each monk is different. Some monks don't even think about enlightenment."

"Really? I thought that was our reason for being here."

"It was probably something close to the reason they all became monks in the first place."

"But not the reason they stayed?"

"The impulse to seek enlightenment is rare. When it comes, it's wonderful, but it may not stay long. As I have said before, if you're serious about this quest right now, you can have all the meditation time you want. But I must ask you, right now as we speak, is meditation what you're really after? At this moment, what I think you need is a plan. But you can't make a plan if don't know exactly where you're been, where you are and where you want to go. Are you sure that meditation alone is the right plan for you right now? I mean, as a plan, meditation is a little vague, don't you think? Perhaps your plan should build around a clear definition of your destination."

"Well, yes." I had to pause for a moment. "But doesn't that mean defining the undefinable? The Self is my destination."

"Set a destination that is definable—a definable place that's as close to the Self as you can get. But you have to define this place in a way that you can understand. Then, you have to come up with your own plan for how to get there and stay there long enough for the Self to realize you, which is what actually happens."

"If all of this is up to me, how do I work with you on this?"

"My job is to help you get comfortable with your approach and keep you moving on track in a useful direction. But you have to do your own legwork. Mainly, you have to really *want* this Realization."

"I *do* want it. I'm just a little bit stumped on how to deal with a destination that's spaceless, timeless and formless."

"Being spaceless, timeless and formless doesn't put it out of reach. The Self is not out of reach. It's You. How can You be out of reach? Yet, if the Self *seems* out of reach, set a goal that is reachable."

"I'm still stumped."

"Go with feeling. What's your deepest feeling. Feelings do not require a definition in words. Once you have identified a feeling, that feeling stands as a remembered experience that needs no definition. You don't feel a need to define anger or fear do you?"

"No."

"Why?"

"I remember what they feel like."

"Right. So, what is your deepest feeling. Just give it a name."

"*Being.*"

"Ok. That's your destination. What does *being* mean to you?"

"Sitting still in bliss—mainly."

"That's good enough. However you state it, the feeling you're referring to is the main thing. You know that feeling because you've had it before. Because you've had it before, you can have it again. And you can have it again without having to put it into words. The next thing you have to do is make a plan. So, what's your plan?"

"Sit still in bliss for a long time."

"Sounds almost like your destination."

"Yes it does."

151

"Sounds almost like meditation."

"Yes it does."

"Meditation with a plan."

"Yes."

"Simple."

"Simple, yes—easy, no."

"Yes."

"So, now, it looks like I need more meditation time."

"Actually, what you need is an ultimate desire—an ultimate desire for the ultimate realization of your truest Self."

X Marks the Spot

We had come to a large, flat boulder the monks called Sitting Rock.

Have a seat," Gurudeva said. Once we got settled, Gurudeva continued. "The thinking mind needs to be happy. It needs to have a hook to hang its hat on. It needs a project that will make it feel useful. Otherwise, it's just going to spin its wheels and create confusion. How about if we make a project of our quest for spiritual illumination? How does that sound?"

"That sounds really good."

"Okay, how can we get our mind happily involved in this project of seeking Self? "

"Okay. Well, let's see. I'm thinking, thinking, thinking .... Okay, here's a helpful thought, I think: 'The Self has to be realized to be known.' How's that for a thought that works *with* us rather than *against* us."

"That's a good thought. The Self is also God. Right?"

"Yes, right, of course. Sorry, I can't believe I forgot that. So we're attempting to define the undefinable for the purpose of using the mind to set a goal of God Realization. Correct?"

"Yes, an intellectual idea can be like a photo of a place you've never been but would like to visit. No one would deny that a photo of something is not that something. But it *is* a hint. And a hint is all the mind needs to initiate a decision. With regard to Self Realization, what we need most from the mind is a decision to proceed on the spiritual path into the unknown."

"All right. So Gurudeva, how would *you* use the mind in a quest for Self Realization?"

"I would use thought to describe Self Realization after the fact—as if it had already come to pass. Leaning on what I had learned from someone who had merged with Self, I would think something like this: 'After the realization of God as my Self, I will not be able to define or explain God or Self any more adequately than I can now, nor will I be inclined to try, for I just won't see any need for it. Coming out of that transcendent merging, I'll see life as it is—a dreamlike manifestation of my deepest Self, all occurring in the now. From that point of view, I'll live differently than I did before. How could I not? The Absolute Reality of my own Divine Self will have taken its rightful place at the center of all my values. Everything I considered of importance before will now stand subordinate and relative to this ultimate essence of all that I have just discovered. I'll seek no security or permanence in the dream of life, for I'll know such qualities aren't there to be found. I'll be a far different person than I was before.' That's how I would think."

"Good, Gurudeva. Really good. What can I say? I am stunned. But I would be lying if I said I could think that way not having been where you have been."

"Act like you have. Think like you have. Soon you will have."

"Okay. Good. Let me work with that."

"Yes, think and act with that kind of confidence and your mind will get out of your way. Not only that, it will help lead you along."

"There's something else my mind wants to know, Gurudeva."

"What's that?"

"It wants to know how it helps to desire what can only be achieved in a state of desirelessness?"

"You are following desire to its end in desirelessness. The desire for the ultimate Samadhi is the last desire. And the only thing keeping you from fulfilling that last desire is some other desire you're chasing instead. If you *really* wanted this ultimate Realization, you would have it right now. It doesn't take time, it takes will. More specifically, it takes an ultimate desire, which triggers an ultimate use of will."

"Gurudeva, when I went home to complete my religious severance, all my friends and family kept asking me why I was doing this. They wanted to know why I was so dead set on living this life of a monk seeking enlightenment. Although I had never doubted what I was

153

doing, I was surprised at what a difficult time I was having answering that question. What had motivated me to live this life had always been a feeling rather than a thought. And I had been quite happy with just that feeling. Even when I was put on the spot with my family and managed to come up with lots of good solid reasons for doing what I was doing, my favorite reason was that I just *felt* a calling."

"Very good. Yes, desires are *felt*. But desires can be tricky. Most of them work subconsciously. That means you aren't always aware of them. They're there, but hidden, as far as your conscious mind is concerned. You *think* you desire only the Self, but actually that's not quite true. Yet simply remembering that the Self is there—and occasionally thinking and talking about it, just enough to keep it in the forefront of your mind—helps you build an all-consuming desire for it."

"Are we supposed to poke a stick around and aggravate those other desires to come out into the open?"

"No, no." Gurudeva laughed. "That's not necessary. They'll come looking for you soon enough. And we'll deal with them then."

"Okay. Back to the plan. Any plan should have things to do. Right? I hope it's not wrong to want things to do in the pursuit of our goal here. Things to do like meditation, for instance."

"No. It's not wrong for your plan to have things to do. But you are doing a lot of things right now. You are working here in this place, striving to be of selfless service, striving to face your shortcomings, striving to relinquish your ego in humble worship, praying for blessings and meditating for enlightenment. That's a lot, isn't it?"

"You're making me feel a lot better."

"When we begin a journey, we can only start from where we are, not elsewhere. And this starting point is different for each person."

"I think I have at least learned that much."

"That's why only you can make your plan."

"Right."

"So, you know where you want to go. As you come to know your subconscious, you'll know where you've been. The current question is, "Where are you now?" Where are you in relationship to where you want to be. Meditate on this. Make a problem of it. Draw it out on paper. Conceive it like a treasure map. Make an 'X' to mark the treasure you want to find. Be a kid about this thing. Have fun. Having fun will keep

154

your thoughts healthy, happy and helpful. Take your time. This is your homework assignment in the classroom of life."

Gurudeva stood up. So did I. He looked around. I did too, even though I had no idea what we were looking for. "This will do," he said, finally, as he picked up a stick about the size of a small walking cane and sauntered over to a patch of bare dirt about three feet square.

"This is the mind of manifestation," he said, as he drew a large sloppy circle in the dirt with the stick. "The mind is all this area here inside the circle. The Self is all the area outside." Now, he handed me the stick. "Where are you in the mind?" he asked. I took the stick and marked a point right in the center of the circle. Gurudeva laughed. "Now's not a time to be humble. Now's a time to be honest. Where are you really?" I made another mark just off center. Again, he laughed. "I'd put you about here," he said as he took the stick from my hands and made a mark flatteringly close to the edge. "You've got your ducks in a row and you're ready to go."

"Can I quote you on that?" I couldn't help asking.

"Please do." We both chuckled politely. "Okay, now let's draw another map," he said as he scrubbed the circle out of the dirt with his foot. Now, he took the stick and poked a small hole right in the center of the patch of soil. "This is the Self," he said, as he handed me the stick. "Where are you?" I hesitated. I really had no idea where to make my mark. "Keep in mind," Gurudeva said, "you may or you may *not* feel a need to leave yourself enough room to do what you think you have to do to get from where you think you are to where you think you want to be. You've said you wanted Self Realization. What stands in your way?"

"Other desires."

"What are those other desires?"

"I guess I'm not really sure what they are at this very moment."

"When you figure that out, put those desires in your map if you think you need to. For now, just give it a crude shot. Where will you make your mark?"

With great hesitation, I softly pressed the stick into the ground as far away from Gurudeva's dot as I could get and still be within the patch of bare soil. Gurudeva just looked at me without much expression.

"Well—I'm leaving myself enough room to do what I think I might have to do," I said, almost apologetically.

"Or maybe you are just being cautious. Cautious is good. There's nothing wrong with being cautious, but let me ask you this. What's keeping you from just putting your mark right here in the middle, right on top of the Self? You are the Self right now. Right?"

"But I haven't realized it."

"Still, you are the Self right here and now, whether you have realized it or not. And nobody can take that away from you. Why don't you just be who you are?"

"Good question."

"What's your answer?"

"I have tried to do this. I have tried to just be my Self."

"Keep trying."

"It doesn't feel like it's working."

"It is."

"But the distractions …."

"So what! Let them be. What do you see?"

"A mishmash of stuff. Some of it's fascinating. Some of it's not."

"Either way it's the imagery of karma created by desire. You are either being attracted to new karmas in their initial development or you are being repelled by old karmas you can't avoid resolving. Positive or negative, your distractions are nothing but karma—your karma. Claim your karma and look at it squarely in one of two ways: as ignorance on the wane or wisdom in the making. You can approach your burden either positively or negatively. Is your glass half full or half empty?"

"It would be half full if I could understand how facing all these karmas would resolve them."

"As we face the karmas that arise as distractions in meditation, we begin to experience mentally what we would experience physically if those karmas were allowed to play themselves out in everyday life.

"What would be an example of that?"

"Say, for instance, a man insults you. Right in front of a group of distinguished guests you deeply respect, he says you look funny with a shaven head and monk's robes. As you're standing there before him, you endure his insults with dignity. Yet later, as you sit meditating in the temple, you react. At first that reaction is but a faint memory of the insult. But it doesn't go away. It lingers on the outer periphery of your consciousness. As your meditation continues, that memory becomes more vivid. Soon enough, it balloons into a fantasy of anger. In this mental fantasy you are consumed in an abusive criticism of the person who insulted you. As your thought feeds your emotion and your emotion feeds your thought, you become more and more distraught. At some point you realize you've forgotten you are meditating. Then you start mentally criticizing yourself for getting so consumed in distraction. Have you ever had an experience like this?"

"Oh yes," I said softly. "More than once."

"Although you feel awful in that moment, you are actually in a position of great opportunity—a crossroads of sorts. You can either end your meditation in frustration, or you can remain in your meditation and simply allow the fantasy you are observing to play itself out as you watch from a distance in detachment. In this watching, you'll find your fantasy ending itself almost immediately. This is because—since the very existence of a fantasy is dependent upon your full involvement with it—no fantasy can exist for you if you are the detached observer and therefore are not experiencing that full involvement.

"And when the fantasy dies, there should be some bit of practical wisdom there waiting for you. This wouldn't be a wisdom you'd have to seek out. It would just be there. And it would pertain to what you had just been through. Is this making sense?"

"Perfect sense."

"By observing these karmas before they have a chance to manifest physically, we not only circumvent the creation of new karmas, we expedite the resolution of old karmas."

"Working smarter mentally instead of harder physically."

"Yes. There you go. Go with it. Let the forces play themselves out. Everything works more quickly on the mental plane. Experience is still the teacher. But the experience is mental rather than physical.

"The usual tendency is to follow a surging forth of impulses out into physical action where a resolution occurs much more slowly and there is the creation of other karmas in the process. So, the challenge here is to resist the pull toward the physical."

"Now *that's* news I can use."

"Yes, remember, you're only at the mercy of what you don't quite understand. Your distractions are not your enemies. They're your friends. They're nothing but your own confusions seeking clarification.

Give them what they want: resolution. All of this can happen in that simple detachment of observation that occurs in true meditation.

"If you are worried about not having enough time for meditation, why not meditate all the time—as in being the detached observer all the time, rather than just when you are sitting in meditation?"

Keeping it Simple

"What about the original meditation?" I asked, wondering if this question was supposed to have an obvious answer. There was a pause. "Back there in your example of the anger fantasy, I was supposed to be in the temple meditating, right?"

"Yes?" Gurudeva replied.

"So, when all this anger drama came up to distract me during meditation, where was my focus supposed to be, on my original concentration point or the distraction?"

"Either is acceptable if *you* remain in charge. Conscious control is the important element here. A distraction is like a person walking up to you when you're talking with someone else. You can either tell this person, 'Have a seat. I'll be with you in a minute.' Or you can excuse yourself from your conversation to focus on him completely."

"So *being, focus* and *distraction*," I said after some deliberation. "These three make sense separately, but not together. Our *distractions* are supposed to represent karmas that need to be looked at. Yet our first instruction in yoga indicates we are not supposed to turn our attention toward distractions during meditation. *Focus* brings eventual oneness with what we're focusing upon, but the one thing we want, the Self, is the one thing we cannot focus upon because it is not a thing of the mind that can be made a point of focus. Hence, whatever we focus on is going to be a distraction from the Self, because it's something other than the Self. Apart from all this, *being* seems most easily felt when we're in a mindless zone, not concerned with distraction or focus either one. I hope I'm not getting to crazy here."

Gurudeva laughed. I can't say I was surprised. I even sounded silly to myself.

"Keep it simple," he said. "Thinking is good but it has a tendency to get carried away with itself. So, keep thinking, but not too much.

Now, what were those three points?"

"Being, focus and distraction."

"Mystics always put the Self first. Then nothing can get too complicated. Complication equals externalization. We don't want to get any more externalized than we have to. Our objective is to go within. The further in we go within, the simpler things get. The *end* of *in* is the Self within. And the Self within is the simplest of the simple. So applying this approach to your three points which were ...."

"Being, focus and distraction."

"Yes, right. So, say those three points backwards and add Self at the end."

"Distraction, focus, being, Self."

"That's the path."

"That's it?

"That's it. From the Self looking out into the world, that's the way the path looks. From the world looking into the Self, of course, it looks differently. It looks far more complex."

"Okay. Well ... you sure did make it simple. And I'm feeling kind of foolish."

"If you take all the various questions of life as they come up and try to answer them from the inside out—from the Self looking out—I think you will be pleased with the outcome. Any more questions?"

"Well, I think we pretty much covered it, except I would like to know a little more about how the practice of *vasana daha tantra* fits into the resolution of karma."

"Excellent. Now we are bringing all of this talk down to Earth. *Vasana daha tantra* is a great thing to discuss.

Burning It Up

Vasana daha tantra is a Sanskrit phrase that names the mystical practice of "writing down and burning up confessions," as Gurudeva would most often put it. But these "confessions" could include any sort of negative memory. In Sanskrit, *Daha* means "to burn" and *tantra* means "method." A *vasana* is a deep-seated, subconscious impression manifesting as a trait or tendency that shapes one's attitudes and motivations.

"Every question is hooked to its answer." Gurudeva said. "How

159

would you say *vasana daha tantra* works with karma?"

"First, I would say *vasana daha tantra* is something we would be most likely to perform after a subconscious issue has disturbed our meditation as a distraction, probably more than once."

"Right."

"Writing these problems down and burning them up gives us a physical method for dealing with those issues."

"Yes, it helps by releasing the suppressed emotion associated with a problem. More than anything else, it is emotion that muddles our ability to understand."

"Once we have our emotion out of the way, are we supposed to think about the issue that came up?"

"Thinking is good at asking. Intuition is good at answering. As far as resolving karma is concerned, you don't need to force-feed a lot of extra thought into the process. The intuitive wisdom that naturally arises from having gone through the experience should be enough, even though that experience might roust out some thought of its own along the way. The understanding we're after here is a been-there-done-that kind of thing. When the soul has been-there-done-that with all the mind has to offer, its deepest essence then becomes self-evident."

"So, if reaction indicates unresolved karma, then conversely, non-reaction should indicate karma resolved. Is that correct?"

"That sounds like good thinking asking a good question. What's your answer?"

"YES."

"Right."

"So what we react to, we've yet to go through."

"Right again. How do you distinguish a reaction when you first perceive it in meditation?"

"It has a certain edginess."

"What do you mean by edginess?"

"Discontent. Dissatisfaction."

"What about non-reaction?"

"In non-reaction, there is peace."

"Very good. When the mind is at peace, it doesn't feel a need to think more than it has to, even though thinking is its function. So thought is primarily a product of discontent. Discontent is the hallmark of reaction, and reaction indicates unresolved karma. Therefore, a wise man knows more and thinks less because his mind is at peace as a consequence of having been-there-done-that with at lot of life."

"It still seems to me that thought is an important part of fully resolving karma."

"It is, but helpful thought occurs spontaneously. Experiences force you to think, and thinking draws forth intuition when it's needed. Thought and intuition are like brother and sister. We don't want to short-change thought. But we don't want to overly extol him either. Intuition has a mind of her own, so to speak, and thought should let her have her say. Thought and intuition work well together when given a chance to do so. That's why it's so important to get in the habit of clearly thinking things through as we deal with the challenges of life, so that intuition can have a good shot at helping out. But again, what we want to avoid is excessive thought. What about the next point? What was it?"

"Focus."

"Yes, focus. What bothered you about focus?"

"Asked and answered, pretty much."

"You're getting pretty good at answering your own questions. I'm starting to feel unneeded."

"Never, Gurudeva.

"Focus has its own agenda. Say, for instance, we're focusing on a flower—that poor flower. But while we are focusing on that flower, we are getting lots of other stuff from the side. Call it distraction if you want. But all this side stuff, this distraction, is actually a healthy consequence of focus. Intuitive understanding of one thing almost always comes when we are focusing on something else. This is the way even enlightenment comes—indirectly. Through a side door in a sense." Now, Gurudeva paused to let me respond in my own timing.

"Yes, as I look back, I can see that all my best meditations were surprises. During those meditations, nothing happened exactly as I thought it would. Often, even during those meditations, I had to alter my approach because of what I was learning in the moment. It is now quite apparent to me how those who stay with the practice of meditation and yoga for a long time get their minds forced open. Isn't that true?"

"Indeed it is."

"You sort of get to a place where you dare not make an assertion lest it be tweaked by intuition, which sort of puts you in what seems like a holding pattern of waiting in life as you live it." I paused. "This waiting wouldn't be a negative state by any means. It would be something like a vigilant state of openness maintained even during intense activity. This is *being*. Right? *Being* was the third point I was trying to tie in."

"*Being* in doing."

"Yes, *being* in doing. That's exactly it."

"Yogaswami talked a lot about this. And the *Shastras* refer to it as 'living with the feeling that nothing is happening.'"

"Gurudeva, how would you define *being*?"

"You tell me."

"Dwelling in your natural state."

"As opposed to what?"

"Your unnatural state ...."

"Which is ...."

"Hold on." I had to pause before responding. "Actually, it is just now occurring to me that I'm very close to my natural state right now. I'm not thinking. I'm not trying to put forward any particular image of myself to you. I'm just here trying to be really open to a fresh insight about what an 'unnatural state' of existence might be. But I'm getting stumped on the implication of the word, "unnatural." In this context, "unnatural" means something like misplaced identity doesn't it?"

"Yes. Good."

"Yet no man has only one identity. Life is too complex for that. Just living requires multiple identities. I mean, perhaps you're a banker at work, a golfer at the country club and a father at home. There shouldn't be anything wrong with that, right? That's just going through life."

"Yes, but where is your home base?"

"Well, of course, your ultimate home base would be the Self. But what if the Self is not yet realized?"

"After 'Self Realization,' you won't be the Self any more than you are right now."

"Okay."

"Why not be your Self now—consciously?"

"Didn't we just go through this?"

"We did."

"The only thing left to do is do it."

"Be it."

"Yes."

"Very good."

"Just one more quick question. If *being* brings enlightenment, can *being* be intensified in some manner so that enlightenment might be achieved more quickly? Oh boy, I'm just feeling through and through this is a wrong question to ask."

A Long Walk's End

"Enlightenment can't be rushed," Gurudeva said patiently. "Enlightenment is what awaits you at the end of *your* path. Each step on that path must be walked. Frustration is all you'll realize if you try to skip steps or quicken the process. *Being* will deepen of its own accord as your desires become more refined and your karmas fade into resolution."

"So, it's just a matter of waiting?"

"To say *being* is not *doing* does not mean *being* doesn't take some *doing*. It does. The work of *being,* which is *dwelling* in the *feeling* that nothing is happening, is to resist following mental distraction out into physical action. This is where one-pointed focus comes in. With one-pointed focus, we lock down in concentration, which grows into meditation, which finally blossoms into the *being* of contemplation, where there we sit and stay, awaiting Samadhi, the 'end of ends.'"

"So we've just walked the path in our heads: *distraction, focus, being, Self.*"

"Indeed we have. Congratulations on keeping continuity."

"Is *being* meditation?"

"More like contemplation—sort of like advanced meditation."

"So, to meditate is to intuit."

"Yes."

"Would you like to add something to that?"

"Not really."

"I guess what's bothering me is that *being* is so simple while meditation can sometimes seem complex."

"What do you find complex about meditation?" Because I did not answer right away, Gurudeva continued, "Even if a book's worth of information is intuited during meditation, the intuiting itself remains simple, does it not?"

"Yes it does."

"So, who's intuiting?"

"The meditator."

"Who's the meditator?"

"The Self?"

"The Self is the source of all manifestation. Although Self is *not* tangible, what it manifests *is*. Its first manifestation is pure life force. Pure life force consists of existence, consciousness and bliss."

"S*atchitananda*."

"Exactly, what can you say about *satchitananda*?"

"It's *being*, and *being* is just existence."

"Yes, but we cannot experience *existence* without experiencing *consciousness* and *bliss*, for these three qualities are inseparably linked. When we experience *satchitananda*, we are experiencing life at its first level of manifestation. When we merge with Self, we have discovered the source of life but we have not had an experience. An experience must include an experiencer and a situation experienced. There is no experience in spiritual illumination. There is only the Self."

"I must say it's a little frustrating to not be able to talk straight about the main goal of life."

"Say more."

"I mean, the Self is unmanifest so it can't be experienced, or even described, explained or adequately named. Yet we *do* stick a label on it, even though we say this label can't adequately do it justice. We call it the Self, I guess, so we can make it a goal of yoga and life. And we say we can merge with this Self in a 'nonexperience' that changes our life forever. I don't know. I just find it all frustratingly vague when I really want it to be satisfyingly clear."

"Yet you're still here?"

"Yes, more than ever."

"Why is that?"

"I don' know. I'm driven. That's all I can say."

"Although you might like it to be another way, you just have to admit that frustration can have a positive effect. It can goad you on. This very minute, frustration is goading you on. Otherwise, you'd just be an armchair yogi."

"An armchair yogi?"

"A person who talks about yoga but doesn't practice it."

"Talking without practice seems like a waste of time."

"Talking is a step along the way."

"I can see that. When I first read about yoga I was intellectually stimulated. And I couldn't stop talking about it."

"Then the novelty wore off."

"Exactly."

"But you stayed with it."

"Yes."

"That tells me a lot."

"Gurudeva, I know we don't usually talk about our past, but I would like to share one thing from my childhood which has relevance to what we have been discussing here. Would that be okay?"

"Sure."

"When I was about twelve years of age, I kept a box of five-by-seven note cards. The first card was entitled, 'The Most Important Thing.' The second card, 'The Second Most Important Thing.' The third card, 'The Third Most Important Thing.' And on and on. I had probably 25 of these cards. On the first card I named and briefly described my life's highest priority. On the second card, I did the same thing with my second priority, and so on throughout the cards. I assumed that at least the first few of these cards would stay the same. But they didn't. For about a week, the first card read 'music.' The second week it read 'art.' The third week it read 'philosophy.' The other cards were also forever changing, some daily. I kept working with these cards into my college years until I started studying your yoga teachings. Only then did I throw these cards out. There just came a time when I didn't feel I needed them any more. When the first card read 'enlightenment,' and the other cards remained fixed for about a month or so, I figured I was about ready to live my life without having to remember how to from a set of cards. I know this is probably sounding like a silly story, but what I'm trying to say is yoga has already transformed me in a most significant way."

"So, you were twelve when you started writing those cards?"

"Yes."

"Amazing."

At this point, we stopped talking for a while and just walked.

165

After about five minutes of moving clumsily through jungle brush, we came upon a flat piece of ground with an expansive view. The sun was in the last stages of setting, and everything everywhere was caste in a red-orange glow. It was beautiful.

"The Self just is what it is," Gurudeva said. "We talk about Self Realization and call it a non-experience. Actually, that's not completely accurate. The realization that we are now and always have been the Self is an experience that follows the non-experience of Self. That realization is a revelation after a fact. We don't usually say it this way because it makes the whole thing sound a lot more complicated than it really is. At some point, probably when you least expect it, you'll find yourself just coming back from this non-experience and you won't even remember that you were once frustrated that it couldn't be labeled."

"Something to look forward to."

"Could happen any time. You were once that armchair yogi. Not driven. Not feeling an urgency. At that point, a lot of your desire was consumed in other things. 'Enlightenment' was for conversation. The pursuit of the one and only non-experience had not yet become your highest priority. Now it has. Now your every thought is shadowed by an itch you can't scratch—an urge to give up all for nothing. And you can't quite explain it. And that's okay."

"You're reading me perfectly."

"What you are experiencing is a stirring of the soul."

"We haven't talked about the soul here. And the soul seems so central to everything we've said."

"God created souls like he created all of this." Gurudeva said as he waved his arm gracefully across the sky. "We don't know how or why. Only the thinking mind cares about that sort of thing. It's only the thinking mind that makes life a baffling predicament as it rattles around in its own cage asking hypothetical questions it can never really answer. In the end, there are only two things to know about thought. It's limited, and it's a tool. You are a soul. I am a soul. We share the same life, and we share the same essence. In a deep love, we acknowledge a one all-pervasive life force. In Self Realization, we acknowledge having merged with the essence of that life force."

"How about realizing the soul?"

"Too easy for words."

166

"Not a goal?"

"If it is, it's one you have attained many, many times. To *be* is to sit in the bliss of soul realization, immersed in *satchitananda. Being* is quite a tangible thing—very much within the reach of even those who aren't too interested in it. But to intentionally hold yourself in *being* for a long period of time. That's difficult. That's yoga. That's the path."

"And if simple dwelling in *being* becomes difficult, we fall back into the focus of concentration leading into meditation."

"Yes, and meditation has other uses as well. It's a master problem solver. I think of meditation as applied *being*."

"How so?"

"In meditation, we sit in *being,* considering options from a safe distance. This way and that we go, in accordance with questions raised or problems posed. Subtract the questions and problems—what's left?"

"*Being.*"

"Yes. But we all need to start with a point of focus. In attention, we establish that point. In concentration, we hold a focus on that point by will. In meditation, we become absorbed in that focus due to interest. All the while a sense of *being* is building. By the time we finally get to contemplation, our absorption in the bliss of *being* is strong enough that an external focal point is no longer needed."

"*Being* builds?"

"An awareness of *being* builds through focus. Focus intensifies energy. Lack of focus dissipates energy. Focus is like a magnifying glass used to beam sunlight onto a leaf to burn a hole. Eventually, your own subconscious mind will assist you in this art of focus. Once you develop a subconscious habit of focus, yoga will pervade a greater percentage of your daily life, and its benefits will multiply. Your subconscious is not always negative, you know. It can be wonderfully positive."

"Well yes, I have had moments here and there when I could see that kind of thing starting to happen. But let me ask you this. If focus is so important, what's to keep a person that has a job requiring a great deal of focus from becoming spiritually enlightened? I mean, such a job would require intense focus all day long, right? Wouldn't all that focus yield a yoga of sorts?"

"Certainly it would to a certain extent. But there are other forces that come into play in the work place, and those forces keep yoga from fully developing. Then, of course, there's desire. No amount of concentration can pull you within if you don't want to go within."

"So here we are, back at desire."

"Yes, remember, realization can only occur in a state of desirelessness. And desire is bound up in ego. With the death of ego comes the death of desire in Self Realization. All of that is a little too much to expect from the work place, wouldn't you say?"

"Certainly it is."

Now we started to walk again. Orchid Mandapam was near.

"Gurudeva, what did you mean when you made that comment about love being a realization of a connection we all share?"

"Actually, you just put it better than I did. A deep love is a sense of a connection we all share."

"But love is such a thrown-around word, isn't it?"

"It's a general word with lots of meanings. Take the emotion out of it and you have something close to what I hear some people these days referring to as an 'unconditional love.' A love without conditions. I like that. A love based more on understanding and unselfishness than emotion, neediness and personal preference. Have you ever observed someone else's pain and felt it as your own."

"Yes."

"That's a good deep love. Next comes discrimination—carefully discerning when and how to act on compassion, and when and how not to. Being wise in the implementation of a deep love comes late on the path of unfoldment, but come it does. You can be sure of that."

Our long conversation was winding down. I could feel it. "Thank you, Gurudeva, for spending all this time with me," I said. "It has been such an unexpected blessing. You've helped me a lot."

"Good. Keep the faith."

Finally, we arrived at the Orchid Mandapam. The sun had set. It was now as dark as it was going to get. Yet, in the peaceful glow of a most auspicious full moon, there was plenty of light for us to see as we walked the six-foot-wide strip of bleached white concrete that stretched from the Orchid Mandapam back to the monastery. We were moving quickly now. Kauai's evening mosquitoes had commenced their hunt for blood and were showing us no mercy.

As we entered the monastery, I made a mental note to write down what I could remember of the inspiring walk and talk I had just enjoyed with Gurudeva. I knew then as I know now, something special had just occurred. Of the great many conversations I had with Gurudeva through the years, this one was one of the most important.

Minority Control

During the next several days, I tried hard to recall what I assumed would be unforgettable. But I just couldn't manage it—not in the way I thought I would be able to. Although I did get it all back, it was at random, in odd moments popping up here and there, like snapshots taken out of sequence. Even then, it took work to hold those memories long enough to write them down or to allow myself a perception of them that wasn't overly influenced by my current mood.

As I was going through all of this and thinking to myself, "What a masterful invention the tape recorder is," I concluded that perhaps my documenting idea was not so smart. How strange is it that now, as I am writing this book 30 years later, I can remember that entire evening as if it just occurred yesterday?

Right after our walk, what I recalled most vividly was Gurudeva scrawling those meditation maps in the dirt. That memory was what inspired me to draw out my own maps on paper as soon as possible. But first things first. Monastic life was demanding and personal projects like this had to get fitted in as time allowed.

Our monastery day began at 5:30 in the morning with an hour-long *puja* (a Hindu worship ceremony) performed in Kadavul Temple. All the monks had to be there for this ceremony—shaved, showered and dressed in formal monastic robes. After *puja* everyone adjourned to the Guru Temple, a room adjoining Kadavul, for another hour of group meditation, singing and chanting. All of this concluded with a short talk delivered by Gurudeva.

From about 7:30 on, our day proceeded pretty much like any workday anywhere. Following a light breakfast served buffet-style, each monk clocked in eight hours of service, punctuated by a vegetarian rice-and-curry lunch at noon, followed by a delicious though brief siesta.

Evenings were free. During that time, some monks exercised. Other monks worked on creative projects. A buffet dinner was set out

169

around 7:00. After dinner, those who wanted could watch a limited amount of strictly monitored TV. Sometimes classes were scheduled during this time. Bedtime was 9:00 pm.

The duties of the monastery were performed by monks working in five *kulams* (families). Each *kulam* was given a name of Ganesha, "the lord of auspiciousness and good fortune." Like other Hindu gods and goddesses, Ganesha has many names, each of which signifies some specific aspect of his personality. The name of Ganesha chosen for each *kulam* was based on the nature of the duties performed by that kulam.

The duties of the first *kulam*—presided over by Lombodara, the "full-bellied one"—were to prepare food, care for the animals and see to the performance of ritual in the temple.

The duties of the second *kulam*—presided over by Ekadanta, the "single-tusked scribe and first patron of literature"—were to care for the guests and provide secretarial assistance to the guru.

The duties of the third *kulam*—presided over by Pilliyar, the "pure child"—were to supervise and record the expenditure of money, and assure that the use of time by all kulams was efficient.

The duties of the fourth *kulam*—presided over by Siddidhatta, the "giver of success and creator of abundance"—were to to handle all of the monastery and temple building and maintenance.

The duties of the fifth *kulam*—presided over by Ganapati, the "lord of the servants of Siva"—were to write, design and produce all of the monastery publications as well as oversee all monastery Web and media communication. I served in the Ganapati Kulam.

The *kulam* managers, or *talavar,* were appointed by Gurudeva, not because of their monastic seniority but because of their ability to perform their *kulam* tasks well. Through the five *talavar,* Gurudeva managed the monastery in a practical way on a daily basis. In his refined performance of this duty, he was masterful.

The hierarchical importance of each *kulam* was established by the need it fulfilled. This meant the last two *kulams,* responsible for building and publication—considered "outreach"—might not be able to function at all if the first three kulams in charge of food, teaching and finance—considered "stability"—were not doing well.

This was why our printing, a function of the Ganapati Kulam, was shut down for five years from 1973 to 1978. During that time, we all

170

withdrew into the first three *kulams* to fortify the foundational strength of the monastery.

Although most of our daily duties were *kulam*-oriented, there was one absolutely necessary monastic responsibility that was not. We called this responsibility the "three hour vigil." Officially, this vigil was a temple guard duty. Unofficially, it was a time for individual worship and meditation.

Through every moment of every day since 1973, there has been a monk performing a three hour vigil in Kadavul Hindu Temple. To even be assigned one of these vigils was considered a sacred blessing—and serious business! If a monk on vigil inadvertently stepped outside the temple boundaries, even for an instant, he had to remain in the temple through the next three-hour shift to "reestablish the continuity of the temple's power."

Although Gurudeva exerted a gentle control over the monk's day-to-day activity through his *kulam talivar*, he managed their conduct and spiritual life through a secret governing body known as the OTM.

"OTM" is an acronym for "one third minority." With regard to the population of the monastery, it referred to the one third of the monks with the longest physical residency. The acronym, "OTM," named the group of monks who comprised the "one third minority" as well as the governmental system they administered.

A monk's monastery residency was the length of time he had lived within the monastery without leaving for more than nine days in a row. If, in determining residency, there was a tie, an older monastic age took precedence. Monastic age began when monastic vows were taken. If there was a tie in monastic age, "brahmacharya age" was the deciding factor. Brahmacharya age was specified by the length of time that had passed since the monk had his last sexual encounter with a woman. If, after all of this, there was *still* a tie—and this has happened—physical age determined the order.

The identity of those on the OTM was supposed to be a carefully guarded secret. Conveniently, this was a secret easily kept. With the monks perpetually traveling on mission, it was all but impossible to calculate the monastery's current residency hierarchy. Although monks not on the OTM never tired of trying to figure out who was a part of this group, they were almost always foiled by the monastery's convoluted

171

tie-breaking procedures.

The OTM calendar-log harbored the final decree on the determination of the OTM membership. Even if, due to some sort of miscalculation, this membership was incorrectly figured, it was considered correct, since all such miscalculation was attributed to divine providence. In the beginning this log was kept in a hand-written book. After 1985, it was maintained on a computer spreadsheet.

The OTM, also known as the Senior Minority Group, did not manage the monastery. That was the guru's job. The OTM's function was simply to assist the guru in his subtle administration of monastery discipline. Not surprisingly, the OTM's implementation of this function was as secret as the identity of its members.

When the OTM met, its members sat in a circle. The formation of this circle was determined by residency. The most senior person in this circle was the Umaganesh. The next was the Hanuman. The youngest was the Umadeva. The Hanuman sat to the left of the Umaganesh—the Umadeva to his right. The rest of the circle, extended from the left of the Hanuman on around and down in seniority to the Umadeva.

The Umaganesh's duty was to maintain the OTM calendar-log, to preside over OTM meetings and to act as a channel between the guru and the OTM. The only OTM identities known to the monastery were those of the Hanuman and the Umadeva.

The Hanuman worked with groups and the Umadeva worked with individuals. It was the Hanuman's job to host guests and address the monastery on behalf of the OTM. The Umadeva was the carrier of the OTM's messages to individuals.

The Umaganesh would begin an OTM meeting by initiating a group chanting of a Sanskrit *sloka* (verse) invoking divine protection and assistance. Then, the Umaganesh would ask for an update from the Hanuman and the Umadeva on tasks they had been assigned to perform during a previous meeting. Following these reports, the Umaganesh would request the group's assessment of "monastery transparency," and "ashram sadhana." "Monastery transparency" meant monastic conduct. "Ashram sadhana" referred to monastery cleanliness.

After carefully noting observations from the group pertaining to these matters, the Umaganesh would initiate a group meditation saying, "Now we will hold the *darshan*." Although the word *darshan* literally means "divine sight," it referred here to the practice of sitting in group meditation to intensify the spiritual power of the monastery as well as to invoke the presence of the *devas* and the blessings of God.

Following this *darshan* session, the Umaganesh shared his last conversations with the guru. At this point, the group came to understand how the guru responded to the various monastic requests, suggestions and complaints that had most recently come in, as well as any specific thoughts the guru had or instructions he wanted to give. Any responsive action initiated by the guru was then given as a duty to be accomplished by the Hanuman or the Umadeva.

All the monks of the monastery were encouraged to communicate with the guru freely, either in person or through the OTM. The correct procedure for a communication through the OTM was to leave a note in the "OTM drop box." From 1975 through 1990, this drop box was just that: a box with a slot in the top under a sign that read, "OTM." After 1990, when every monk had a computer for work purposes, it was an email address.

Through the OTM system, the guru was able to work with a monk's personal issues impersonally—and therefore more efficiently. This divinely conceived method allowed the guru to focus more directly upon the spiritual life of the monks without getting overly drawn out into the confusion of unnecessary emotional drama.

Because there was no apparent status associated with being on the OTM—membership could be gained or lost at a moment's notice—and because being on the OTM often required performing anonymous tasks, ego was not likely to surface among OTM members.

With regard to receiving correction and instruction from the OTM, no one knew whom to blame if blame was sought. No one could know for sure, for instance, whether a correction or an instruction had originally come from the guru's wisdom or a monk's complaint.

Also, if a monk complained to the OTM, he would often receive some sort of a disciplinary reprimand from the OTM, which would be dispensed along with any action taken by the OTM in response to his complaint. As a modus operandi, the OTM was self-balancing.

Interestingly, because physical age was the last determinant of a monk's resident seniority and because new monks were less likely to do much traveling, it was easily possible for a young monk to become the

Umaganesh. Because the Umaganesh worked directly with the guru in a duty that flourished if it was performed with the childlike innocence a young monk was likely to have, young Umaganeshs usually performed quite well, allowing the OTM to function at its optimum level.

I had extensive experience working as Umaganesh, Hanuman and Umadeva. Being Umaganesh was by far the easiest job of the three — and the most fun, if I might dare to make such a comment. For one thing, it provided an official reason for spending a lot of time with Gurudeva. Being Hanuman or Umadeva was much more work.

When I was Hanuman, I had to hustle, especially if there were lots of guests to host. When I was Umadeva, I had to convey sometimes embarrassing messages like, "Your brother monks would deeply appreciate it if you ate with your mouth closed." Or "It was felt that fewer monks would encounter surprises in the bathroom if you would be so kind as to lift the toilet seat before taking a pee."

Night Flight

I finally got around to drawing my own meditation map with the Self at its center. This map was composed in the *Shum* language—mostly. It also had some art. Its four *Shum* words were written large and designed aesthetically along with a rather intricate colored drawing.

In the upper right corner of the page, I printed out the *Shum* word *imkaif*, which means "no awareness." This was the map's "treasure." Toward the bottom left corner of the page, I used colored pencils to draw a picture of a blue-green ocean at sunset in a cove bordered by palm trees and a beach of white sand. This hint of tropical paradise was the map's starting point.

In the center of the page, I wrote three *Shum* words in a vertical column. *Kalibasa*, "breath control," was at the bottom. *Rehvumsirehli*, "letting go," was in the middle. And *kaif*, "pure awareness," was on top.

All of these elements—the picture in the lower, left corner of the page, the three words in the center of the page and the one word in the upper, right corner of the page—were all connected by *nimf* lines. In *Shum*, *nimf* means "flowing awareness."

In English, the meaning of this map, when read from the bottom to the top, would be something like, "Calm down. Control your mind by controlling your breath. Release everything but awareness aware of itself. Then hold awareness aware of itself until it dissolves into itself."

In the end, this little piece of art did indeed look like a treasure map. As I drew it, I felt like I was the playing child Gurudeva wanted us to be in our inner search for Self. In Gurudeva's view, a child's loose and free look at life was a great perspective to hold at the beginning of a meditation, especially when that meditation centered upon seeking something as deceptively simple as "the life of our life," as Gurudeva was so fond of calling the Self.

Little did I know that my own *thought* would attack this map again and again, tearing it apart, reconstructing it over and over until the poor thing finally ended up like it started: one picture and four images.

I was sure this map would be the first of many. What it turned out to be was something like a visual version of my one-page yoga journal—a one thing I just kept trying to get right.

It was nine o'clock at night when I finished my first version of this map. As has been mentioned, nine o'clock was bed time.

I fell asleep normally enough. Yet, somewhere just beyond the twilight zone of transition from waking to sleep, I woke up. At least, I thought I woke up. It felt like it. By no intentional effort of my own, yogic or otherwise, I was suddenly conscious of being suspended about five our six feet above my bed, lying parallel to the ground on my back in the air. In this position, I was looking up and studying the detail of my hut's cement ceiling, which was about two feet away—even though it should have been too dark for me to be seeing what I was seeing. Also, I was vibrating, forward and back, like a car revving its motor, getting ready to move. As I raised my head to look down at my feet, I could see I was pointed toward the wall of my hut. Somehow, I just knew—I could feel it—I just knew I was going to go straight through that wall.

And so I did. Right through that wall I went. Slowly at first, as if I were being kindly guided. Then faster. There was no resistance in the wall's cement block, not even a little. All I felt was a slight tingle.

As soon as I was outside my twelve-foot cube of a hut, I kept moving—faster and faster—even though I was still lying flat. It was like I was a bobsledder leaned way back in a downhill race. Although it felt like I had no control over what was happening, I had no sense of being aggressively forced to do what seemed to be done through me. It was

175

as if the very life of me now had a mind of its own that had suddenly decided to take me for a most impressive ride.

Now I was flying over dense tropical jungle, heading feet-first toward Mount Waialeale about five miles away. The distance seemed like nothing. As the speed of my flight increased, my heart raced.

"No!" I thought to myself. "I do *not* want to go through that mountain." Yet, as soon as I had that thought, I was. I was moving right through Mount Waialeale, feeling its mass as new life.

That mountain was *alive* and it was a *he*. If he felt within himself like he felt to me, he was a blissful and happy being who wanted for nothing — a grand old man who had survived a tumultuous youth and was now settled in peace. Fearless contentment was his prize possession and fearless contentment is what he gave to me.

As soon as I moved out the other side of that magnificent old mountain, I flipped forward from feet-first to head-first to fly the ocean like a jet. Now, I was moving smoothly, not like in the beginning just outside my hut where I vibrated and shook. Now, I was fearless and content, moving elegantly — enjoying myself completely.

Through all of this, I was not so aware of sights, sounds and smells. I was more conscious of feelings. And I was feeling from vastly different vantage points. I was feeling air as air feels to air, feeling the mountain as the mountain feels to the mountain. During this strangely multidimensional experience, I was not myself, or the self I was used to being, shall we say. It was exhilarating to say the least.

Even in thoughts, I was feeling. I was feeling thoughts. I could feel the thoughts of the air and the thoughts of the mountain. And in these thoughts there were messages for me. In the air, there were messages that felt like freedom. In the mountain, there were messages that felt like courage, peace and stability.

I crossed the 2,500 miles from Kauai to California as quickly as I flew the five miles from the monastery to Mount Waialeale. There was no sense of passing time really. For one timeless instant I was just flying the ocean — racing over its water, perhaps 200 feet above its surface.

Then suddenly I was in downtown San Francisco gliding along a busy street, *through* people. And as I moved through these people, I could feel their thoughts — thoughts of me as I moved through them. They felt me as a tingle. And this tingle was in their thoughts. And in

176

their thoughts were messages for me—boring messages compared to those of the air and the mountain. Perhaps these human thoughts were boring because I, a human, was just so accustomed to them. Yet now I was human with the fearless contentment of a mountain and the grand, untouchable freedom of air.

I think I was somewhere on Union Street close to Van Ness. Many people were out and about, and everyone was happy. I was enjoying this, and learning so much. I loved feeling the happiness of the people.

Then I moved quickly up Union Street to Presidio Park where there were trees. Suddenly, I was at the base of one tree in particular, deep inside its trunk, and moving up through the fibers of its wooden body right to its top. And I could feel the life of this tree and all of its wisdom. It had been there so long and knew so much. It felt rich and abundant, but not like the mountain, and not like the air.

Up toward the top of this tree, there was a house. Not a house really. More like a mansion. A vast mansion in a tree, much larger than any mansion could possibly be if it were in a tree. Yet there it was, and there I was in it, looking out through one of its windows.

In this mansion, there were many rooms with many windows opening out in many directions. And through each window there was a one-and-only view. All the wisdom of this tree was in its mansion. But its mansion contained nothing—not even furniture. Just windows. Yet each of these windows framed an overview of some wondrous something this tree wanted to give to me, if I was ready enough to receive it. But I wasn't. Such a supreme disappointment. There I was, wanting to learn but not being able to. And so, for now, this tree gave me but one gift: the gift of humility.

There in that mansion, looking out just one of its windows, I wondered to myself, "How did I come to be in this tree?" And with that asking thought I felt an almost violent slam, like I had been thrown against a wall in a fight.

I was back. Back in my body in my bed on Kauai. Wondering if I had died but knowing I hadn't, I sat up and pointed my flashlight toward my alarm clock. Ten o'clock. All of this had happened within the short space of an hour? Trying to grasp my bearings, I looked at the meditation map I had just drawn. What did my astral adventure have to do with: *kalibasa, rehvumsirehli, kaif, imkaif?*

177

Tethered Freedom

When the time was right, I told Gurudeva about my night travels through Mount Waialeale to San Francisco. I had to be patient. The right time took its time in coming.

In the impersonal life of the monastery, it was not cool to make a big deal, or even a small deal, of personal experiences, be they inner, outer or other. This impersonal aspect of monastic living was important. It kept life unsticky and therefore a little more rarefied than it might have been otherwise. To live on Earth like *devas* in heaven was the idea.

Sooner or later, we all came to understand that inner life gets deepened through the development of an impersonality. And in this fine discovery, we learned how the emotion of living personally produced a drag on the efficiency of our yoga and service.

Aside from being impersonal, monastic life was gloriously streamlined. Everything in it was funneled toward an ultimate Samadhi. In this focus upon Samadhi, there was a lot of reference to "the path" and "distractions on the path."

Gurudeva referred to "the path" in two ways. In a general sense, he talked about it as the overall trajectory of the soul's evolutionary journey from its divine conception to its final return to and full merging with God. In a more specific context, he described it as the way of the mystic, the way of a life committed to the fullest experience of *being* and the ultimate attainment of Samadhi.

For Gurudeva's monks, "the path" was an impersonal life that was strapped into a perpetual practice of yoga by a strict work routine overseen by Gurudeva functioning through the *talivar*, and a strict lifestyle overseen by Gurudeva functioning through the OTM.

For monastics, walking straight on this path meant not getting distracted. Becoming overly involved with anything not established in our monastic program was considered a distraction. This included astral projection. As Gurudeva put it in his book, *Living with Siva*, monks "may spontaneously experience but do not practice clairvoyance, clairaudience, astral projection, lucid dreaming, trance mediumship, mind-reading, fortune-telling, magic or other distracting occult arts."

I was safe, sort of. I was *spontaneously experiencing* astral projection, not *practicing* it. Nevertheless, I was bound by conscience to share my night flight with Gurudeva. Yet such sharing had to happen in good timing. As much as it was proper to keep Gurudeva informed, it was just as proper to inform him in the right way at the right time. Good monastic living was qualified as much by *how* we did what we did as *what* we did and *why* we did it.

My next good chance to freely talk with Gurudeva about my nocturnal adventure on the astral plane came on a plane to India.

There were only three of us on that trip. Gurudeva preferred to travel with two monks instead of one. When he was once asked why he chose to incur the extra expense of including a second monk on his blitzkrieg journeys, he said, "If one wears out, I'll have a spare." From personal experience, I can say this reply was less funny than true.

But this trip was different from Gurudeva's customary journeys, which generally focused on him teaching. Its main event was a spiritual initiation. Veera and I were receiving our vows of Hindu monasticism in a ceremony called *sannyas diksha* on the holy Ganges River in Hardwar, India, near the foothills of the Himalayas. Still, it would to be a busy trip. It could not be otherwise with Gurudeva. He knew people all around the world. And these people always wanted to see him when he traveled.

Because the central purpose of our journey was spiritual, we were referring to it as a pilgrimage, but a pilgrimage that would take us not only to India but also to Japan, Sri Lanka and Malaysia. I had never traveled with Gurudeva like this. It was exciting.

We left for India on May 5, 1980, and returned to Kauai on the second of June. Although we were gone almost a month, we accomplished our primary objective only five days into the journey. So much happened on the trip *after* our Ganges initiation, that initiation itself seemed almost like a past-life memory by the time we arrived back at our garden island home.

Before we even got to India, we spent two glorious days in Japan traveling by first-class train up through the island's mountainous interior to the famous Nikko Temple north of Tokyo. Japan was an interesting prelude to India. Unlike India, it was sharp, clean, neat, tidy, efficient, modern and meticulously manicured.

Gurudeva was tactfully wise in crafting this little diversion at the beginning of our journey. He wanted to vivify by contrast our first perception of India. In this effort, he was masterfully successful.

I will never forget my first step onto Indian soil. We landed in

New Delhi late at night, and it was hot, very hot. One single, muscular blast of India's dry summer air gave me not only my first exposure to her oppressive heat but also my first awareness of her scent. The air was full of many smells all blended together into a one fragrance that was decidedly Indian. Trying to pick out the different components of this one aroma was fun. There was incense, diesel, perfume, dried cow dung and the smoke of family cooking fires. More, to be sure. Much more. But nothing Japanese.

Gurudeva did not waste any time in moving us along. Before sunrise the next morning, after about three hours of sleep, we traveled four hours by car to Hardwar for our monastic initiation. Although the ride was as bumpy and arduous as any travel in India almost always is, it was worth it. The sights along the way were magnificent.

When we arrived in Hardwar about nine in the morning, we bought orange robes and rudraksha beads in a marketplace. Then we found a spot by the Ganges that was somewhat private. There, almost before I realized what was going on, Gurudeva began our initiation.

First, he asked us to chant an ancient Sanskrit *sloka* to invoke blessings and protection. Then he shaved our heads, but just on top, leaving a samurai-like strip of bare scalp about five inches wide and six inches long, extending back from the forehead hairline. This rather cumbersome task took nearly half an hour to complete. When the deed was done, Gurudeva had Veera gather up our cut hair and throw it into the Ganges. The current was devilishly strong.

Next was the hard part. Veera and I had to go into the water.

As we waded into the Ganges up to our waists, we had to work hard to keep our balance. Although the weather was summer hot, that Ganges water straight out of the mountains was icy cold. And its current *was* strong.

Once we got stable in the water, we had to undress. Getting out of our shirts was easy compared to taking off our pants. We both stumbled awkwardly through all of this, nearly loosing our footing a number of times. When we had finally escaped our clothes and released them downstream, we turned upstream to pray toward the Himalayas.

In that moment of devotion, I was suddenly private inside my head where I could sense having prayed in this manner so many times before. Strange. I never considered myself the worshipful type. Yet there I was feeling tears well up as I was learning how devotion doesn't always fall upon a type.

I looked at Veera. He was over to my left, splashing around. It took me a minute to discern whether or not he was in trouble. As soon as I could see he was just trying to get out of the water, I blundered to catch up. Together, we emerged from the Ganges wearing only loincloths.

By this time, we had attracted quite an audience of local people. They were staring at us. There is no other way to put this. They were just staring. We tried to ignore them.

Gurudeva gave us our new orange robes and beads, which we attempted to receive graciously in our wet and shivering self-consciousness. After we dried off and dressed, we sat with Gurudeva in silence. I'm not sure how long we were there, resting in a timeless peace. When I opened my eyes, our audience had gone and we were alone except for a few ardent bathers nearby.

Gurudeva and Veera were looking at me. Apparently, they had been waiting quite a while for me to come around. As soon as I looked alert, Gurudeva leaned over to each of us—Veera first, then me—to whisper a mantra. This mantra was an important gift. It was the magic part of the initiation that would later influence our yoga practice favorably. When this mantra transfer was done, the ceremony was over.

Before returning to New Delhi to conclude one of the longest days of our trip, we traveled fifteen miles upstream to Rishikesh where we ambled about for a while at the "gateway to the Himalayas."

Recently nicknamed "the world-capital of Yoga" because of its growing popularity with westerners, Rishikesh had long been extolled as a significant Hindu pilgrimage destination as well as an important way station for stalwart devotees advancing further into the mountains to the ancient and legendary Hindu temples of Badrinath, Kedarnath, Gangotri, and Yamunotri.

The rest of our trip was a heady amalgam of diverse activity spiked with fast-paced intensity. We never lingered long anywhere. In Agra, we toured the Taj Mahal. In Varanasi, we rode boats on the river Ganges by the fires of the cremation ghats where ashes of the dead were being thrown upon the water. In Palani Hills, we climbed 697 steps to attend a festival at Lord Muruga's hilltop temple overlooking the dry plains of Tamil Nadu. Here, Gurudeva was honored as a saint. Hundreds touched his feet. In Chennai, we visited Swami Chinmayananda, who was famous among Hindus and a long-time friend of Gurudeva's. All along the way, we worshipped in more temples than I can remember.

Three weeks into our trip, we left India for the small, southern Island of Sri Lanka. Little did we know then, a tragic civil war was brewing behind the scenes in that delightfully inviting place of great spiritual heritage. For the time being, however, all was well. Or so it seemed. We were blissfully ignorant, of course. I was, at least. Certainly, Gurudeva knew more than he was saying.

Yet nothing could have stopped us from having a most enjoyable time: first, in Colombo, the largest city on the island where we stayed in the old Galle Face Hotel perched near the shores of the Indian Ocean; next, in the middle of the island at Annuradhapura, where we faced our fears as vicious monkeys half our size ran us ragged; and finally, in the far north at Alaveddy on the Jaffna peninsula, where we worshipped at Nallur Temple, the sacred haunt of Yogaswami, his guru and the guru of his guru. We also spent some time at Gurudeva's three-story Alaveddy Ashram, which included a school for 200 children.

Before leaving Jaffna, we traveled for about an hour through narrow side streets to visit a sagely old man named Markanduswami. This venerable gentleman, then in his nineties, had been a lifelong devotee of Yogaswami and had known Gurudeva 30 years before.

Because Markanduswami rarely spoke, our meeting with him was brief. After gazing at us long enough to make me feel uncomfortable—about five minutes—he said in English, "Realize the Self, yourself." Then he got up and left.

Although that short encounter seemed little more than awkward at the time, it has dogged me all my life. Even now, whenever I sense myself becoming silly or trite, I see Markanduswami's stoic face locked in that five-minute gaze.

The day after we met Markanduswami, we drove to Colombo. From there, we flew to Kuala Lumpur in Malaysia, then home.

Traveling with Gurudeva was revealing in a number of ways. It gave me a chance to know another side of him, actually several other sides of him. The phrase "multi-dimensional" fits well in a description of this most unusual man who, living freely, easily and happily with no dead-set way of doing things, could morph like a chameleon in adapting to the ever-shifting world of people and circumstance.

When I finally told him about my astral journey to San Francisco, he listened like a child with rapt attention and countered with similar stories of his own. He even told me how to induce astral projection right before sleep. This was not what I had expected. What about all those rules? My mind was full of questions.

Like most anyone, I had gained a sense of security in life by working out a way of living that fostered a sense of *self*-confidence. I had devised a *me* I could live in with a sense of being protected. Or so I thought. Then, of course, that *me* got so solid I forgot I made it up.

But with Gurudeva, it wasn't like this. He had no such *me* he felt he had to be to get by in the world. He derived all his confidence and security from his discovery of Self, the ultimate *me*, and so could spin on a dime as he moved through life, changing his persona as required, very much like an actor on stage. It was such a joy to be with him as he danced nimbly along—austere one moment, genial the next, forever spontaneous, yet never vulnerable. Truly, he was a living example of yoga's greater potential. And his Self left no "personality quirks" to tip-toe around, no personal eccentricities to avoid.

Yet, what inspired me most about Gurudeva was not that he had optimized his life through yoga, but that he had given me a sense *I could do that too*. This inspiration, fortified by Markanduswami's command to "realize the Self, yourself," is what I brought home from India.

Back within monastery walls, back within those many OTM and *kulam* confines, I felt like a bird caged. I should have been happy, but wasn't. Happy was what I was when I was traveling with Gurudeva.

Sitting there in the aftermath of that magnificent journey, I was just barely able to resist despondency in the inescapable thought that a monastery's home-and-hearth safety only barely justified its tethered freedom. And in that thought I could see how far I was from Gurudeva's transcendent detachment, and how far I had to go.

That night I wrote two verses in my yoga journal.

The trap-like grip of time and space
Is born of acts that bind,
For souls tied down in earthbound lace
Are surely flying blind.

Calling back unraveled threads
Brings home the force to rise
Through yogi's hearts into their heads
As ego slowly dies.

Busting Seals

There were moments here and there when Gurudeva could be coaxed into conversing casually about mystical things. Unlike those evening, Sun Palace talks, which were scheduled and anticipated, these chats occurred spontaneously and leisurely when time constraints were least rigid, like just after lunch.

During that relaxed afternoon time, Gurudeva would frequently nap on a couch just outside his downstairs office. That nap was always short. Soon enough—too soon, some might say—those monks for whom nap time was rap time would gather 'round—two, three, four or more—quietly waiting for Gurudeva to wake up. And when he did, there would always be talk of a mystical sort.

During one such post-lunch chat, shortly after we got back from India, Mular had just asked Gurudeva about charkas as I was arriving. Gurudeva was responding.

"In yoga, the fiery force of life rises to the top of the head," he was saying. "As it rises, it bursts through the seals of the *chakras*, four, five, six and seven. These chakras are not physical. They are astral. But the experiences are very real. And the breaking of these seals affects a permanent change in the psyche."

"So should we work to break these seals?" asked Mular.

"They will open themselves," replied Gurudeva. "They know what to do. Our's is the path of not only striving to awaken our higher nature, but also consciously acknowledging and patiently transmuting those remnants of our lower nature we must admit are still there."

"How does all of this change after Self Realization?"

"In Nirvikalpa Samadhi, awareness merges with the formless, causeless, spaceless Self. When awareness returns to the experiences of form, life is as it was, except for one thing. It's not binding. Where there was automatic attachment before, now there is automatic detachment. This makes all that business of dealing with the lower nature a lot easier. Also, after Samadhi there is an outpouring of energy. There is this unique effulgence—a natural consequence of having merged with the essence of all. Others feel this effulgence as blessings. As far as the Self-Realized yogi is concerned, there is only bliss."

"Does this Self-Realized yogi feel sort of extraordinary. And if he feels extraordinary, how can he be humble?"

"How extraordinary can Self Realization be if every soul, without one single exception, *is* that Self and destined to realize this most fundamental of all facts. At some point, when many have merged with Self in Samadhi, Self Realization won't seem *extra* ordinary at all. It will be quite ordinary."

"So everyone should set Samadhi as an eventual goal?"

"Yes, but *now* is the time. This is the way we should think of our pursuit—as something that can happen *now*. The path to enlightenment can only exist now. In the lower realms of the mind, where time and space seem real, most people live in a perpetual regret of the past and fear of the future. This limits their experience of the now."

"But we talk about past and future all the time."

"Looking forward and back intentionally and usefully is okay. But *living* out of the now in any fashion is a problem. Dwelling in the past, as in constantly reliving old memories—mainly the negative ones, for they are most vividly remembered—clouds our enjoyment of the present and our constructive planning for a positive future. Living in the future over-activates our thoughts, emotions and desires, for the future is little more than a mental fantasy. Idle wandering into the past or the future is detrimental to an effortless spiritual unfoldment."

"Sounds to me like anyone living in the past or the future just thinks too much."

Gurudeva laughed. "True enough. A person who intentionally looks forward or back for good reason, has control of his mind. Such a person is naturally happy. He lives each moment with full attention, and the excellent quality of his life reveals the usefulness of that approach. And he's never bored. Everything he does is interesting. Fulfillment is never an issue for him. He's plenty fulfilled in the moment and needs nothing but what he has right now."

"So does everyone work toward Samadhi in the same way? I mean, each person is at a different point on the path. Right?"

185

"In the yoga I was taught, love is the secret. On this path of love, you don't have to be a great rishi or a highly disciplined yogi. You don't have to be a great philosopher. You don't have to know Sanskrit. All you need is love. Everything else comes as a result of that."

"Even this breaking of chakra seals?"

"Even that."

"And by love, here, you mean devotion."

"Love is not a mushy thing. It's Life, the life that's the same in everyone. To realize God as the life within everyone is to realize God as the love that binds us all. And to love in this way, we must become very simple, very uncomplicated, so that a perception of a one life flowing through all can become obvious."

"So where is the yoga in this work of becoming uncomplicated and simple? Is it in purification? Self discipline?"

"The life of a thought doesn't care if that thought is good or bad. Take away the thought and you are left with its life, which is love. But remaining conscious of life and love, requires self-discipline. The very perception that life is love dawns on you as an unfoldment. But you need discipline to enjoy this unfoldment and quicken it on into the next unfoldment, and the next, and the next. This is where the yoga comes in. You *love* on the outside, *realize* on the inside. Love plus realization equals transformation. You become a different, better."

As this discussion was going on, I was enjoying what Gurudeva would refer to as a "psychological moment," one of those nice points in time when something previously heard, witnessed or experienced rings true. I was finally getting what Gurudeva had been trying to tell me some years before when he said, "You've just never been in love," in response to my confession that I was having trouble feeling devotion.

When he made that comment, I assumed he was reprimanding me for being selfish, and maybe he was, but he was also trying to tell me that love is not just an emotional feeling dressed in poetry. It's an awakening that starts with a sense of getting swept away into a larger life than one person can fill.

Gurudeva was trying to tell me, whether love first dawns as an fondness of a man for a woman, a woman for a pet, or a father for a son, it eventually becomes something that is the same for all: an enjoyment of a primal force that ignores the prison walls of a personal life.

186

What was it that had changed so that now I was understanding this and before I wasn't? Who knows what brings on the slow dawn of perception? Not I. All I know is, right then and there, I got it.

Later that night, while writing in my journal just before sleep, I happened upon what I think were the thoughts of *devas*, or perhaps they were my own thoughts as I looked at myself from another place. Either way, those thoughts were these:

Looking long and hard for thee
We chanced upon the dead,
For you had lost what you would be
While seeking in your head.

You felt that loss and begged it back.
We did not honor thee.
You tugged and squirmed like cat in sack.
We would not set you free.

We've come for you. It's time you know
A secret bed of peace.
The life you lived so long ago
Now begs for your release.

Three Earth-Shaking Events

In 1982, two years after my monastic initiation, I returned to India on one of our monastery Innersearch programs. During that trip, I was "the coordinator." An Innersearch coordinator is the point man of a monastic staff responsible for moving 60 to 90 people through about a month of fairly complicated international travel. Although the job of coordinator had always been considered a somewhat difficult assignment, it was especially so for me. Put simply, I was just not well suited for it. This is to say: I did it poorly and was not asked to do it again.

I barely remember the India part of that pilgrimage. For me, the whole trip was just one long string of emergencies dealing with passports, cash currency, schedules, vehicle transportation, hotel accommodations, health problems, petty personal concerns and more. When I got back to Kauai, I just felt lucky to be alive.

Happily, my experience of that Innersearch was not the norm. Most of the travelers, I was told later, had a great time.

A typical Innersearch day would usually begin with an hour of hatha yoga followed by breakfast and a pleasant assortment of yoga and meditation classes. After a light lunch, there would generally be some sort of sightseeing adventure. In the evening, everyone enjoyed an abundant rice-and-curry dinner followed by a cultural event of some sort. The classes in the morning were fun, easy-going and informative. The sights seen during the afternoon were almost always of a spiritual nature—temples, ashrams, sacred places and the like. The entertainment following the evening feast was usually worth happy anticipation— something like a concert or a dance performance.

In and through all of this, Innersearchers had a rare opportunity to visit and talk casually with Gurudeva and the monks who were, in most other venues, not so available for socializing.

Quite an assortment of people signed up for Innersearch. At one extreme there were the serious seekers. At the other extreme there were the curious adventurers. Although it was the duty of the monastic staff to keep everyone happy doing pretty much whatever they wanted to do, the yoga and spiritual side of life was generally emphasized, as much as was politely possible. This usually worked pretty well. When it didn't, guess who got to handle the fallout? Yes, *the coordinator*.

"Fallout" could and would include anything from "I'm sick. I need a doctor;" to "I'm sick of temples. I want to go shopping;" to "I'm sick of life. Can you help me?"

When the trip was all over and I was happily easing my way back into the "tethered freedom" of monastery life, thinking nothing could be as hectic as Innersearch, along comes Iwa.

Iwa, a Hawaiian word meaning "thief," is commonly used to name a specific kind of frigate bird that steals other bird's babies. The Iwa I'm referring to here was a Hurricane.

Iwa, the hurricane, flew over Hawaii on November 25, 1982. Devastating the islands of Niihau, Kauai and Oahu, she wreaked more than 300 million dollars worth of damage. Had there not been advanced weather reporting providing ample warning of her arrival, she would have killed far more than the four poor mortals who perished in her wake. As bad as Iwa was, however, she was nothing but a lightweight dress rehearsal for Iniki, ten years later.

Billowing her wings only a few weeks after Florida's devastating Hurricane Andrew, Iniki began her pummeling of Hawaii on September 11, 1992. *This was the same day terrorists would fly two planes into the twin towers of the World Trade Center in New York nine years later.*

When she was done with her fun, Iniki left 1.8 billion dollars worth of damage across the state. As with Hurricane Iwa, she killed few only because of well-deployed warnings. For the residents of Kauai, who were positioned right under her eye, she was most destructive.

As Iniki approached, we took cover in the Sun Palace. This had worked well with Iwa. But the winds of Iwa were nothing like those of Iniki. Within the first ten minutes of Iniki's initial fury, all of the sun palace windows were blown out, even though they had been covered with four-by-eight-foot sheets of half-inch-thick plywood.

The storm winds were so viciously powerful they whipped around and behind those plywood masks, suddenly billowing them out like spinnaker sails. This created a contained pressure that shattered and projected fragmented glass back into the Sun Palace like shrapnel thrown from an exploding bomb. It was all we could do to tip toe down the shard-strewn stairs and run for cover in the temple.

With its three-foot-thick walls built of lava rock and concrete block, the temple was as sturdy as a fallout shelter. Although we were safe there, it didn't feel like it. Tall coconut trees stripped of their branches slapped at the temple walls like cracking whips.

Had I been deaf, the whole event might have seemed peacefully surreal. It was the horrifying racket of it all that made the drama of Iniki such an in-your-face event so permeated with a sense of impending peril. The last thing I remember before entering the temple was hearing a loud, rifle-like sound and seeing the roof of a nearby building lift up and whip away like Kleenex in a summer breeze.

Two hours after the storm began, the winds stopped suddenly. We thought it was all over. When we went outside, everything was dead still. As I think back now, I can't be sure how long this stillness lasted—perhaps about five minutes from the time we became aware of it. All I can remember with full clarity is this: When those terrible winds began again, I was only thirty feet from the temple door—a safe distance, I thought. But this second half of the hurricane came up so rapidly and with such vicious might, I was almost literally blown away before I could stumble back into the safety of the temple.

When we finally emerged from shelter to witness what nature's fury had left behind, we were appalled at what we saw. Large fallen trees, covered with mountains of debris, now had us completely trapped.

We wanted to walk from the temple to the press shop to see if our computers were ok. Even though the press shop was only about a hundred yards away, we couldn't get there. We couldn't even *see* there.

Looking out over a once familiar landscape, unrecognizable now in its desolation, we tried to pick out familiar landmarks. Only big things looked the same—the mountains in the distance, the river below. Otherwise, there was only "witch's hair," leafless trees now bent and broken all around us, and "open graves," vast and barren stretches of red Kauai clay.

Iniki had only lasted about four hours. Although it started with violence sometime late on a dark, stormy afternoon, it ended in the dreamlike peace of an uncommonly beautiful sunset.

We chose to sleep in the temple during the night following the hurricane, mainly because, on our property, the temple was the only building that was virtually undamaged. Although this was a wise move in theory, it was not practical. Because it was a hot and humid night, the temple had no windows, and there was no electricity to run fans, sleeping in that confined space was all but impossible.

I just moved outside to rest amongst the debris.

What I saw was quite a sight. A bright, full moon kept watch over a spooky scene that played tricks on perception. In the pale glow of a ghostly light, the mounded heaps of lifeless rubbish around me looked like dead bodies piled up.

One interesting thing: No mosquitoes. A blessing of sorts. Not for the mosquitoes, of course. They were gone—blown off the island. Kauai had always been famous for its mosquitoes. Now, it would be famous for their absence.

Gurudeva was wise throughout this entire drama. The monks were especially impressed by how he saved our vehicles from damage. When we asked him where we should park our cars, trucks and trailers in preparation for Iniki, he said, "follow the cows."

As Iwa was making its approach nine years before, Gurudeva had observed how our cows had moved out into a shallow valley in the middle of an open field where they could huddle together in relative safety from both falling trees and strong winds.

In the imminent danger of an approaching Iniki, Gurudeva just had us do as our cows did as they did again what they had done during Iwa. After having dutifully followed Gurudeva's instructions, and after Iniki had passed, we were pleased to discover that every single one of our vehicles had survived the hurricane without a single scratch, as had our cows.

Although Iwa had done well in teaching us a great deal about disaster survival, she could never have fully prepared us for the aftermath of Iniki. It would be no exaggeration to say it took us two years to recuperate from our second, stronger dose of hurricane fury. Actually, to this day, some of that damage has never been repaired.

Immediately after the hurricane, limited time and manpower forced us to deal only with high-priority emergencies, like hundreds of dead koi fish rotting on a stream bed that was dry because fallen trees had blocked its water; and piles of debris clogging our driveways, and gaping holes in our roofs, and wet, smelly carpets in our press shop.

Because Iniki had been classified as a national disaster, federal aid was being rushed to Kauai. During the first two weeks of the storm's aftermath, when there was no running water or electrical power, the military was there in full force. They drove mammoth trucks carrying water balloons the size of elephants to places that were accessible. To points unreachable by road, they flew water and other supplies via ground-shaking, double-propeller, Sea Knight Helicopters.

Although there were no public utilities, we did have power of our own making. Like many on the island, we had purchased a generator right after Iwa. Now we were driving that unmuzzled demon petal-to-the-metal at least 12 hours a day.

If you're not familiar with the sound-level of a high-powered generator, think of a chain saw and lawn mower running together at full throttle. The blare of all the island's generators combined with the thunderous rumble of the military's Sea Knights let Kauai roar her intense indignation in the fading wake of Iniki's dissipation like a dwarf bravely taunting a vanished dragon.

191

During my 37 years as a monastic, there were three significant natural disasters that affected our properties. Although a fine monastic protocol emphasizing modesty leaves me somewhat disinclined to tout personal distinctions, I do feel impelled to assert here that I was the only monk present at all three of these events. I can say this with full assurance because there were only two of us at our temple in California when the 1989 Bay Area earthquake occurred, and the other monk there with me was not present in Kauai for Iniki. So there. I'm distinct.

The Quake of '89, officially named the Loma Prieta earthquake, occurred on October 17, 1989, at 5:04 p.m. It lasted approximately 15 seconds, measured 7.1 on the Richter Magnitude Scale, killed 67 people and left more than 12,000 homeless. Because it took place during the warm up for the third game of the 1989 World Series and news cameras were already rolling, it was the first major earthquake in America to be broadcast on live television.

When it happened, I was in our temple teaching a class to about fifteen children from eight to twelve years of age. The building shook. Dishes fell and broke. Bookshelves collapsed. And the ground under us rolled like a blanket slowly flapping in the wind. When it was all over, one little girl turned to me and said, "Whooaaa .... Cool!"

Four Fames
It took the second half of the seventies for us to transition into a way of living that incorporated that portion of the *Shastras* we had decided to accept into a lifestyle. This was an exciting time of trial and error. Every day was a creative investigation and life was a lab for experimenting with new ideas.

Much of the *Shastric* principles we put into practice, like the OTM and *kulam* policies, were quite effective. What we didn't implement from the *Shastras* could have filled several books.

Through the eighties, our guidelines for living got quite solidly established as we settled into a one way of doing things. By then, having clocked in more than a decade of residency on Kauai, we had become established as one of the island's more respected spiritual organizations, as well as one of its more dignified tourist destinations.

We had not anticipated this popularity. From the very beginning, it had been our intention to live quietly behind the scenes. Now, we were being called upon to host and handle a variety of people from beyond our monastery walls. Many of the monks perceived this unexpected task as an imposition. Gurudeva adopted another perspective.

"Each person we meet has something important to teach us," he would often say, "because each person we meet is God in form." As is often the case with good teachers, Gurudeva was a good student.

As Gurudeva opened his arms to the public, the public sent its emissaries. And when we lavished those emissaries with all the polite cordiality we could muster, they left our presence buzzing much praise for Gurudeva, the monks and the monastery. Through all of this, the monastery gradually gained fame for what was perceived to be virtuous conduct and gracious dignity.

Having been indoctrinated with the idea that public recognition could all too easily garnish ego, we were learning now, for an institution like ours, it could work in an opposite way. It could be a conduit for service. The most valuable commodity we had to offer in service was our example. From experience, we came to understand that our collective example could be and remain favorable only if we intentionally and continually worked to mold it that way. This was something we had to learn and remember. It kept us vigilant.

For us, there were two publics. One was on the island. The other was off. Through Gurudeva's wise affiliation with these two publics in the early years of the monastery's development, he—and we along with him—earned two fames, one near and one far.

The near fame brought us a peaceful integration into the local community. The far fame brought us an opportunity to teach internationally, primarily among Hindus. Both opened positive channels for communication, productivity and healthy coexistence.

When the roots of these two fames had become well established and were growing strongly, Gurudeva began the careful building of walls. This brought a third fame primarily among institutions similar to ours where successfully establishing and maintaining an ever-so-tricky balance of private seclusion and public exposure was respected as a major achievement.

Although some of these walls were constructed of wood, wire and cement, most were made of rules. These rules were less plastered on signs than they were written into our church doctrine as procedures for dealing with guests, friends, students and church families.

Although hosting guests had become an unavoidable part of our daily life and had therefore been assigned as a routine duty to some of the monks, Gurudeva would often participate. I think he felt impelled to do this—impelled by what he saw and felt more than what he thought or was taught. From his point of view, it was not the good fortune of our guests to be served by us; it was our good fortune to serve them.

In particular, Gurudeva liked to chat with visitors and pilgrims after they had been given a tour of our monastery and grounds. At this time, he would answer any questions they might have.

One or two monks tried to always be present with some kind of recording device during these question-and-answer sessions, for they were invariably packed to the brim with Gurudeva's particular blend of practical advise, gut-level humor and spiritual wisdom.

During these sessions, Gurudeva's comments were always good, sometimes extraordinary. He had this fascinating ability to respond to even mundane questions with surprise answers that would emerge from unanticipated perspectives. Even more compelling than his uncommonly savvy insight was his uncanny knack for spontaneously wording his answers in always simple and sometimes amusing ways that couldn't be improved upon later in careful editing.

During one discussion, a lady asked, "How does a vegetarian diet affect meditation?"

"A vegetarian diet is a big help on the spiritual path," Gurudeva responded. "I've worked out a simple look at food. Basically, there are four types: fresh food, dead food, clean food and dirty food. The objective of our vegetarian diet, which we call "Nutrition for Meditation," is to eat clean, fresh food and avoid eating dead, dirty food. Now, next time you have a delicious looking meal in front of you, ask yourself, 'Is this fresh, clean food or dead, dirty food? Or, is this clean, dead food or dirty, fresh food?' Then have a wonderful dinner, if you can!"

Service was a central theme of our monastic life. Like the word *love, service*—even if only perceived in a religious or spiritual context—is a general term with many meanings. It can refer to acts of compassion born of an impulse to give. It can even refer to good deeds performed as recompense for selfishness. From a yogi's loftiest perspective, service is a doorway to enlightenment.

Through Gurudeva's eyes, all perceptions of service were true from different points of view. On one occasion I heard him say, "Even though the highest service is performed for no reason but to serve, it is quite possible to perform good service selfishly.

"There are two kinds of selfish. One selfish serves I, me and mine. This kind of selfish would never serve another. It would never want to. The other selfish serves another knowing the server and the served are one and any service done for anyone benefits all. Then of course, there is the law of karma, the principle that any good deed done comes back to the doer. In the end, great service comes from great intention. What intent could be greater than a selfless urge to serve?"

On another occasion, when talking with cloistered monks, he said, "It is a privilege to live in the monastery as a renunciate monk, exempt from many of the laws of the world. We must give back to the world for this privilege of living apart from it. This we must do through service. Everything we do is service in one form or another, but our main service as a monastery is through *Hinduism Today*."

Since 1991, *Hinduism Today* has been a glossy, full-color, international news-and-religious magazine. Before it was a magazine, it was a newspaper entitled *The New Saivite World*.

When Gurudeva first brought up the idea of publishing a newspaper in January of 1979, we were somewhat surprised—even though we had grown accustomed to the fact that Gurudeva's ideas often came from inspiration impossible to anticipate.

"Hinduism needs a shot in the arm," Gurudeva said. "It needs an international newspaper."

Gurudeva was committed first to yoga, then to Hinduism. His love for Hinduism flowered out of his respect for the historical fact that yoga developed in the Vedic culture that preceded the practice of Hinduism as it is known today. Thus, embedded in his dedication to yoga was his loyalty to Hinduism.

The service Gurudeva was striving to render in publishing first a Hindu newspaper, then a Hindu magazine, was not just intended for Hindus. It was meant for everyone. Because of this broad intention, it was *Hinduism Today* that provided Gurudeva with his most efficient service to the world, as well as his fourth and most powerful fame.

For non-Hindus, Gurudeva wanted to help dispel illusions, myths and misinformation about Hinduism. For Hindus, he wanted to assist in fostering "Hindu solidarity" through "unity in diversity." This latter aim he hoped to accomplish by highlighting the common ground all Hindus shared so that Hinduism as a whole might be respected as a unified force in the world.

Although *Hinduism Today* was primarily a news vehicle, each of its issues featured a center section, approximately one third of the magazine's total text, clarifying some aspect of the Hindu philosophy and lifestyle.

When we were laying out the basic design format of the magazine, our first goal was to establish a comfortable balance of news and religious education. What we didn't realize then was how needed that religious education was, even for Hindus.

To say it was rewarding to watch *Hinduism Today* blossom into something far beyond our original expectation would be an understatement. Perhaps Gurudeva was the only person not amazed when this simple magazine became almost like scripture for many, whether they were Hindu or not.

Guests Are God

Even today, the monastery property wouldn't appear to have changed much compared with the way it looked when it was the Tropical Inn Resort, or even long before that. Although we disentangled and refashioned its thickly overgrown 58 acres into an all-new tropical labyrinth of elegant gardens, paths, ponds and waterways, we couldn't decorate away the basic fact it was and always has been a green-covered chunk of red clay on a river, saturated by rain on the shadow-side of a mountain crest that had come to be known as "the wettest place on earth."

With all the construction projects we were forever pursuing, we somehow managed to avoid renovating eighty percent of the main building on the property. The twenty percent we altered was at that building's main entrance. This is where we added Kadavul temple.

By the time we finished building Kadavul, we had successfully Indianized our look, even though we had structured the outer façade of the temple with local lava rock to maintain a Hawaiian appearance.

Standing inside the temple as it looks today, a visitor might think he was in Tamil Nadu, India. At center stage in the main sanctum, Lord Siva stands majestically, four-armed, one foot raised—an exquisitely rendered, two-hundred-and-fifty-year-old, six-foot-tall bronze sculpture of Nataraja, "the king of dancers." Flanking him left and right in shrines of their own are black granite statues, each also six feet tall, of Lord Ganesha, the elephant-headed God of good luck and fortune, and Lord Muruga, the beautiful God of yoga.

Just inside the temple's front entrance, an intricately detailed bronze of the "half-man/half-woman" God/Goddess, Ardhanarishvara, strikes a graceful pose to remind us that we, as pure souls, are a perfect balance of masculine and feminine force. Across the way on the other side of the entrance, an eight-foot-tall silver trident stands menacingly, symbolizing Lord Siva's three powers of desire, action and wisdom.

Lining the main walls of the temple, a rare collection of 108 sixteen-inch-tall bronze icons covered with gold leaf represent Lord Siva's *tandava* dance poses. Just outside the entryway is a pavilion for Nandi the bull, Siva's mount and greatest devotee, a giant granite sculpture weighing 32,000 pounds, carved in India from a single stone.

As Hawaiian as the property holding our temple was said to be and as Indian as we tried to make it, this sacred land had its own identity. It was the identity of an entity, ancient and wise—older than man. Yet there was this impermanence about it, a vague instability teetering on the possibility that years of history could be undone during ten seconds of a major earthquake. Yet there we were living on that island—one of eight little land dots in the Pacific, assuming that one day would go on into the next forever.

God kept coming as guests to our little temple and monastery. Most of these people were at least respectful, but a few were not. Yet, Gurudeva assured us that even those few who came without respect were no less Godly, no less worthy of our listening ear should they have something they wanted to tell us.

Some pure-blooded Polynesian Hawaiians told us the land we were living on was not really ours. They said it didn't and couldn't be owned by anyone because it was an ancient *heiau* (temple), the fifth of seven built up the Wailua River from its end in the sea to its source at the top of Mount Waialeale. And they told us the story of a great battle that

197

was fought at the site of our Kadavul Temple next to the river that "ran red with blood." And with great and noble pride, they proclaimed Kauai was the only Hawaiian island not lost in war. They said we should be proud of this, as they were, and we should let them roam our land freely as was their want.

Some delegates of the New Age told us we were graced to be living on a spiritual vortex. They said the energy funneling through this vortex would bring about a great change on Earth, a change quite soon to come. They assured us that we, because we were living on this vortex, would serve as a channel for this change; and because we were to be this channel, we should prepare; and, if we looked within our hearts, we would know we should let them assist us in this preparation.

Some teachers from India, Hindu and not, told us Kauai was an ancient mountaintop as sacred to the yogis of India as Mount Kailas. With proper guidance, they assured us, we could cultivate this special place to become again what it once was long ago, a great center for spiritual learning. With this end in mind, they proclaimed, they would be most happy to share with us their considerable knowledge—if we would get them green cards, provide them with servants, pay them a worthy stipend and give them free room and board.

The monks began to become jaded. But Gurudeva kept saying, "Guests are God."

A lot of eccentrics came—like UFO enthusiasts, with stories of outer space. On one occasion, I was cornered in the temple for about hour by a lady who was telling me we were being infiltrated by people from a group of six planets called "the Pleiades." These people, she said, were living among us to study us for the purpose of helping us. I could be one of them and not know it, she was telling me, or maybe I did know it and I was studying her. And if that were the case, she wondered, did I have any advice for her?

When I shared this conversation with Gurudeva, feeling a little silly as I did, he surprised me by responding that she might have been right. "Are you sure you aren't from the Pleiades?" he asked me. Then, of course, I surprised myself by answering, "I dunno. Maybe I am."

A week after that, I got really sick. For three days I lay in a fever, in and out of cold sweats. On the fourth night, I was awake at about midnight, aching all over and feeling miserable, yet unable to sleep.

Suddenly, I found myself sitting on the ground by a river, tightly hugging my knees to my chest and shivering. As I gazed across this river at the sparkling night-lights of a quaint little town of some sort, I saw a nearly imperceptible flash of light darting from right to left over the water right in front of me. Yet, just as soon as that light flashed by, it was back, like it was doing some kind of a roadrunner-cartoon screech-halt-and-reverse maneuver just to have a look at me — or perhaps for me to have a look at it.

Rather than speculating that this thing I saw was a space ship, I'll just try to describe it.

What it looked like was a soup bowl with windows turned up-side-down on another soup bowl with more windows. But the look of this thing wasn't as significant as its presence. It had an unearthly feeling of being perfectly still. This is to say it was very much like a photograph superimposed on a motion picture.

It couldn't have been a dream because I had not been able to get to sleep. If it was an astral projection, where was I going? All I knew for sure was ... I was there. That thing was there. And suddenly, I was inside it, sitting on a bed-table in a starkly simple but spotlessly clean room, wearing a tied-in-the-back patient gown.

As I was looking around wondering where I was, the door opened and a charming, silver-haired lady, perhaps 65 years of age, walked in wearing a white smock and carrying a clipboard.

She smiled ever so sweetly and said, "Well, it looks like you're feeling better now."

I briefly checked myself out to feel how I was feeling and indeed discovered I *was* feeling better — just fine, as a matter of fact, really fine. The next thing I knew, I was back in my bed in my hut, filled and thrilled with bliss. My sickness was gone like it had never existed.

The monks were quite surprised to witness my sudden and some-what miraculous recovery, of course. I was too. I had been really sick. I didn't tell anybody about my nighttime excursion — except, of course, for Gurudeva a little later that day. My timing wasn't so great though. He was on his way somewhere and couldn't really talk. But he certainly wasn't surprised by what I had to say.

When I had a chance, I made the following entry in my journal.

Mountains gilded red aloft,
And spattered by the rain
Rise like towers painted soft
All made of window pane.

Billows white and made of glass
Chance a question: "Why?"
Before that thought has time to pass
Into a deeper sky.

Who's a friend? Who's a foe?
Which way's right or wrong?
Which end's up, down, fast or slow?
What's worth rhyme in song?

We'll catch and match and thatch some things
That wander lost and found,
Then patch together golden rings
On fingers of a sound.

A fractal flavor understands
The flight of arrows shot
That grow a garden on dry sands
To make a magic spot.

Scrutinized

The one hundred years of British occupation and rule in India, from the mid-1800's until India's achievement of independence on August 15, 1947, dealt a far more devastating blow to the integrity of Hinduism than the preceding 300 years of Mughal oppression. A Britisher named Thomas Babington Macaulay was responsible for a lion's share of this.

In 1834, Macaulay was assigned the task of educating India in the ways of the West. Working on the premise that most Asian Indian Hindus were irredeemable heathens, he established a English speaking educational system that focused only on India's rich, upper-class youth. His intention was to inculcate in these young people the elitist beliefs and attitudes of a modern, Christian West, well fortified with a healthy disdain for what he considered to be a primitive, Hindu East, then train this relatively small group of highly influential youngsters to spread this thinking throughout the rest of India.

We must assume he considered his venture to be successful, even though even he ended up admitting that all he really accomplished by surreptitiously attacking the core of India's Hindu culture, philosophy and integrity was to create a generation of disoriented Indian Hindus who spoke English with a heavy British accent and were ashamed of their cultural heritage.

In truth, Macaulay never really hoped to completely westernize India. He was convinced that was impossible. All he wanted to do was humiliate her with enough of Britain's version of western aristocracy that she would be susceptible to a dominating British influence in trade and business. As he himself put this in a religious context: "We may not be able to make them good Christians, but we can most certainly make them bad Hindus."

At least partially because of Macaulayism, many Indian Hindus, as well as Hindus who left India to live elsewhere, entered the twentieth century embarrassed to be Hindu.

As time passed, Macaulay's seed of contamination flourished in the minds of the children of the Indian Hindus who were the very first recipients of Macaulay's influence. Because these kids could see in their parent's faces no deeply ingrained reverence for Hinduism *or* acquired respect for Christianity, they learned to live without religion at all. This was devastating to a people whose spiritual faith was also a lifestyle.

Several generations of accumulating shame created a great many Indians who were Hindu in name only. If these Hindus practiced their faith at all, it was by habit devoid of faith and knowledge.

When Gurudeva started publishing *Hinduism Today*, he was only trying to provide a service. His only intention was to give the world a well designed magazine that featured some Hindu news, flavored with some Hindu religiousness.

Naturally, we were pleased when our Indian Hindu readership responded favorably to *Hinduism Today*. "This is what we need," our readers kept saying. "Keep it coming." And so we did.

Not only were the readers of *Hinduism Today* happy to receive the little bit of religious information we were providing in the magazine during the first years of its formation, they were honored by the very fact that Gurudeva, a "westerner," had chosen to produce an international magazine built on no intent but to extol Hinduism. And they were deeply impressed by Gurudeva himself. His history. His yoga. His life. He appealed to all Hindus, young and old alike.

Many Hindus who left their motherland of India through the sixties, seventies and eighties, hell-bent on moving west to the United States to live the "good life" and make a lot of money, did just that. Yet as these migrated Hindus observed the consequences of their move in the lives of their children who had no choice but to grow up without a healthy exposure to Hinduism in a land far away and far different from India, they realized their "good life" wasn't that great. When they finally came around to wanting back the ways of their forefathers, they found those ways had become illusively distant.

Where could these American Hindu parents go to find answers to the questions their kids were asking? And how were they to deal with the suffering their kid's endured when they were asked sarcastic questions by their peers at school like, "What does a Hin-doooooooo?"?

These young, first-generation, American Hindu children were just too smart to simply parrot what they had been taught: wild stories about gods and demons fighting battles in the sky. So they said nothing until they got home where they lamented to their parents how stupid they felt not being able to say something sensible about Hinduism.

Gurudeva was a unique presence amidst all this. Here was this strikingly handsome white man who looked like a Himalayan sage and exuded a sense of mystic strength and self-confidence that he seemed to be deriving from the very faith born Hindus in America were embarrassed to claim as their own.

"Why?" these Americanized Hindus were asking themselves. "What does Gurudeva see in Hinduism?"

They found their answers to these questions and more in the magazine, *Hinduism Today*. And when they asked more questions and again got more than they asked for, yet still asked for more, they pushed us to research even further in response to their asking. All of this was healthy and good for all involved.

Hinduism Today's greatest distinction emerged from the most auspicious timing of its initial publication. As I compose these words now, *Hinduism Today* is *still* Hinduism's *only* international magazine. All credit for this timing, and the very idea to create such a publication in the first place, goes to Gurudeva.

The historical basis for *Hinduism Today's* spiritual content was derived primarily from good old-fashioned research, performed by the monks, reviewed by Gurudeva and validated by the growing number of Indian scholars we were becoming affiliated with through the years. Although much of this research was being done for Gurudeva's books, it was just as useful for the magazine.

The final version of Gurudeva's books, referred to as the *Trilogy* and consisting of *Dancing with Siva, Living with Siva* and *Merging with Siva*, evolved out of Gurudeva's teaching program called *The Master Course*. Although the essential message of *The Master Course* has never been altered from its inception in 1957, it has enjoyed much benefit through the years from all of the research we were always doing, as well as from the experience we were accruing as we put what we were learning into practice.

Dancing with Siva lays out the elaborate history and philosophy of Hinduism. *Living with Siva* suggests a lifestyle designed to put this philosophy into practice. And *Merging with Siva* presents a system of yoga that originated from within this philosophy and lifestyle.

When born Hindus were first immigrating to the United States, most of them were gleaning their religious identity not from their perception and practice but from their bloodline and homeland. In their minds, they were Hindu because they were born into a Hindu family in India. Second generation Indians in America lost at least half of that identity. They were born Hindu, but not in India. When a first generation Indian Hindu came to America and married outside his or her religion, the child of that marriage had almost no Hindu identity.

This forced Hindus to think differently about who they were and, in that changed thinking, more readily accept Gurudeva into their fold, especially since his message about identity was what it was: *the one true identity of all is the one Self of all.*

When asked for advice, Gurudeva encouraged America's first generation of immigrated Indian Hindus to develop Hindu societies and build temples. As these societies and temples emerged, Gurudeva was often invited to participate in their various festivals and functions.

Through all of this, Gurudeva's service to the Hindu community became more crystallized. As Gurudeva's agents, we monks prepared to be scrutinized in the light of an old Indian adage: "If you want to understand the value of a teacher, look to the quality of his students."

Now, Hindus were coming to Kauai not just to see Gurudeva but to have a look at us as well. As we learned to encounter this scrutiny and grow in the new knowledge it sometimes drew forth from within us, we came to understand that living through this examination was itself part of the training being around Gurudeva enticed.

As we tried to be good examples of good monks, we attracted the attention and respect of America's second generation of born Hindus. This was an unexpected but inspiring accomplishment, for these kids were and are bright lights — brilliant, willing and wanting to accomplish something significant in the revitalization of their ancient faith.

This was all occurring through the first part of the nineties. In addition to producing quarterly issues of *Hinduism Today,* we were also working on Gurudeva's books.

During this time, questions we received indicated that a growing group of Indian Hindus in America as well as a curious American public sought to understand that which made Hinduism look so wonderfully ambiguous. Questions like: Why does Hinduism have so many gods? (Hindus believe in a one God who created the many gods like He created all souls.) Why do Hindus worship the cow? (The cow unselfishly gives life-sustaining milk and is perceived as a symbol of service) Are Hindus idol worshipers? (No. They worship God *through* a symbolic image of Him.) Are Hindus forbidden to eat meat? (Hinduism does advocate vegetarianism, but all Hindus are not vegetarian.) Do Hindus have a Bible? (Yes. The *Vedas*.) Why do many Hindus wear a dot on their forehead? (The "pottu," as this forehead dot is called, indicates a Hindu identity and symbolizes divine insight. It is also a beauty mark for women.) Are the gods and goddesses of Hinduism married? (No. Only in stories.) What is the Hindu caste system and why is there "untouchability" in India? (The caste system was originally conceived by a Hindu named Manu as a natural division of society according to occupation. Although today discrimination against "outcasts," or "untouchables," is illegal in India, it exists there as it does everywhere in the world.)

When Gurudeva was challenged, as he quite frequently was, to respond to the claim that Hinduism is a superstitious religion, he would simply say, "all religions are superstitious to at least some extent, as are all matters of faith?" Although this was Gurudeva's intuitive response in the moment, it made a great deal of sense when checked later against his monk's research.

The *New Oxford American Dictionary* defines *religion* as "the belief in and worship of a superhuman controlling power, especially a personal God or gods," and *superstition* as "an excessively credulous belief in and reverence for supernatural beings." Neither of these beliefs can be scientifically proven. Thus, both require faith.

The main difference between these two beliefs is indicated in the definition of *superstition,* which includes the phrase, "excessively credulous." Yet, if the followers of *religion* are "excessively credulous," which frequently they are, what separates them from the followers of *superstition*?

Even if we can justify answering this last question with, "not much," we would have to concede that *religion* and *superstition* differ more in their implied meanings than in their literal definitions.

The word *superstition* bears a negative connotation that implies a superstitious person is a heathen. (A heathen is by definition "a person who is not a follower of a widely accepted religion." Hinduism is widely accepted. Like Catholicism, it has a billion followers worldwide.)

This negative connotation also implies that a superstitious person is a demon worshipper. This last implication is derived from a logic that states, "If a heathen does not worship the God or gods of an established religion, he must be worshipping the devil or demons of a superstition."

In Hinduism there is a practice called *Kavadi*, a Hindu *sadhana* sometimes considered superstitious by non-Hindus.

In understanding *kavadi*, it is helpful to understand how Hindus perceive *penance*. From a karmic point of view, which would be the view of the Hindu, repenting for wrong doing through the voluntary self-punishment of penance is not a practice meant to propitiate a wrathful or vengeful God. It's simply an early payment of debt, a purposeful bringing on of a natural consequence for the sake of accelerating karmic closure. Certainly, God, gods and *devas* smile upon such recompense and respond with blessings.

205

Kavadi

Kavadi is a walking pilgrimage, performed while bearing a "burden" on the head or shoulders. The destination of this pilgrimage is usually a temple, and the "burden" carried can be any object symbolizing the weight of negative karma. The intent of the practice of *kavadi* is to bring the karma of past misdeeds to the feet of God, there to be dissolved by God's grace into experiential wisdom gained, or as Gurudeva would put it, "lessons learned." At its simplest, this practice might entail walking a short distance carrying a pot of milk. More elaborate versions of *kavadi* could include walking further, carrying greater weight and piercing the skin, tongue and cheeks with skewers.

The skewers of *kavadi* are commonly referred to as *vels*, miniature versions of the sacred spear that Lord Muruga carries. Muruga's *vel* is a weapon to be sure, but it is a weapon symbolizing wisdom wielded in a battle against ignorance. In a song composed to describe and extol Lord Muruga to children, Muruga's *vel* is referred to as a "lance-like spear that's wide, long, keen like pointed wisdom, broad and deep." The shape of the *vel's* point is distinctive. It looks like a teardrop.

The *vels* used as skewers in the practice of *kavadi* can be from two inches to ten feet long with shafts as thin as a sewing needle or as thick as a gun barrel. The base of the shaft is what gets pierced through the skin, not the teardrop tip. This shaft base is filed to a point, the sharper the better. A sharp point produces less pain going in.

Usually, the tongue and cheeks are pierced first. After this, any number of skewers may be inserted all over the body. When the cheeks are pierced, the *vel* is penetrated in and through the right cheek, over the tongue and out through the left cheek. To pierce a *vel* into the tongue, the tongue must be pulled forward out of the mouth as far as possible (by the *kavadi* priest) so the *vel* can be inserted downward through it outside the mouth.

The word *kavadi* refers to the practice of this austerity as well as the object carried during the practice. The most common *kavadi* object is a semicircular canopy, decorated with flowers and supported by a wooden rod carried across the shoulders, behind the neck.

Devotees commonly prepare for *kavadi* during ten days of prayer and fasting. All through the night before the day of the event, they forego sleep to build their *kavadi*. On the morning of the event, they gather at a spot designated as the origin of the *kavadi* pilgrimage. There, the *kavadi* priest, a person who has been specifically trained to pierce, will "install the *vels*." The carrying of *kavadi* generally occurs as part of a festival dedicated to the performance of *kavadi*.

During the culmination of the Muruga festival of Thaipusam in Nandi, Fiji, I watched at least a hundred devotees line up for the grand piercing of the *vels*. The priest performing this function, inserted from three to twenty *vels* per person. For every *vel* he pierced into a devotee, he pierced one into himself as well.

Like many Hindu observances, the practice of *kavadi* is based on a mythological story:

On Mount Kailas in the Himalayas, Lord Siva gave a rotund sage named Agastya two small hills to haul to and install somewhere in Tamil Nadu (South India) to be revered as places of worship. Busy with his prayers and yoga practices and knowing full well the task would be a strenuous one, Agastya passed the job along to his disciple, Idumban, who embarked upon the journey with dutiful glee. As might be expected, Idumban became tired during the trip and needed to rest. So, near the town of Palani in Tamil Nadu, he set the two hills down to take a nap. When he woke up and attempted to continue his journey, he found his hills had taken root and could not be moved. Somewhat perplexed but highly motivated to proceed with his assigned task, he asked a nearby youth to help him lift the hills.

As it turned out, this youth was more of a hindrance than a help. He claimed the hills belonged to him. In the tussle that ensued, Idumban came to realize the fellow he was fighting was actually Lord Muruga, and the place he had reached was the destined location of the hills.

In commemoration of this whole ordeal, Lord Muruga decreed that anyone who approached these two hills with devotion and with any object similar to two hillocks suspended by a rod would be forgiven his or her past misdeeds. Today, the famous Palani Hills Muruga Temple stands atop one of those hills. And *kavadi* is a common practice there.

I carried *kavadi* twice—both times in the comfortable privacy of our monastery on Kauai.

When I carried *kavadi*, I was a swami. Gurudeva felt swamis should perform *kavadi* only in private since at least some of the public, Hindu or not, might assume such penance should not be necessary for a

207

swami. Then, of course, there was also the perception that *kavadi* was a superstitious practice. This was a stigma that was *Kavadi's* burden to bear—as well as our's.

Since my two experiences of carrying kavadi were for the most part identical, I will share only the first one here, since it was unique in being first, there being only one first experience of anything. This, my first carrying of *kavadi*, occurred during Thaipusam in 1987.

Thaipusam is a ten-day Hindu festival celebrated mainly by the Saivite Hindu Tamils of South India. It occurs in January/February and commemorates that birthday during which Lord Muruga received his signature *vel* as a present from his father, Lord Siva.

For ten days, I fasted on fruit juice, wrote and burned confessions and did more than a thousand prostrations to Lord Muruga. On the fourth day, I performed what we called the "walking prostration."

During a *walking prostration,* a pilgrim moves along a path by prostrating, full body to the ground, then rising and striding forward one body length to prostrate again. My quarter-mile version of this discipline took about three hours to complete. Since I was counting each prostration on a string of 108 beads as I proceeded and had just concluded my third cycle through the beads when I finished, I figure I had performed at least 324 prostrations.

By the time I was done, my clothes were so muddy they were beyond cleaning; my legs were rubbery like I had run five miles; my hands and knees were raw and slightly bleeding from small cuts and my chest was aggravated red through the thin shirt I was wearing. It wasn't for gallantry or devotion that I had not worn the vest, gloves and knee-pads I had been advised to use. I had just forgotten. Had I remembered to don these protections, this small story within a story might not have been worth telling.

On the night of the ninth day, I drank coffee to stay up, thinking to myself, "Tonight, coffee is a fruit juice." At about nine o'clock, we started building our *kavadi*. "We" was me plus one other swami and four younger monks. The three of us for whom this was a first experience followed the lead of the three who had performed *kavadi* before.

Although building a *kavadi* is a bit of a process, we had plenty of time. The piercing was to take place at four o'clock the next morning.

I had dreaded staying up all night after ten days of fasting on juice. As it turned out, that night was quite enjoyable. The enjoyment was of the sort that comes from keeping busy being creative, when the alternative — trying to stay awake doing nothing — would most certainly have been a miserable experience.

During our night of creativity, I was successful in not thinking forward to the piercing of the skewers the next morning. That was the point, pardon the pun, of staying occupied building our *kavadi*: to not think forward to the piercing of the skewers.

At the appointed time, the six of us gathered at the river where the *kavadi* priest directed us to sit by the water's edge. As the priest lavishly showered us with buckets of river water, icier than usual, even for January, we shivered wet and cold amidst the mad racket of drums beating, bells ringing, and monks screaming, "Vel Vel Muruga," over and over again. Somewhere in all of that, we got pierced with the *vels*. Of that piercing, I have no memory.

I felt warm, peaceful and oblivious to my surroundings as I walked barefoot with the other *kavadi* carriers in a ragtag parade up the jungle path from the river to the monastery. My *kavadi*, which felt heavy and awkward coming down to the river, now sat free, easy and light on my shoulders. The ground, which was painfully rocky under my bare feet before the event, now felt soft — almost cushioned. The night, which had been inconveniently dark through all of our preparations, now seemed somehow lit enough for me to see where I was going, even though I had no flashlight and the sun would not rise for another hour. Our walk up the hill and three times around the monastery had to have taken at least a half hour. Yet it seemed to last less than a few minutes.

I couldn't even feel the *vels* — except for the one in my tongue. Because that particular *vel* held my tongue forward and out of my mouth, I was not able to swallow, which forced me to slobber a bit. This made me look like I was in some sort of oblivious trance, which I wasn't — I don't think.

When Gurudeva first saw me during the *kavadi* procession, he turned away. This bothered me a little. I think he thought I was in pain. I wasn't, except at the end, when the *vels* came out. That was painful!

When the priest pulled out my *vels*, those who were watching wrenched. As I was told later, my facial skin stretched out about four inches from my jaw as the priest pulled out the two-foot-long *vel* that had been inserted through my cheeks.

The removal of the *vel* from my tongue was not too uncomfortable, even though it was at least a foot long and had a shaft about the thickness of an ice pick. For some reason, the three *vels* inserted through skin that had been pinched and pulled out from my throat really hurt as they came out. I don't know why. Compared to the other two, those three *vels* were small—something like five-inch sewing needles.

Because the whole event took place before dawn, the only time anybody saw the *kavadi* I spent all night building was a few days later in photographs taken with a flash exposure. Actually, that was good. My *kavadi* was not pretty. It was a flowered thing made of chicken-wire mesh pressed into the shape of an arch and tied onto a five-foot pole that was designed to sit on my shoulders with buckets of milk hanging off its ends. The whole thing weighed about 40 pounds at the beginning of the parade—maybe ten pounds less at the parade's end when I was wearing most of the milk that was supposed to be in the buckets.

The main Thaipusam *puja* began as our procession from the river ended. As soon as our *vels* had been extracted, the temple priest began a ceremony that would go on for two hours. During the ceremony, the six of us set in front of Lord Muruga like guests of honor.

All I can remember of that long, elaborate ritual was a feeling of tranquility. All I can remember about the rest of that day was a calm sense of being fearlessly detached with a cool sense of purpose, like I had something important to do but was in no hurry to do it.

The next year, I carried *kavadi* again. After that, we did it no more. *Kavadi* was a guest who lived with us for only two years. I don't know that he ever fell out of favor. He was just there. Then he wasn't.

Our experience of *kavadi* exemplifies something important about what one of the monks referred to as "Gurudeva's experiments in living." These experiments were like chapters of a book—daringly unpredictable in the moment of their occurrence yet cohesively purposeful as they helped mold our future in the *now*.

In this approach to our monastic life, we were forever bringing on one challenge after another, stimulating adventures that seemed like they could go in any direction as they happened yet settled into history like they were obeying a script written long ago.

The Life Ends

A Call

Come to the fore of life to chance
A dance long meant to be,
A dance sprung wide in vast expanse,
Unfolding mystery.
Then spread out silk-white robes of soul
For future plans to make
A sturdy life of dreams lived whole
That sadness cannot shake.

All full of joy, a poet spawned
A song he sang with flare
For gladness bursting fully dawned
Where some might fear to dare.
He told of greater life to come
From spaces in between
That made a total in their sum
Of good times not yet seen.

Anchored past a time of trial
And gearing up for more
That poet climbed a mountain while
Great angels rose to soar.
Above the highest waves of breeze
That crash upon lost shores
Those angels built a house with ease
All filled with secret doors.

But still that poet sought a star
Far out of reach or touch.
He tried so hard to see that far,
Yet meanwhile saw so much.
Who was that soul so set on sight
He could not see that place
That angels built for him in light,
All filled with God's sweet grace?

213

To hesitate a chance embrace
For love sung in a song
Might sadden grace met face to face
For fear of living wrong.
This is to say that moments lost
May soon not come again
While such times caught might pay the cost
Of what some might call sin.

Dance beneath a crest of fire
As thunder rolls the sky
Sparkle lights of pure desire
With little wonder why.
Then lastly look, yet not too late,
To see what has been done
Compared with all that planned-out fate
Of future's best to come.

The gods support a rendezvous
With willingness to change.
To this they'll yield a kindly view
That falls in reason's range.
Looking in a laser glass
Calls forth a knowledge gained.
Looking up the crownward pass
Unfolds the Self sustained.

Come to the fore of life to chance
A dance long meant to be,
A dance sprung wide in vast expanse,
Unfolding mystery.
Then spread out silk-white robes of soul
For future plans to make
A sturdy life of dreams lived whole
That sadness cannot shake.

The Beginning of the End

My lone pilgrimage to India in 1994 came as a surprise, a gift and a blessing. Just after I learned I was going, I went to Gurudeva to thank him for providing me with such a once-in-a-lifetime opportunity and making arrangements for my duties to be covered while I was gone.

He smiled and told me several things:

He said the journey would be life changing, yet challenging.

He said now was a good time for me to be making a pilgrimage like this because I was 45 years of age—old enough to appreciate such a journey yet young enough to endure its hardship.

He said I would soon be experiencing what he referred to as "male menopause," a sensitive time, mainly psychological, when a man realizes he has just passed what is touted as the "prime of life," faces what has occurred thus far—almost always with some degree of regret— and gets himself set for his last years on earth.

He said, even though it was a monk's discipline to not recollect a past, I would. I would, he said, unavoidably bear witness to memories of a life seemingly long gone and apparently forgotten. He said this had happened to him when he was my age, and now it would happen to me. When it did happen, he said, India would be a good place to be.

He was right. All of this did come to pass—all through the next year, as I traveled through India.

With regard to esoteric issues like providence and fate, I believe my "dance long meant to be" is a destiny not forced upon me, but one I've built myself. This is to say I believe my life today was yesterday's foreseeable future, because of decisions I made during my long-ago.

Yet in this "me" I've gradually come to be on my way to a final destiny, I've also had unseen help. A lot of good help, to be sure. And for this grand assistance, which I will refer to here as divine grace, I am forever thankful. Although I take responsibility for what I've done and do, I feel through and through each decision I have made or make, even should it be unwise, is supported by divine aid in a way that immediately or eventually bends its consequence toward positive growth.

I also acknowledge I couldn't easily live life this way, thinking these kinds of thoughts, had I not enjoyed a happy birth to good parents in a place like America during relatively peaceful times. Thus, I thank God I'm free in a land of liberty, even though such freedom itself, like all things, is of karmic origin and consequence.

All of these reflections were drifting through my head as I prepared myself for my pilgrimage through India. During this time of
preparation, I fashioned my thoughts as questions without immediate
answers, using these questions to hold my mind open so as to make
the future as pliable as possible. And in this openness, I let the bud of a
flower begin to blossom.

When a twinge of fear began to surface, such as in a worried
anticipation of traveling alone in a distant land, I found great strength
in Gurudeva's assurance that we can't be confronted with situations we
do not have the capacity to handle. From the fortitude this assurance
awakened within me, I gained the courage to be bold.

Also helpful was Gurudeva's previous "surprise training"—all
that forced "quick thinking" demanded in those situations he created
for our learning benefit. In such predicaments, we discovered "quick
thought" was more like thought deferring to intuition out of need.

"Who can think quickly?" Gurudeva used to ask us. "It can't be
done. Thought is slow by nature, compared with intuition."

When Gurudeva put us on the spot, we surprised ourselves by
knowing what to do as we did it. Later, in looking back on doing what
we did, we realized we had been allowed to find not only "intuitive
wisdom in the moment," as Gurudeva liked to call it, but also an almost
magical transcendence of fear.

Gurudeva's central instruction for my year of travel in India was,
"Don't make any plans. Let intuition guide you from within."

By the time I was told of my trip, my plane ticket had been
purchased and arrangements had been made for me to obtain, during
my travels, any amount of money I needed, as I needed it, through our
temple work site in Bangalore.

The Bangalore work site was on land gifted to us by a famous and
influential South Indian swami who had known and respected Gurudeva
for years. This site was managed by a person Gurudeva had hired to take
on the long-term project of overseeing the hand-carving of our Iraivan
Temple in India and getting it shipped to America. I knew both of these
men well. They were, one might say, something like duly professional
but exceptionally friendly associates. Fortunately for me, Gurudeva had
asked these men to assist me in my travels.

Before I knew it, I was in the air. Because I had packed only what I could carry on foot, I survived the long and arduous sequence of somewhat complicated flight connections without checking luggage.

When I arrived in New Delhi, I was met by two fellow monks from Kauai who were just finishing their own one-month pilgrimage through India. Together, we stayed in the ashram of a local swami.

Our stay with this swami, another one of Gurudeva's close friends, began on the first day of popular Hindu festival called Navaratri. This nine-day, religious event, dedicated to the worship of the Divine Mother, culminated with a celebration of yet another Hindu festival called Vijaya Dasami. Because it would have been impolite as well as culturally improper to leave the ashram before these two auspiciously important events had concluded, we took our three-day train ride south to Bangalore nearly two weeks after I had arrived in India.

After our long journey to the south, we spent three easy days in Bangalore. During this time, we got to know the family of the fine man Gurudeva had hired to manage the building of our temple. We also got to marvel at the progress being made on the stone carving.

Then the three of us traveled east across India to the coastal town of Chennai, again by train. There, we parted ways as the two of them boarded a plane for Kauai and I headed for Palani Hills. Finally, I was alone in India. As soon as I could, I wrote in my journal:

Powdered power under feet
Peppered on the range
Grows a fruit that's strangely sweet
Yet rings a chime for change.

The cage of age that wonders last
On fading willow mist
Sees a ship at sea, half mast,
All wilted, wet and kissed.

Prance a dance. Enhance a chance.
So say a lonely few
Who look ahead, see in advance
A bigger, better view.

A Temple on a Hill

When a South Indian Tamil tells you he's going on pilgrimage to Palani Hills, he's being vague at best. This is to say, you would probably have to have done what he is about to do to know what he's telling you. Palani Hills is a big place, a rather extensive mountain range covering about 800 square miles of South India.

In its non-literal and usual sense, a "pilgrimage to Palani Hills" refers to a spiritual journey to a small but famous temple on a hill, just outside the town of Palani in Tamil Nadu. There, Lord Muruga is worshipped as Dandayudhapani, the lord of yoga and austerity.

The Palani Muruga Temple, which is the destination of this most famous pilgrimage, is far more popular than the other temple in the town of Palani called the Tiru Avinankudi Temple. Nobody knows exactly when these temples were built. They're too old. All anybody knows for sure is the "hill temple" is the younger of the two.

A note of clarification: When Saivite Hindus of South India worship Lord Muruga—also known by at least 1,008 other names like Veylan, Subrahmanya, Shanmugan, Swaminatha, Arumuga, Saravana, Palani and Dandayudhapani—they are communing with one of many gods, even though they also worship a one supreme God Siva who, quite confusingly, also has many names. They see no inconsistency or contradiction in this perception because they regard the many gods and goddesses, each with their many names, as children of the a one Lord.

Hindus believe gods and goddesses are as real as people. To put this a little more accurately, they believe gods and goddesses *are* people without bodies—bodiless people who are distinctive because of their advanced spiritual development and superhuman love. They also believe these resplendent entities are in a uniquely beneficial position to be of service, not only because they are spiritually advanced, but also because they live in ethereal realms less veiled to wisdom than the physical world. Therefore, it could be said Hindus worship gods and goddesses with the conviction they would have in communicating with people they can see, hear and touch, but with a devotion they could only express to a transcendent divinity.

A Hindu who worships a god or a goddess chooses that deity in the same way and for the same reasons he or she would choose another person to be a friend, a business partner or a lover. Perhaps there is a

218

special feeling of affinity. Perhaps there is a special respect.

We monks were taught to worship Lord Siva as the one supreme God and, of the many gods and goddesses, Ganesha and Muruga as Siva's primary spiritual assistants.

When we needed help in handling the practical matters of life, like solving personal disputes or finding parking spots, we approached Lord Ganesha for his expertise in dealing with worldly matters. When we needed help in the practice of yoga, such as assistance in developing *faith* to keep up the mystical pursuit of meditation, or *will* to maintain a one-pointed focus, we prayed to Lord Muruga for his skill in effecting personal transformation and purification. When we weren't sure whose jurisdiction the solution of a problem or the satisfaction of a desire might fall into, we worshipped Siva just to cover all the bases.

Before I left for India—besides telling me, "Don't make any plans. Let intuition guide you from within."—Gurudeva said, "Mix and mingle with the swamis and *sadhus* (wandering Hindu holy men) while you are there. They will take care of you because Lord Muruga takes care of them."

When I got back from India, I was surprised that Gurudeva was surprised I had done just what he said. I had stayed in ashrams with swamis everywhere I went.

I guess I had somehow misconstrued what he meant by "mix and mingle." I had assumed, even though I had been assured again and again that the high value of the American dollar in India made it feasible for me to stay in high-quality hotels at a low cost everywhere I went, Gurudeva would have been more pleased if I had managed to live with *sadhus* in ashrams.

"How did you get into all those ashrams?" Gurudeva casually asked me after I had returned from India.

"I just asked," I replied. "I thought you were hinting this was what I should be doing."

"Well, yes. But I didn't think you would actually be able to do it. Congratulations."

"It was all Muruga," I replied, trying to be humble, yet perhaps inadvertently blurting out what could have been truer than I realized.

When I was in Palani town, I stayed at a place called Swami Ashram. This retreat center for *sadhus*, which became my home for over

219

two months, consisted of a monastery building with perhaps 30 small apartments for resident monks and a large dining hall that provided free daily meals. This ashram, which was sponsored by rich, local patrons, was also the base boarding station for a tram built for pilgrims who were too old or disabled to walk up the stairs to the Muruga temple.

At Swami Ashram, I was given a small room with about eight square feet of floor space and a ceiling some 14 feet up. Although this was certainly a strangely constructed chamber, it was more than suitable for my meager needs.

I took my meals in the eating hall and spent my nights sleeping outside on the ashram veranda, like most of the other resident swamis.

I washed at the ashram well as I had learned to do on previous trips to India, using the first bucket of water to discreetly soap and scrub my body under a sarong-like cloth wrapped loosely around my waist, then the second and perhaps a third bucket for dousing, rinsing and teeth brushing. After this, if no one was waiting for the well, I would use a forth and fifth bucket to wash yesterday's clothes.

Water in Palani is too much or too little—too much during a two-month monsoon season, too little during the other ten months of a year.

Sometime during the 1950's, a public well was dug and a pump for its water was built on the backside of the temple hill. From this pump, a large pipe was extended along the road encircling the hill. At points along this pipe, perhaps 100 yards apart, there were faucets.

As I circumambulated the temple hill every morning, which was a little less than a mile of walking, I would see ten to a hundred people lining up at each of these faucets, holding empty buckets, bottles and pales for their first water of the day. This water, unlike most of the water in South India, was safe to drink. It didn't come from a polluted river.

Although the Palani Muruga temple enjoys a certain amount of international prestige, it is primarily a Tamil temple in a Tamil town for the Tamil people of Tamil Nadu. For the most part, these Tamil people are very religious and very devotional. But many are also proud. And for good reason, some might say.

The Tamil language is one of the oldest in the world. In 2004, the government of India formally acknowledged and designated Tamil as a classical language even older than Sanskrit.

Also, more than two thousand years worth of rich Tamil literature indicates that today's Tamil lifestyle stems from the ancient culture of the Dravidians, the first inhabitants of the land now known as India.

Had I learned the Tamil language, I would have suffered more than I did from the many insults of discrimination I received in Palani. Should you be asking, "Does a verbal insult exist if its words can't be understood?" my answer would be, "Yes," for I felt those words and saw their meanings on the faces of many. Yet, my inability to speak Tamil also attracted a compassionate sort of assistance, a kind of help that comes from benevolent souls blessed with an urge to serve.

This pilgrimage visit to Palani was my fourth and longest of five. During my other four visits, which occurred with Gurudeva and his many bilingual friends, the language barrier had not been such a problem. Now, as I was living there alone, communication wasn't a luxury. It was a necessity. Out of a desperate need, I finally found a few people who could speak English well.

To my surprise, some of those few spoke English better than I did. These older, distinguished alumni of schools like Yale and Harvard had made their fortunes abroad and returned to their homes in Palani to humbly finish out their lives in religiousness.

Although all of these dignified elite were kind, sweet and helpful, each one of them offered me one specific pronouncement that was worded as if it had been memorized from a one script they all shared.

I was not the Hindu I thought I was, they each told me kindly, because I was not born Indian, which was, they said, an incontestable requirement for even *understanding* Hinduism.

Although, at the time, I was both ill-equipped and polite enough to not get drawn into a lengthy debate on religious conversion, I *did* think of a reply—months later—that might have had carried substance, had I used it. I could have asked, "What about Kalanginatha?"

Kalanginatha was the spiritual preceptor of the man who established the Palani Muruga temple. Kalanginatha was respected in India as a Hindu sage. Yet, he was born and raised in China.

According to one version of Indian history, characteristically vague with dates, Kalanginatha was a respected alchemist who pilgrimaged to India from China for yogic enlightenment. After achieving his spiritual goal, he gained eminence in India as one of Tamil Nadu's 18 siddhars, or "accomplished ones." One of his disciples was Bhogar.

When Kalanginatha sent Bhogar to Palani to worship at the Tiru Avinankudi temple as part of his training, he instructed him to purify himself in *tapas* before entering the town of Palani.

While Bhogar was sitting high on a hill outside Palani dutifully performing this *tapas*, he had a profound mystical experience. During this experience, he was instructed to fashion an image of Muruga that would save mankind from disease.

Since Bhogar had been trained by Kalanginatha in alchemy as well as yoga, he made this icon out of nine poisonous substances, which together formed a panacea for all ills. It was Bhogar's intention that this universal remedy should be received by devotees as an ingredient of the *prashadam* (food made sacred during Hindu worship) offered after a *puja* performed for Lord Muruga. This *prashadam* consisted of milk, fruit and honey that had been poured over the deity during the worship ceremony and had therefore picked up traces of the magical substance from which the form of the deity had been made. In addition to restoring perfect health, this elixir was said to bestow perfect loveliness of form, not unlike that of Muruga, the god of beauty and youth.

Up the backside of the temple hill, there is a little-known foot-path used today only by small, tough muscle men hired to carry milk and *puja* supplies up to the temple. The priest who showed me this trail told me it was the path originally established and used by Bhogar.

This made sense. Before the construction of the current front temple stairs, the likely approach to the top of the temple hill, perhaps the only one, would have been up what is now considered the hill's rocky backside.

That hill, as I refer to it now for lack of a better word (What's the word for bundle of boulders jutting up out of the ground like the nose of a rocket?) was almost unclimbable. It was steeply sloped on one side with a drop-off bluff on the other. Interestingly, the main front stairs up to the temple were carved out of the rock of the bluff side.

Off Bhogar's trail, there were many side paths leading to caves and rock overhangs here and there. Following these paths and occasion-ally venturing off of them, I found a few great spots to meditate.

One morning, as I was preparing to sit at one of those spots, I was literally stormed by hundreds of monkeys, each of them half my size and baring teeth, or so it seemed.

I should pause here to share a tidbit of information with those of you who think monkeys are cute, cuddly little things nice to give as pets to five-year-olds for Christmas. At least ninety percent of India's monkeys are vicious, aggressive and often dangerous scavengers who *will* attack and bite. And those bites should be taken seriously. Some of these primates have rabies, and many spread diseases like tuberculosis.

Back to the story. As this army of monkeys approached me, I dropped to the ground, rolled into a ball, buried my head in my arms and prepared to die. Yet, not a single one of these little primages even touched me. All they did was pass around me as they continued on up the hill. As suddenly as they were there, they were gone.

Obviously, these monkeys had a plan that didn't involve me. As it turned out, they were on their way up to a breakfast they were able to extract from the coconut husks and banana peels that got hurled over the back temple wall every morning at nine o'clock after *prashadam* (food offerings) had been prepared for the morning temple *puja*.

Long story short: Although I was able to enjoy lots of meditation time on that mountain, I was not able to do so at nine in the morning.

For a great many reasons, the year I lived in India—my twenty-fourth in a monastery and my forty-fifth in a physical body—was not like any of the other thirty-six years I spent as a monk. For one thing, my schedule was different.

Like never before, I was waking up to days that were completely unstructured. Much to my dismay, I found this disconcerting. I *wanted* structure. But more importantly, I could see why structuring the use of time was helpful in the practice of yoga. I could see—like I couldn't see in the monastery—how a creatively structured day offered a natural support for a well-engaged mind. Now it made sense to me why Gurudeva worked that way, structuring his day to help structure his mind.

So I got up every morning before sunrise to be at the well getting ready for a day all structured with stuff I had decided was important to do. And I was surprised at how busy I became happily living this life I had created for myself with meditation at its front and center.

What I was striving for in meditation at that time was to simply sustain a sense of *being*. Because this approach had touched me into Self many times before, method was no longer a mystery. I had long since stopped window-shopping for ways and means and was now just down

223

to the business of keeping the peace—the business of holding that peace of *being* for as long as possible before it broke like fragile glass. And break it would, for work it was, this work of keeping the peace.

Work it is, because, although *being* is not *doing*, it takes a bit of *doing* to *be*. If you don't believe me. Try it and see. Try to hold the waters of your mind still as the waves of thought and emotion rise, even in the first minutes of trying.

So as I proceeded in this way with my day, working with this simple meditation in *being*, I watched in amazement as this one practice blossomed of its own accord into a multi-faceted kaleidoscope of many practices. When my body ached from sitting too long in one position, I took a break to stretch in hatha yoga. When it felt heavy and congested, I ate less food and drank more water. When it got sleepy, I took it for a walk. When it quivered with emotion, I measured its breath.

From all of this multiplicity developing out of a one simple practice, my body gained my respect. And with that respect, it became less demanding of my mind and let that mind rest. And while my mind rested, there was bliss until regrets for past misdeeds rose before me like debtors at my door, forcing me into prayer and the humility of realizing I needed the help of beings greater than myself to survive the messes of my own making. And this drove me around Lord Muruga's mountain and up the stairs to the temple for its *pujas* in the morning and at noon, and for its parade of the Golden Chariot in the evening, and for the sense of alrightness I discovered in worshipping with others.

Soon enough, I was living a schedule as busy as any I had ever experienced at home on Kauai. And I was happy for it. Like a mother delighting in observing her child learn something new and useful, I was observing myself build good habits for a solid spiritual life. I knew the longer I could stay with a schedule like this, the better my world would be. But staying with this schedule was not meant to be, for it was early June and the skies were shifting their colors.

I must admit I thought it was a bit odd that all the street *sadhus* were leaving town. By the time I figured out the monsoons were on their way, relentless rains had already arrived, and too much water was everywhere. My robes were so muddy I couldn't even think of keeping them clean, even though I never stopped washing them.

After three days of continual rain, I decided to conclude my stay at Swami Ashram in Palani, and move on to some place, any place, where the sun might shine at least a little bit. With this plan in mind, I made arrangements to meet with the head monk of Swami Ashram to say good-bye.

When I waded my way to see him, looking like a wet rat, his lovely daughter—perhaps thirty something—was there with him to most graciously receive me. This was a surprise.

Way back at the beginning of my stay there, when I had first tried to talk to Swami, I had communicated through a translator, for Swami didn't speak a word of English. At that time, Swami had offered me a place to stay even before I had asked for it and had seemed to take more of an interest in my personal welfare then was logical, given the fact he did not know me. I had assumed that something about my appearance had impressed him. I was right, but wrong. There *was* something in me that he liked, but that "something" wasn't what I thought it was.

The way I looked in India was the way I looked on Kauai. A foot-long beard. Three feet of hair tied back in a bun. Head shaved just on top. Robes. Obviously, I was a monk. Right? Apparently not. What Swami saw in me, apparently, was an American who would soon be returning to America.

Now, the same translator I had communicated with before, whose English was only slightly better than my Tamil, was trying his best to explain to me that Swami had led a long and happy family life before renouncing the world, and that he now wanted me to meet his daughter whom he had long-shot hopes might someday marry an American like me. Suddenly, I realized I was in an extremely awkward situation.

After about fifteen minutes of uncomfortable clumsiness during which no one present communicated well at all, I tried to give Swami some rupees for room and board, which he refused ever so sweetly. At least, I thought he was refusing. Confusing is what it was. Was I supposed to insist on paying? What I needed was a protocol coach, and a better translator. Having neither, I finally just sort of abruptly thanked Swami, said good-bye to his daughter and stumbled out into the rain.

An Ashram on a Mountain

There is a point in a long meditation when the energies within the body coalesce, flow up into the head and become quite intense. Curiously, this powerful intensity unfailingly follows a state of contemplative tranquility that's almost like sleep. Some might suppose such a development from peace to power would not seem likely. Perhaps peace begetting more peace, or power subsiding into peace, would make more sense. Yet peace to power is what it has always been for me, and I can't put it here any other way.

And it never seemed to matter what method of meditation got me there. After having meditated regularly for a number of years, it became clear to me that about a half hour to forty minutes of any sort of focusing effort would consistently bring about this same ascending intensity.

When I asked Gurudeva about this, he said calmly, "It's like moths flying close to a flame. They get excited."

I found this assuring, especially when he also confided to me that he had experienced this same flow of energy in the same way, and with the same consistency.

"This is just one of those things it wouldn't have done any good for me to tell you about before it happened for you," Gurudeva said. "After you experience that intensification of energy, I don't have to say anything except, 'You're on the right track, just keep going.'"

And so I did. I took his words as encouragement to stick it out with that potent headiness to see where it would lead.

My first discovery was that this upward thrust moved on a pulse that had its own rhythm. My second discovery was that I could alter the rhythm of this pulse through breath control—by simply regulating the in-breath so it was of the same duration as the out-breath. In this control of breath, I found that a natural pause of the breath occurred at a full inhalation and at a full exhalation. At first, this pause was short. Later it was longer.

My third discovery was this: the longer the pause was at the breath's height and depth, the stiller the breath became in general. And vice versa. The stiller the breath in general, the longer the pause, high and low. My fourth discovery was, the stiller the breath became, the more I could sense a solid energy, high in the head. This heady energy felt as if it were made of something like a physical substance that was

226

stouter than steel. My fifth discovery was, if I could stay in this solidness, the breath would stop effortlessly for long periods of time.

In this pausing of breath, I was still experiencing a subtle reflex motion of lung expansion and contraction even though there was no real inhalation and exhalation of air. Although I am sure there is a good scientific explanation for this, it seemed to me the purpose of this reflex movement was to keep my mind from panicking in a fear of death.

Sitting in this breathless state brought its own fulfillment: a sense of the direct relationship of *being* to Self. Because my previous experiences of "touching into the Self" had occurred unexpectedly and lasted for only a second or two, I had never been able to catch and cognize this connection. Now, I was discovering this missing link was not only perceivable, it could be studied as a solidness in which breathlessness elongated my transition from experience to non-experience and back.

And so it was that sitting solid became my new yoga, and I was filled with great joy. Here is how I described this in my journal:

Riding breath that's measured strong
Well locked into a count,
I cross a bridge. I can't go wrong.
I trust my mighty mount.

Soon enough, my breathing stops.
I linger like the dead.
Soon enough, a bubble pops
As power floods the head.

Yet how is this the peace I seek,
That sweetest bliss within?
"Can this be right, this power peak?"
I ask myself again.

Then soon enough, that force planes out,
Imploded from within.
Inside out. It turns about.
The lion backs in his den.

I escaped the rains of Palani in a place some 5,000 feet above sea level, a little tourist town named Yercaud. There, in that mountainous spot on the border between northern Tamil Nadu and Kerala, I stayed another two months in the ashram of Swami Poornanandagiri.

Although I have managed to refrain from using real names thus far (except for Gurudeva's) in the telling of this story, I am sharing Swami Poornanandagiri's name with you now because he asked me to.

He said, "If you ever write a book, can you mention my name?" Then, he carefully spelled his name for me and watched me write it down. Then, he checked my spelling of it—and reminded me, yet again, to include him in the book he seemed sure I was going to write.

After all that, how can I not mention Swami Poornanandagiri's name, correctly spelled? Truth be told, his name is here because his story is worth telling.

By his own admission, Swami Poornanandagiri had no specific intuition that I would be writing this book (nor did I). He just thought every westerner he met was a writer doing research. Otherwise, why in the world would they come to a place like India?

I had heard about Swami Poornanandagiri from an American friend of mine who had been traveling through India and had just happened to run into me in Palani during the monsoon rains (What are the chances of that?). I don't know how my friend came to know of Swami Poornanandagiri, but he spoke highly of him, insisted I would like him and offered to guide me to Yercaud for a meet-and-greet. I consented.

My first encounter with Swami occurred with such ease and in such good timing, I could only assume it was yet another one of those many little Muruga miracles that always seemed to be happening here and there to move my pilgrimage along in just the right direction in just the right way.

To my surprise, I did not even have to ask Swami if I could stay with him. My friend had already done that for me. I don't know how or when, or even why he assumed I *wanted* to stay there. All I know is, suddenly, it had all been taken care of and Swami was asking me—in perfect English—when I would be coming back with "my stuff." The only information I had to convey to Swami was that I didn't have to go anywhere to get my stuff. I had it.

"That's it?" he asked me, looking at my one dumpy duffle bag half filled with practical things—a few books, some toiletries, two sets of robes, two kurta shirts, one pair of traveling pants and a blanket.

"This is it," I replied. "This is my travel kit."

As I looked around at Swami's utopian mountain palace, I thought to myself, "What a perfect retreat from too much monsoon rain! What an ideal environment for the practice of yoga! What a warm-hearted welcome I am receiving! How can this be? Too many good things all at once. Why?" Slipping into a jaded frame of mind, just for a moment, I mentally asked myself, "What's in this for Swami? Nobody does something for nothing."

My unspoken question was answered soon enough. That which Swami would get out of me being there would be a poodle on a leash to be trotted out every time dignitaries come around—which was fairly often. Swami, I came to discover, was somewhat famous in that part of India. And I was his curiosity, a white American who said he was a Hindu, claimed to be a monk and wore his hair and beard sage long.

Don't get me wrong. Swami wasn't just a social butterfly. He was a deeply mystical man with a lot of power accrued from his long practice of yoga. But he was also the head of an Indian ashram doing what most swamis in India do when they are in that position.

A lot of the dignitaries who came to the ashram were high up in government. During their chats with Swami, they *sometimes* discussed spiritual matters, but they *always* talked politics. This was not unusual.

India is full of ashrams. Some are spiritual. Some are not. Some are in between. Yet they are all so woven into the fabric of the land it would be unrealistic to assume any of the swamis presiding over them would or even could stay out of politics altogether. Some *mutt* heads (*mutt* means "ashram") have an overt interest in and influence upon politics. In certain parts of India, they are the very political backbone of all that occurs. Although these monastery pontiffs don't usually work together, the very existence of their many ashrams exerts a formidable influence on both a religious and secular India.

The relative esteem of each of these ashrams is determined by factors that fluctuate, sometimes in unforeseeable ways. For instance, an ashram's longevity is a growing constant, but its revenue and property value might vary unpredictably. The strongest determinant of an ashram's stability, and the most difficult if not impossible one to predict into a distant future, is the reputation of the various swamis who take its charge in succession through the years. And the good name of these leaders hinges primarily upon the merit and rectitude of their followers, mainly their ashram residents.

Swami Poornanandagiri was in the early stages of building a name for himself and his ashram. Remote yet accessible, the location of his monastery was unique. Nestled deep in a jungle several miles outside Yercaud, it sat majestically on a cliff overlooking the only road linking a sparsely populated highland to a heavily populated lowland.

Beautifully designed, long against the rock face of a steep bluff, it featured a large kitchen, a full library, a trinket shop, a meeting hall, a covered front porch, and four rather large apartments, each with an adjoining bathroom. All in all, there were ample living quarters for as many as ten people.

The ashram's temple was a separate building, small but also quite elegantly designed and constructed. It featured a mammoth Shakti (feminine) deity, beautifully rendered.

The three permanent residents of the ashram were more like Swami's children than his devotees. One was a bright young man, about 24 years of age. He was a Sanskrit scholar who had been well trained in a local *padasala*, a school specializing in preparing boys to become temple priests. His job was to perform *pujas* in the ashram temple.

The other two residents, a man and a woman, both about 45, had lived on the streets as beggars until Swami took them in. The man was a bit of a simpleton with no family and no place to go. The woman, abused and abandoned by her husband, had been left with nothing, could not find employment and had no relatives willing to take her in. With Swami, these two had a roof over their heads and useful work to do. The lady cooked. The man cleaned and served in simple ways, wherever he was needed.

We were a strange crew, these three and I. Our only common bond was our respect for Swami, a man who was humorous, kind and intelligent. In Yercaud as well as in several towns around the mountain upon which we lived, Swami was known for his compassion.

The ashram income was derived from several sources: a number of "donation boxes" conspicuously placed in the ashram and temple; the sale of gift shop items—precious and semiprecious gemstones as

230

well as religious accessories like *japa malas* (prayer beads), incense and *kum kum* (red powder for making the forehead dot)—and the numerous temple *pujas* performed by the ashram's resident priest for local towns-people, travelers crossing the mountains and even a few tourists.

Swami Poornanandagiri had been married. I found this to be a common scenario with swamis in India where vows of renunciation are most often taken toward the end of life. When older householders become swamis, they are generally careful their familial responsibilities have been properly handled lest they reap what they understand all too well would be a backlash of negative karma.

Swami's wife and three grown children occasionally came to visit him in the ashram. They lived in Salem about an hour's drive away. Indications were they had been well taken care of and were happy with Swami's chosen path of renunciation.

Around Yercaud, most of the resident population consisted of tribal villagers who worked on coffee plantations and in orange groves deep in the mountain jungles. Many of these people came to Swami for advice and council. While I was there, I witnessed Swami settle quite a few local disputes. Most of these conflicts he was able to resolve peace-fully. Some he could not.

One morning, I couldn't help but overhear a storm of yelling and screaming, all in the Tamil language. After it was all over and the six or seven upset visitors had left, I asked Swami what the racket was all about. I knew it couldn't be good.

He explained that a boy from one village had married a girl from another village against the wishes of the girl's parents. Later, after the marriage, the father of the bride had invited the couple to his village to reconcile residual ill feelings and celebrate the marriage after the fact. When the new bride and groom arrived, the villagers, led by the bride's father, surrounded the couple and brutally killed them both. Now, some of the family of the groom wanted revenge.

When I asked Swami what advice he had given, he said that giving advice had not been an option. All they wanted from him was an empathy they could read as permission to wreak vengeance.

There was no formal law there in the mountains. For many who lived in the area, the only law was Swami's word. And Swami's word here in this situation would not be heard. Yet his silence said, "No! You should not do what you know you should not do."

Swami was about 65 years old and huge. By "huge" I mean fat. He said he got that way unintentionally by performing a hatha yoga breathing exercise called *plavini pranayama,* a somewhat obscure practice of swallowing rather than inhaling air for the purpose of cleansing the stomach and intestines. Although he showed me how to perform this "air gulping," as he called it, I never did it. Nor do I intend to. He also showed me the "death breath" that he said could end life within 24 hours. I never performed that one either, obviously. Nor do I intend to.

Every morning, Swami and I took a walk together. Although he told me this walk was his exercise to get his weight down, he added, with a mocking smile, "fat chance." This led me to assume that what he really wanted to do on these walks was talk. He wanted to talk because he liked to talk—and because, as I came to understand, very much to my surprise, he was lonely.

He rarely spent time talking with the permanent residents of his ashram except to help them with their personal problems or explain the chores they were expected to do. He took a liking to me, I think, because I had a thirst for his knowledge about yoga, I asked sincere questions while taking careful notes, and I was willing to help him host guests.

As we strolled a half-mile down a hill to a gorgeous lookout where we sat for a while before hiking back up to the ashram, we were forever talking. I should say: *He* was forever talking. After watching me scramble to scribble on paper the gist of what he was saying as we walked, he lent me his hand-held tape recorder, which worked wonderfully until its batteries died almost as soon as I started using it.

A side note here: In India it is surprisingly difficult to accomplish seemingly small tasks like mailing letters, washing long hair, and buying small items like dental floss (impossible), cheese (difficult) and AA batteries for a tape recorder (no where in or near Yercaud).

I really got to know Swami on those walks. He was a brilliant man, fluent in at least five languages. And funny. Hilariously funny.

Swami was Shakta. I was Saivite. Of the three primary sects of Hinduism—Saivism, Shaktism and Vaishnavism—the first two have more in common with each other than either has with the third. In search of Siva, Saivites discover Shakti. Through worship of Shakti, Shaktas discover Siva. Although these latter two sentences are most admittedly

232

simplistic, they begin what could be a long explanation of the difference between two theologies that are more alike than not.

Shaktas perceive Shakti and Siva as a Goddess and a God. They believe they must worship an active Shakti to achieve spiritual illumination in a quiescent Siva.

Saivites perceive Siva and Shakti as a one deity. They believe they must worship Siva through Shakti to achieve spiritual illumination in a merging with the one Self and source of all.

Many of the worship and yoga practices of these two sects are the same, the only significant difference being their emphasis. It has been said, for instance, that Saivites are a little more contemplative then the Shaktas because they emphasize *being* over *doing*. Yet the Shaktas say, as would the Saivites, it takes some *doing* to *be*. So, there you have it. Not much difference.

All of this is to say Swami and I were more or less on the same page, philosophically, and therefore had an easy time talking with each other. Of course, our conversations also benefited greatly from Swami's mastery of the English language.

I kept a separate notebook for recording what Swami said. A lot of what I wrote down had to do with yoga techniques, ways of coordinating *pranayama* with *japa* and the like. With regard to *japa*, Swami spent a great deal of time carefully explaining the powers of specific mantras, and the different results that could be expected when these mantras were repeated in different ways.

He also talked about the potency of visualization, how "visualization can invoke visions," as he put it. Although he said visualization *can* invoke visions, he also made it clear they *might not*. Elaborating, he explained that visualizations were controlled by man while visions were gifts from God. Because of this, he said, visions were not likely to come to a person who learned to visualize for selfish or personal reasons — like building a reputation as a "seer," for instance.

I found Swami's way of thinking to be much like Gurudeva's. Even his sense of humor was similar. Yet, like Gurudeva, his humor was never wasted in frivolousness. Every funny story he told had a point aimed high. This impressed me and fortified my faith in what he said.

I wrote a lot in the notebook I had dedicated to Swami. Much of it I even wrote twice, copying it a second time in the same notebook just so it would be more easily readable later. I wrote and wrote and wrote. Then later, sometime after I left Yercaud, I lost that notebook. I couldn't believe it. All that work. Lost. Just like that. The whole notebook.

I know there is some deep significance in that loss. Yet, to this day I'm hoping I'll open some dusty box in a closet somewhere and there it will be, waiting for me. It hasn't happened yet. If it does, there will be enough material there for another book. Swami Poornanandagiri would be so happy. Two books extolling him, both with his name quite properly spelled.

In Swami's mountain ashram, it was easy to begin again those long meditations I had so enjoyed in Palani. In a room I had to myself, I spent as much time as I could, cycling through various practices of pranayama, hatha yoga and meditation. My on-going experimentation with sitting solid kept me enthralled in eager anticipation like a scientist immersed in research.

Also, there in that little room, I discovered how foresight could be attained through hindsight. I arrived at this insight by looking into memory to see that none of my uncontrolled worrying about a future was ever beneficial. This simple epiphany left me contentedly firm in a *now* that was flavored with an earned respect for the experiences that had brought me to that point. In this peaceful contentedness, I felt no tendency to force a desired future. Instead, I found myself quite willing to let my future create itself, as a natural consequence of my optimal absorption in the present moment. All of this was my intuition leading me into the realization that *now* is the only time there is and that past and future are just ideas. I was arriving at this breakthrough not from having read about it in books or having heard others talk about it. I was realizing it directly through my own *now* experience.

The language of *Shum* came in handy here.

There are single words in *Shum* that describe entire groups of experiences. One such word is *nalif*. To experience *nalif* is to enjoy the power of one meditation building into the power of another meditation without a break in continuity. By contrast, if *nalif* does not exist, there is a necessity for revitalizing spiritual energy at the beginning of each new meditation.

For a serious yogi, *nalif* is important because a continual cultivation of a building spiritual force is important. It's *nalif* that generates the intensity necessary for a genuine spiritual transformation. In *nalif*, each of our meditations starts where the last one left off, not where it began.

As I looked back on my time in Palani, I could see how a *nalif* was beginning to develop there but got stopped when I had to travel. Now I was seeing a chance to reestablish a *nalif* in Yercaud.

For anyone practicing meditation long enough for it to become a habit, this *nalif* would occur of its own accord to a certain extent. Yet an intense *nalif* is created intentionally.

Three conditions are necessary for this intentional establishment of *nalif*. First, there must be a comfortable atmosphere of aloneness, a protected space where yoga can be practiced in safety and without unnecessary interruption. Second, there must be enough time available for the practice of yoga so that one meditation can soon be followed by another. Third, the demands of external life must be minimal since externalized thought and emotion tend to dissipate the power of meditation and break the continuity of *nalif*.

At Swami's ashram, these conditions were present enough for me to be able to easily continue what I had started in Palani. As I look back on my time in Yercaud now, I realize my most significant achievement there—and this was the result of intentionally cultivating *nalif*—was in establishing what in *Shum* would be referred to as *tyamuif*.

A person who is experiencing a powerful *tyamuif* performs even the everyday chores of ordinary life in a consciousness that is rooted two thirds within. Yet *tyamuif* is not a "spaced out" state. A person experiencing *tyamuif* is vitally alive and alert, yet calmly poised in focus.

In *tyamuif*, we are—without effort—the solver of problems, the settler of disputes and the giver of blessings. In *tyamuif*, we are not only more easily able to access positive inner resources—like intuition, will, compassion, selflessness and serenity—we are also less likely to be drawn out into negative emotions like anger, resentment, depression and fear. Experiencing *tyamuif* is like living in the more refined realms of both inner and outer worlds, "taking the best and leaving the rest," as Gurudeva would so often say.

Every time I moved from one place to another on my pilgrimage through India, some event would occur to bookmark that point in time for easy reference later.

On the morning of my last day at Swami's ashram in Yercaud, I

235

went into the washroom to bathe. This washroom was a six-foot cube with a door, a faucet, a bucket and a drain. To facilitate drainage, its concrete floor slanted toward a corner hole in the wall.

In a dim predawn light, I filled the bucket with water from the faucet and leaned over it to wet my face. As I was hovering and splashing, the bucket moved. Then it moved again. And again. As I moved back to have a better look at what was going on, I saw, curled over the back upper rim of the bucket and looking straight at me, the head of a snake. I froze. Happily, so did he—or she. I'll call it a "she."

She and I stayed that way for what seemed like a very long time—actually probably only about five seconds. During that interval of stillness, I screamed mentally, "Get out!"

To my delighted surprise, the snake did just that. She slowly and gracefully lowered her head, slid across the floor and disappeared through the drain hole in the corner of the room. Only as she left, could I see how really long she was. She had wound herself several times around the base of the water bucket.

I couldn't resist going outside to have a better look at this girl. As it turned out, she was at least fifteen feet long. I am sure of this size because, as she was slithering up and over an eight-foot wall with her head out of sight on the other side of that wall, she was still at least half on the ground in front of the wall.

Swami laughed as I told him what happened. When I asked him what kind of snake it was, he replied, "She didn't get you did she?" That wasn't the answer I was looking for, but it was enough to let me know I was probably never in any real danger.

Just before I left his ashram, Swami made me promise to come back and see him and his band of three before returning to America. To create some semblance of insurance this might occur, he gave me a more durable carrying bag than the one I had and made me vow to return it. Sadly, this was a commitment I was not able to honor.

That was the last I saw of Swami. He died a year later. So did the swami who took care of me in Palani, by the way. My bridges were burning, as the pages of my life were turning.

A Haven in the Himalayas

Three days after I left Yercaud, I was back at our Bangalore work site, sitting comfortably in my home away from home. As sweet as this was, my pilgrimage was not meant for lingering long at any sort of home base. I would soon have to be traveling again.

Because I had now been in India five of the six months my visa allowed, it was time to start thinking about doing what now had to be done to stay in the country longer. My general plan was to cross the Indian border at some point so I could obtain another six-month visa as I re-entered the country.

There were only two feasible places I could accomplish this going-and-coming. One was down south, into Sri Lanka and back. The other was up north, into Nepal and back. Although I wanted to go to Sri Lanka, the home of my teacher's teacher, I was strongly advised not to do so because of a civil war that was then raging there between the Tamil Tigers and the Sinhalese army. So, focusing upon the only logical course of action, I set my sights up toward Nepal.

After a few days of pilgrimaging to temples in the Bangalore area, I was back on a three-day train ride up to New Delhi to stay again with the swami who had hosted me when I first arrived in India.

Riding the train into New Delhi and looking out the window of my coach, I was suddenly overcome with nervous anticipation. Strange. During my previous stay in Delhi, I had felt no such anxiety. Then, however, I was not alone. Now I was. Now, I was alone and wondering where my free spirit had gone and why I was feeling myself becoming stoic and geared up for trouble. I kept trying to convince myself the anxiety I was feeling had no merit. Actually, it did.

Indian railway stations are always busy and chaotic, but for those of us who aren't accustomed to traveling in India by train and who can't speak any of the country's 122 languages, these transportation networks can be overwhelmingly confusing. For me, the Delhi station was more than confusing. It was a nightmare.

Just getting from the train to the street was an ordeal. Once I stepped down from my coach and could see I had to get from where I was to the main terminal by crossing over about twelve train tracks on a pedestrian bridge that was some two stories up, I stepped into the people flow and gave myself up to its current.

237

While crossing the bridge, there was a small boy right in front of me. He couldn't have been more than five years of age. The fact he was moving a little more slowly then everyone else didn't really surprise or bother me. I figured it was just because he was little, or maybe he was looking for his mom. Where *was* his mom, I wondered? And what was he doing there in that train station all by himself?

When I finally made a move to pass him, he actually blocked me. Although this certainly seemed a little strange, I didn't have time to give it much thought. We had just arrived at the far end of the bridge and I had to focus all of my attention on getting down a long flight of stairs. Just as I turned to make my descent, I felt a slight tug on the back left corner of my shirt. As I turned around, I saw a little girl, about seven years old, running off into the crowd. When I looked back to the front, the little boy was no longer there.

Suddenly, it dawned upon me. Two pre-pubescent children had been robbing me. This was, enraging, frightening, funny and embarrassing—all at the same time.

"Let's see now," I thought to myself, "What was *I* doing at the age of five? Eating cookies in kindergarten?"

Once I figured out my plight, my only question was: Did they get anything? I couldn't stop to check. The crowd was moving me on.

Finally, I was able to pull out of the people flow into a quiet corner of the main terminal building. After a moment of investigation, I could see I still had my passport and almost all my money. But all the eight zippers of both my bags, had been opened. And the zipper of the money belt, which I had been wearing *underneath* my pants, had also been opened. And all of the paper rupees I was carrying in that money belt had been pulled half out.

Although the little girl had actually gotten only a small bundle of rupees I had kept separately in a side pants pocket for quick access, she had come alarmingly close to snatching my entire cash stash. With just another five seconds she could have altered my pilgrimage through India quite extensively.

When the driver of a three-wheeler (a motorized, two-passenger tricycle commonly used as a taxi in India) saw me counting my money, he asked me if I needed a ride. I said yes. In accordance with my request, he took me to Swami's ashram. When we arrived, he authoritatively ordered me to pay him 200 rupees. I knew from having taken that same ride before that I should only be required to pay 40 rupees. So, instead of paying him money, I gave him a glare.

He seemed genuinely surprised by this. What he couldn't have possibly known, poor fellow, was that my quite recent encounter with those toddlers from hell had frayed my tolerance for thieves down to just about nothing.

Even so, I just couldn't bring myself to get too tough with him. After some careful deliberation and forced resistance of an urge to just turn and walk away without paying anything, I decided to compromise and give him 100 rupees, twice rather than four times the worth of the ride. The driver started to object but didn't. He could see in my face I was in no mood to discuss anything, especially money.

As I sat on the front steps of Swami's ashram around sunset that evening, I felt sort of raped, but not really. I knew I was in the land of lost and found, a magic place where what goes missing somehow manages to eventually get retrieved with gain. So far, in just less than half a year, I had lost a pocket full of rupees, a backache's worth of physical tension, a headache's worth of psychological anxiety and a king's worth of unnecessary self-esteem. Yet, from all that loss, I had gained a slave's worth of humility and a street's worth of smarts. All in all, I figured I had come out ahead.

I stayed in New Delhi just long enough to make a plan for getting in and out of Nepal. Dharma Ajay, one of Swami's devotees, was very helpful in this effort. Dharma was a distinguished and elderly gentleman who had been a successful attorney in New Delhi when he was younger. Now, with his considerable savings, he had moved back to his family home in a small village 500 miles east of New Delhi, and five miles west of Birganj. Situated on India's upper border, Birganj was known as "the gateway to Nepal."

Birganj, I was told, was the best place to perform my border crossing for a visa. And Dharma, who had been visiting Swami in New Delhi when I arrived, had volunteered to escort me through the process. How perfect was this? Things were looking up.

As I sat slumped in a doze during an all-night train ride to Birganj with Dharma, I had almost forgotten the powerless vulnerability I had been forced to feel at the hands of those babies working the Delhi train station. Little did I know I was just about to get shown again just how, at a lower level of Indian society, imaginative petty theft, performed by kids barely old enough to walk and talk, provides a significant amount of income for someone. Who? The parents of the infant thieves? Some sort of street mafia? I had so much to learn, yet was learning so much.

After about an hour of disturbed sleep, a jolting shift of the train shook me awake. An older lady across from me had been lying sideways on a hard bench, sleeping with her head firmly nestled on her one and only carrying bag so as to discourage robbers from taking it. Now, just as I was watching, a little brown arm appeared out of the dark beside the lady's head. Reaching in through horizontal window bars installed about six inches apart to keep thieves out, this little arm slithered like a snake as the fingers of its chubby little hand gracefully unzipped the bag under the sleeping lady's head to slickly extract through the window bars that bag's entire contents, primarily clothes.

Not being close enough to the window to grab the child's arm myself, I screamed, "Hey!" Quicker than immediately, the crime's most unfortunate victim was awake, alert and at the bars, desperately clutching through them at thin air. Too late.

By now, I was over at the window myself, seeing if there was something I could do. There wasn't. It was all over. But I could see what had happened.

As the train had slowed down to pass through a village not large enough to warrant a full stop, about six boys had leapt onto the coach like spiders, grabbing and holding on to the very window bars that were meant to keep thieves like them out. Within the slim two minutes they had before the train sped up again, they had performed their heists, dropped to the ground and leisurely strolled away with a booty they knew was virtually untraceable.

I could hear wailing from other seats in the coach. The lady across from me had not been the only victim. Yet perhaps she was the noblest. This sweet, little, grandmotherly person simply sank back into her seat and looked down, saying nothing, not even crying. Her loss had been substantial. She was obviously poor. Yet there she was, sitting so unobtrusively dignified in the manner of so many in India like her who suffer indignities they know are best endured with forbearance.

My acquisition of a new visa went smoothly, only because

of Dharma's assistance. At the border-gate between India and Nepal, somewhere in the middle of Birganj, Dharma approached a large, pear-shaped man, dressed in a uniform, sitting on a folding chair behind what looked like a card table in a tent by the road.

There was a lot of talk in Hindi, punctuated with some finger pointing in my direction. The uniformed man had a look of seriousness that worried me a little, especially when he turned to Dharma, shook his head and sent us to another tent across the street to another man who was sitting behind another card table. That man then sent us to yet another man in another tent. Eventually, we found our way to a small building where there was finally some nodding of heads amidst a bit of Hindi chat that sounded somewhat positive.

At that place, I was asked, in Hindi, to show my passport. When it became obvious I hadn't understood what had just been said, Dharma casually reached over, pulled my passport out of my shirt pocket and placed it on the table. This initiated some shifting, shuffling and signing of papers. Suddenly, I was out of India and in Nepal.

We walked around a bit. "Stumbled around in shock" would be a better way to put it. Here, just a few feet into Nepal, we were completely surrounded by the sight of blood and the stink of butchery. Along muddy streets in makeshift shops all falling apart, vendors were selling hard liquor, cheap cigarettes, raw eggs and gutted fish—as well as chickens, goats and pigs, dead and alive.

After about twenty minutes, when Dharma could see I had seen enough, we returned to the passport building for more paper work, an exchange of polite nods, and a casual exit from Nepal past all of those same uniformed gentlemen sitting on folded chairs behind card tables in tents, until we got to the last fellow, who was the first fellow we met as we came in. This gentleman—who had been so serious when we first saw him—was now beaming a broad grin, exclaiming to me in exquisite English and with relished enjoyment, "We hope you enjoyed your stay in Nepal."

Back in India, I spent one night in Dharma's home, a fort-like mansion in the town where Dharma had grown up. Now, in the sunset of his life, Dharma was the village headman there, "a big fish in a little pond," as he himself put it.

On the evening of that night, many of the village men gathered around a fire in Dharma's huge cow barn to talk, laugh and host me until we all fell asleep, one by one, amongst the cows. As the guest of honor I had been invited to relax in a hammock, which had been stretched between two of the structural poles of the barn just for me. In this hammock, I slept through that night like a baby.

The next morning, as I emerged from the cow barn, there were about two hundred people gathered in a semicircle to bid me farewell. I was completely surprised. All Dharma had told me was that he had a car waiting to take me to the nearest train station some twenty miles away, As I slowly raised my hands palm to palm in a prayer gesture, Dharma's wife stepped forward from the group to give me a shirt-and-pants set of clothes, which she had begun making for me when she first heard two weeks before that I would be coming. In the strained quiet pervading this sweet goodbye, I felt ill at ease, yet blessed.

On the way to the train station, I asked Dharma why so many of the town's residents had turned out to acknowledge my presence and say goodbye. He said most of the people in his village had never seen a white man. He also mentioned that all of those who had gathered were born in that village and had never left it.

At the train station, Dharma and I parted ways. I thanked him profusely for all of his help in getting me *visafied* for another six months. Truly, he had immeasurably simplified a potentially complex process.

After about twelve rough and raucous hours of travel by train, I arrived in Hardwar for a one-night stay. While I was there, I tried, quite unsuccessfully, to find the spot where Gurudeva had initiated me into *sannyas* just fifteen years before. The whole town had changed so much I could find no familiar landmarks at all.

Tourists, street vendors, beggars, and imposters of all sorts had invaded sweet Hardwar to take her by siege. True seekers of spirit were nowhere to be seen. I could only hope that the sage-types I remembered having been there some fifteen years before had escaped the bright lights, blaring noise, and mundane ordinariness that had so successfully transformed a once holy place into what now looked like a stage set for a movie about India. I couldn't wait to leave.

There were no trains to Rishikesh. I had to take a bus. But it wasn't far—about twenty miles. In Rishikesh, I stayed in the ashram of another swami that Gurudeva knew. My accommodations there were no less than splendid.

The swami in charge of that ashram was quite famous. It was for this reason that I didn't see much of him while I was there. He was almost constantly traveling. But he had his staff take care of me. And take care, they did. I was treated like a king.

Rich patrons supported the ashram and made it the palace it was. These patrons had apartments built on the ashram grounds so they would have places to stay when they came to visit. When these patrons weren't present, their apartments were made available to guests.

The apartment provided for me had a sitting room, a bedroom, a full bathroom, a shower (unusual in India), a kitchenette and a patio.

Although most of the ashram residents ate in a communal hall, I was served my meals privately. This had been set up for my comfort and convenience. Swami had also arranged for my passport and whatever money I didn't want to keep with me to be kept in the ashram safe.

The three months I stayed there in Swami's ashram were quite memorable. It was a high time, spiritually and physically (Rishikesh is nearly three miles above sea level). And it was a place I vowed to come back to, again and again. Even as I am writing this book, I deeply yearn to return to Rishikesh.

There in that ideal ashram setting, again fully immersed in the practice of yoga, I found myself thinking a lot about Gurudeva.

Seeing in Gurudeva a living example of what I was trying to find within myself gave me fortitude to endure the sometimes-uncomfortable circumstances I encountered as I traveled through India. Dealing with these circumstances coupled with enduring a certain amount of psychological overhaul was making my pilgrimage challenging.

Understanding the deeper principles of yoga intellectually—a relatively easy task—is objective. Experiencing those principles in practice—an unquestionably difficult task—is subjective.

Because the central purpose of yoga is to transmute a misplaced sense of identity, each person's experience of yoga will necessarily vary in accordance with that person's sense of who he or she is at any given point in time. This ever-shifting sense of identity is what makes yoga a work in progress until the one Self of all is realized.

Although veteran yogis are not strangers to this view of yoga, they find it more and more revelatory as its validity gets reiterated again and again through their personal experience. Those yogis who continue in their practice over a long period of time become increasingly aware that yoga's end is actually brought about through a constant reformation of the "I," even if this reformation should be occasionally uncomfortable as it occurs.

My experience of this was obvious in my yoga journal where only the last page made sense to me and didn't seem juvenile. However that page was composed, it was the only page that was relevant to my ever-shifting sense of identity.

Gurudeva had mellowed through the years. It was a mellowing that was something like the aging of fine wine. As time passed, his very appearance reflected his frequent merging with *Self*. Sensing *Self* in his presence, we were inspired just being around him. Sensing *Self* in him, we could sense It in ourselves. Sensing *Self* within, we changed. In this changing, we discovered a great *Self*-confidence.

The longer I lived in Gurudeva's presence, the more I came to appreciate why he never made his yoga teachings black-and-white like we all wanted him to, but instead left certain truths "up in the air" for each of us to catch as we could in our own timing. He was smart that way, having gone that way himself and knowing there was really no other way to go.

In beautiful India, I was moved—as my reflections deepened—to more appropriately respect the Gurudeva I could now see I had too often taken for granted through all those years of living shoulder to shoulder with him in his monasteries. Now, my pilgrimage was starting to look like a stepping out to dive more deeply within, like a rubber band being stretched away to snap back with great power.

So I lived day to day in Rishikesh, practicing yoga as I would have practiced yoga most anywhere else. Yet in Rishikesh, it was like nowhere else. Rishikesh is a yoga town, a place where yoga can be practiced without breaking rank, because yoga is the rank.

Not a day went by that I didn't feel a growing gratitude for this year Gurudeva had given me far away from our cloistered monastic life. Because the strict work ethic of our monastery routine had been so very deeply ingrained in me, along with the idea that time was not to be wasted, I could not help but consider such a long, truly happy-go-lucky sojourn in this motherland of yoga as anything but a gift. With this heartfelt acknowledgment and appreciation holding my feet firmly to the ground, I strolled up and down the Ganges as free and untroubled as I have ever been.

It was inspiring to be in the presence of the thin *sadhus* who came down out of the hills in the early morning light, hauling their long matted locks and wearing only a loincloth. I must admit I was surprised to learn that their life—at least the small portion of it that I observed—followed a routine of military regularity and precision.

Just before dawn they were at the river bathing, but not for long. The water was cold. After that bath, each would follow his personal routine, a routine that never varied even a little, morning after morning. These routines consisted of hatha yoga, pranayama and mantra japa—but no meditation that I could see. I never saw a native Indian sadhu meditating. This was something I had not expected.

During the day, the sadhus disappeared, leaving Rishikesh to tourists. Those tourists included me, I guess, much as I hate to admit it. Yet I also withdrew during the day, and for the same reason the *sadhus* did: to do *sadhana*. At least, I would presume *sadhana* was what they were doing. What else? Who could know for sure? They were out of sight, out of mind.

There was a "this side" and a "that side" to the river Ganges as it flowed by Rishikesh. The town of Rishikesh was on "this side." The ashram where I was staying was on "that side." The only access to "that side" was over one of two suspension bridges, each about a quarter mile long, built to deal with the Ganges when it was flowing at its highest and a quarter mile wide, which was the way it was when I was there. One of those bridges was called Ram Jhula, the other, Lakshman Jhula.

Monkeys were always perched atop the bridge's tall suspension pillars. Their sole goal was to throw the rain water that collected in the pillar tops down on tourists—only tourists. They would leave the locals alone. I have no idea how they knew who was who, but they did.

A tea shop owner told me it wasn't rainwater coming down. He said it was monkey pee. I didn't believe this for two reasons. The shopkeeper was smiling when he said it, and I watched the monkeys through binoculars. It was rainwater for sure, I think.

Those monkeys would also often rush anyone carrying the light pink or blue plastic bags sweet shop owners would give their customers for carrying purchased sweets.

I must say it is very disconcerting to be rushed by a snarling monkey. Of course, this kind of thing happened only to tourists. Everyone else knew not to carry light pink or blue plastic bags.

When I first got rushed by monkeys, I was alone on Lakshman Jhula Bridge. During that memorable occasion, monkeys came at me from both ends of the bridge to trap me between them. When I threw my blue bag of half-eaten halva over the railing, one particularly ferocious looking primate, swinging to rise up from underneath the bridge like a savage troll, caught it like a fly baseball. Yet, as he bounded onto the bridge and tried to slip his plunder past his cohorts, he was attacked by two of them, who were, in turn, attacked by four or five more. In the dramatic squabble that then ensued, which sounded far worse than it was, I fell back in hasty retreat and made my happy exit.

I took that monkey business on the bridge as a sign that I should begin the end of my stay in Rishikesh. I'm also choosing here to begin the end of my story of India there where it culminated in those ancient Himalayan foothills. I am taking this approach simply because everything that happened during my pilgrimage after Rishikesh was not as deserving of space in this book as that which happened immediately following my arrival back home in our monastery on Kauai.

During the last three months of my journey, my thoughts were homeward-bound and joyfully so. This doesn't mean my final days in India weren't happy and busy.

After making my way back through Hardwar to New Delhi, I boarded a train and headed, again, three days south to Bangalore. There, I stayed another two months in another ashram. Although my adventures there were different from anything described thus far, they were all well flavored with a heading-for-home determination to get mind and body set and ready for the rigor and regime of monastery life.

All that had happened from the beginning of my journey through my time in Rishikesh had the feel of a blooming up. Now, all of that fabulous momentum was winding down. Little did I know then, I was closing down upon not one but three ends: the end of a pilgrimage, the end of a human life and the end of a way of living.

Three Ends

When I returned to the monastery in March of 1995, everything was as it had been when I left. Or so it seemed.

As is so often the case, appearances can be deceiving. There had been change—just not the sort of change I had expected. While some of the monks appeared to have aged more than the one year I was gone, a choice few seemed to have de-aged, youthified in some fashion. Yet everyone had grown, for everyone had learned from a year's worth of life experience.

During my time away, Gurudeva had changed the most. But not like the others. He didn't seem older or younger, just different—quite different—in a way that was hard to pinpoint. As I looked at him, all I could think was, "something's not right." He talked less, moved less, smiled less and ate less. In general, he was more austere and withdrawn than ever before.

Though such might be considered the expected demeanor of a reclusive sage, it wasn't what any of us would ever have anticipated seeing in Gurudeva. He had always been so dynamically *alive*. Now, there was a distinct air of morbidity about his physical appearance. Worst of all, his famously luminous countenance seemed drained of its magic. That gleaming face that could uplift with a look now looked strangely masklike, washed-out pallid and ghostly white. Something wasn't right.

Of course, I asked around about his health. No one seemed outwardly concerned. This surprised and bothered me greatly. I tried to rationalize this apparent apathy, thinking to myself that Gurudeva's physical condition was more obvious to me only because I had not been around to subliminally adapt to its gradual deterioration.

I didn't say any of this, of course. Such would have been too assertive, I thought, coming from a monk who had been traveling and should now be mostly concerned with humbly adjusting himself back into monastic life.

What I slowly came to realize was that, behind closed doors, there was great concern for Gurudeva's health. And much was being done privately—so as not to overly concern the younger monks.

That which none of us could ignore in Gurudeva was driving us all through a painful education about life and death.

Gurudeva had promised us he would live to be 120. Even had

he not made such a bold commitment, none of us would have dared to consider the possibility of his imminent demise. Such thought would have seemed almost blasphemous.

Even as Gurudeva began working diligently to either automate or systematize as much of the church's day-to-day operating procedure as he could, most of the monks successfully refused to contemplate the idea he might be doing this in preparation for his earthly departure. It was only when he appointed his successor and started withdrawing from the work he would normally do and the trips he would normally take that it became impossible to ignore he was getting ready to die.

Finally, in early 2001, no amount of looking the other way could stave off our full acknowledgement of the stark inevitability none of us had sufficiently been trained to accept unemotionally. It was as plain as the look on his face. Our beloved teacher was leaving us.

Gurudeva never liked doctors. Perhaps it would be fairer to say he never like the business of doctoring. To be even more precise, he saw doctoring as a business generally more focused on wealth than health.

There were, however, two doctors he trusted. They were also his friends. One of those doctors was allopathic. The other was ayurvedic. From 1995 onward, both these doctors repeatedly asked Gurudeva to submit to a full battery of tests at the hospital. Gurudeva's response had always been, "I wouldn't be caught dead in a hospital."

Finally, a few days after "9/11," that fateful day in 2001 when terrorists slammed planes into the World Trade Center in New York City and the Pentagon in Washington D.C., Gurudeva consented to go in to the hospital for an examination. The next day, his impending death due to cancer was officially announced to the monastery over the phone from the very place he was so dead-set on never visiting.

We all took it well, I would say, considering. Against the backdrop of a truly appalling tragedy like the 9/11 terrorist attacks, the bleak drama of Gurudeva's passing was more easily perceived simply for what it was: a much loved teacher's inescapable quietus. Although intensely disheartening, it was bearable, and certainly inevitable.

No one who understood Gurudeva's teachings could really have any excuse for not being at least somewhat prepared to witness a death. Now, this very man who had taught us so well was challenging us to send him off with thoughts like: "death is a door," "only the body dies," "the soul is immortal, an ever living, growing entity that enters and leaves physical form again and again."

When Gurudeva came home from the hospital, we had a special room ready for him. He couldn't walk. So we moved him in a wheel chair. It was also difficult for him to talk.

It was hard to determine how much pain he was feeling. Because of his stolidity and also because of his withdrawal from communication, we had to get creative in determining the level of his suffering. One method we found especially efficient was to show him a piece of paper with drawings of ten cartoon faces rendering a progression of expressions from happy to sad—then ask him to point to the one that most indicated how he felt.

We were supposed to be giving him morphine, but he didn't like being drugged. Even when the pain got intense, he would only accept less than the minimum dosage.

None of us were surprised when he told us he was going to fast to death. We all knew he didn't want to be a burden on us. We also knew he just "didn't want to linger in the door," as one monk once tactfully described a slow demise.

Within the darkness of Gurudeva's impending death, something quite observable was occurring in Gurudeva's life.

More and more obviously, he was enjoying some sort of preliminary exposure to a world beyond death. He managed to describe what he was experiencing as "an overlap," meaning, I think, a transitional state of consciousness affording him simultaneous awareness of the physical world he was in and the astral world he was moving toward.

On the eleventh day of the 31-day death-fast that the hospital doctors speculated would last no more then ten days, Gurudeva insisted we get him up out of bed and into a chair. As we helped him through this painful move, he kept saying, "Yogaswami is sending a car for me." Barely able to sit up, Gurudeva remained in that chair all through the next night. For a full ten hours, he stayed awake and vertical, waiting for the car he was so sure his spiritual teacher was sending for him.

When I saw Gurudeva for the first time the next morning, he beamed a benign smile and said ever so sweetly from his chair, "I'm still here." I wanted to cry but didn't.

After the fifteenth day of his fast, Gurudeva was talking with unseen entities so frequently it stopped being unusual. Often, the people he *couldn't* see in his room were the physical ones.

There were always (physical) monks at his side, seeing to his needs, even at night. For Gurudeva's last two weeks on Earth, this care was intensified and formalized. Each monk assisting Gurudeva served in three-hour shifts and performed duties that were carefully detailed on paper. My shift was from nine to midnight.

In Hinduism, the passing of a saint or a sage is considered a great mystical event. I can say now, looking back in retrospect, this was perhaps true of Gurudeva's last 31 days on earth. Yet, as it was all actually happening, when we were all immersed in the detail of caring for him in his final fading, it didn't usually seem that way.

For me, it was only during my three-hour, care-giving shifts, when I was alone with Gurudeva from 9 to midnight each night, that I could see, now and then, beyond the gut-level toil of it all and realize something deeply spiritual was occurring. During those precious spans of time, I was touched with some bit of magic and mystery that I'm still trying to sort out—even as I write about it now nearly eight years later. In retrospect, what I can say is this:

During the darkest hours of the night, Gurudeva's room was filled with a tenacious vitality. Yet there was also something else. Though not the opposite of this vitality, it was a reforming of it, or a recognition and celebration of its continuance into a new world past a portal just now opening for a limited time.

It was as if, for an elongated moment, the coming of life and the going of death were not working together as one might normally think they would—like tag-team runners touching just long enough to pass a baton. It was more like they were halting in their duties to enjoy each other's company, as old friends might. And in this communion, exuding bliss, they seemed ancient, wise, venerable and godly.

Then, of course, there I was, like a peasant with kings—feeling honored but misplaced, doing my duty yet watching in awe.

I couldn't meditate—or wouldn't, I should say. That would not have been appropriate. I was on duty. And it was a duty requiring great vigilance. I had my assigned tasks, all of which centralized upon being mindfully aware of Gurudeva's needs. Yet, as I sat there doing my duty, what I couldn't ignore was Gurudeva's way of breathing. Right there in his breath was a commingling of life and death like honey and milk in cupped hands.

He was breathing deeply two or three rounds at a time until his breath sighed to a natural stop. Then, after thirty seconds or more, he would gasp to draw in the first of several more deep breaths until again his breathing would stop.

For the longest time, I thought each pause in stillness was his last. But he kept coming back. So I started trying to breathe with him in his pattern until I could stay still as long as he could. And I felt so happy. He was giving me one last instruction, one last *pranayama* that I could treasure, and *do* treasure to this day. I call it "the death breath."

One night, his pauses were particularly long. I counted nearly two minutes in one. I couldn't stay with him. "Wow," I thought. "That's really amazing."

When my care-giving shift ended that night, death—anyone's—was the furthest thing from my mind. As I casually sauntered away from Gurudeva's room feeling unusually joyful, I heard my name called so softly I almost missed it. I turned. It was the monk who had just taken my place on duty. I thought he was going to ask me to bring him a cup of coffee. Instead, he said quietly, "Gurudeva's gone."

It took an hour to get everyone out of bed, dressed and into the Guru Temple. At about one in the morning, we tediously worked our way through the coronation of Gurudeva's successor. This occurred in an autopilot sort of way. Nobody said any more than they had to. Our Gurudeva had died. It was over. At this point, there was no emotion.

Although our life was droid-like for a few days, we eventually came around to dealing with the details of what now had to be done. And there was much to do: the planning and handling of the various temple ceremonies, a cremation, more temple ceremonies, the hosting of guests, and the announcement of an end and a beginning.

A month earlier, when word first got out that Gurudeva was fasting to death, the island was flooded with devotees. Now in the aftermath of his passing, we monks were quickly realizing *we* were the ones who had to yield a sense that all was well, even though we weren't sure it was. So, we walked around smiling, trying to look confident as we talked.

Of course, there was grieving, even though theoretically there shouldn't have been, according to what we had been taught about death, and what we said in our lectures and wrote in our magazine articles about dying and the immortality of the soul. So, we all kept our grieving as private as possible. Sometimes, however, it spilled out.

Shortly after Gurudeva died, I wrote these verses:

Who sets the course? Who sets the pace?
Who sets the mind in thought
To feel remorse, to feel a face
Gone wet with tears not caught.

So asks love in chest of heart
From where she takes a view.
She wonders not where all things start,
She cares not why they do.

She seeks to find a knowing great
That rides on wordless song,
She will not linger long or late
For thought to say she's wrong.

Her sense of right wards off that sin
That might have been her plight.
She trades her thought for rhyme to win
A mystic's graceful flight.

A heart throbs bliss that's hard to miss,
Yet missed it is by some,
A heart that's cold is proof of this.
It can't be felt. It's numb.

Yet numb it's not deep in its core
Where there its source does thrive,
Where every bliss we might ignore
Is there so much alive.

When starts a whipping spin to churn,
A force then spirals up.

The power of that thrust, we learn,
Is hard to interrupt.

It has a mind all of its own.
It seeks not to agree.
It flows in all, yet is alone.
This force so ever free.

I stayed on in the monastery for six more years, mainly because I felt I should. When a handful of monks left right after Gurudeva's passing, I decided the proper thing to do was stay. Then came a day—and it came suddenly—when I just couldn't do it any more and had to leave. It was as simple as that. There was no doubt—no lengthy anguish or emotional turmoil. I just had to leave and did.

Today, I'm a happy man—as happy as I've ever been. I practice all of the spiritual disciplines I learned in the monastery, plus a few more. And I am thankful for having gained and given as a monk. I am also married. End of story.

For those of you who think, "What? This is no end. Say more," I have only these two words to share: *Stay tuned.* Plus …

Walls that fall like worlds apart
That suddenly are one
Are like dark clouds in painted art
That fade before the sun.

Finish up the fight of fright.
Sing bright that sacred song
That hammers down those birds of flight
That claim a right as wrong.

Please claim the death breath. Claim it now,
Before the curtain falls.
Blame the death breath. Blame it now,
For bringing down those walls.

40038631R00151

Made in the USA
Lexington, KY
22 March 2015